UNDER THE YOKE
A ROMANCE OF BULGARIAN LIBERTY BY IVAN VAZOFF WITH AN INTRODUCTION BY EDMUND GOSSE, C.B.

A NEW AND REVISED EDITION

LONDON   MCMXII
WILLIAM HEINEMANN

INTRODUCTION

IF there is a certain gratification in presenting to the English public the first specimen of the literature of a new people, that gratification is lifted above triviality, and grounded upon a serious critical basis, when the book so presented is in itself a masterpiece. I do not think that it will be questioned that *Under the Yoke* is a romance of modern history of a very high class indeed. That it should be the earliest representation of Bulgarian *belles-lettres* translated into a Western tongue may be curious and interesting, but the book rests its claim upon English readers on no such accidental quality. In any language, however hackneyed, the extreme beauty of this heroic novel, so simple and yet so artfully constructed, so full of ideal charm, permeated with so pure and fiery a passion, so human and tender, so modern and yet so direct and primitive, must have been assured among all imaginative readers.

The story is one of false dawn before the sunrise. The action proceeds, as may gradually be discovered, in the years 1875 and 1876, and the scene is laid in that corner of Bulgaria which was not until 1886 completely freed from Turkish rule—the north-west part of Thrace—overshadowed by the Balkan on the north, and then forming part of the anomalous suzerainty of Eastern Roumelia. *Pod Igoto* is the title of the book, and I am instructed that in Bulgarian the three words *Pod Igo-to* mean, literally translated, *Under the Yoke*. The whole story is the chronicle of one of those abortive attempts which were made throughout Bulgaria and Roumelia forty years ago, under the hope of help from Russia, to throw off the intolerable Turkish yoke of tyranny. The tale ends tragically, with the failure of the particular and partial insurrection described, and the martyrdom of the leading patriots who took a part in it ; but the reader is preserved from finding this failure depressing by the consciousness that relief was at hand, and that an end was soon afterwards to be put to all the horrors of bondage, to the incessant zaptié at the door, to the hateful Turkish rapine, to the misery of Christian servitude under a horde of Oriental officials.

For particulars as to the career of the author of *Under the Yoke* I am indebted to the kindness of Professor J. E. Gueshoff of Sofia, whose enthusiasm for English institutions is well known in this country. Ivan Vazoff, by far the most distinguished writer of modern Bulgaria, was born in August 1850, at Sopot, a large South Bulgarian village in what was later known as Eastern Roumelia, at the foot of the Balkan, and about forty miles to the north of Philippopolis. The locality indicated is identical with the centre of the district obviously described in *Under the Yoke*, and I should not be surprised to learn that Bela Cherkva, the little town so lovingly and so picturesquely pictured by M. Vazoff as the centre of his novel, was Sopot under a disguise.

The other scenes of action—Klissoura, Karlovo, Koprivshtitsa, and the rest—appear in the course of this romance under their real names, and are the towns of a lovely pastoral district. The story passes in the heart of the famous Valley of Roses, where the attar is made ; and over those billowy meadows, heavy with the redundant rose, over the hurrying water-courses, the groves of walnut and pear trees, the white cupolas ringed about with poplars, the little sparkling cities—over all this foreground of rich fertility there rises the huge bulwark of the inaccessible Balkan, snow-clad all though the tropic summer, and feeding the flowery plain with the wealth of its cascades and torrents.

M. Ivan Vazoff was educated at the school of his native village. From Sopot his father, a small trader, sent him to Kalofer and then to Philippopolis. At that time, so Professor Gueshoff assures me, Bulgarian literature consisted of nothing but a few school-books and political pamphlets, possessed of no literary pretensions. Like all other Bulgarians who have made their mark in new Bulgaria, M. Vazoff was driven to seek his facts and his ideas from foreign sources. None but works written in alien languages were worthy to be read. He set himself to study Russian and then French, taking advantage of the school libraries existing in the chief centres of population. When the budding spirit of Bulgaria put forth that first tender leaf, *The Periodic Review*, published at Braila, over the frontiers of friendly Roumania, he was one of the first to contribute poems to it.

From 1870 to 1872 M. Vazoff resided, like so many educated Bulgarians of that time, in Roumania. But in the latter year he went back to Sopot, hesitating between the only two employments open to such men as he, teaching and trade. He chose the latter, and entered his father's business. He was not very successful, attending to it, we may believe, not much more closely than his hero, Ognianoff, does to school-work. No doubt, not a little of M. Vazoff's personal history is here mingled with his fiction, for we find that he grew more and more an object of suspicion to the Turkish authorities, until in 1876, the year of smouldering and futile insurrection, he had to fly north across the Balkan for his life. He reached Roumania in safety, and at Bucharest joined the Bulgarian Revolutionary Committee. The three stormy years that followed saw the final development of his genius, and the publication of three volumes of his patriotic lyrical poetry, *The Banner and the Guzla, The Sorrows of Bulgaria, The Deliverance,* in which the progressive story of Bulgarian emancipation may be read in admirable verse.

He returned in 1878 to find Sopot destroyed, and his father murdered by the Bashi-bozouks. The impression made upon his imagination by the horrors of his bleeding country may be clearly marked in the later chapters of *Under the Yoke.* M. Vazoff accepted from the Russians, who were then in occupation of Bulgaria, a judicial appointment. In 1879 he was elected a member of the Permanent Committee of the Provincial Assembly in the new and anomalous country of Eastern Roumelia. He settled in the new capital, Philippopolis, and here he published his earliest prose works, his stories of *Not Long Ago*, *Mitrofan*, *Hadji Akhil*, and *The Outcast*, his comedy of *Mikhalaki*, and issued, besides, two new collections of poetry, entitled *Fields and Woods* and *Italy* respectively. The last-mentioned was published in 1884, after the author had been travelling in the country it celebrated.

During the Serbo-Bulgarian war of 1885, M. Vazoff visited the battle-fields of Slivnitza, Tsaribrod, and Pirot, sang the valour of his countrymen in dithyrambic strains, and inveighed—in a volume entitled *Slivnitza*—against the fratricidal madness of King Milan. Dissatisfied with the turn taken by affairs in the peninsula after the abdication of Prince Alexander of Battenberg, M. Vazoff in 1886 left for Russia. It was while residing in Odessa that he wrote the romance of *Pod Igoto* ("Under the Yoke "), which is generally admitted to be his masterpiece. In 1889 he returned to Bulgaria, and settled in Sofia, where he had inherited some property from an uncle. *Pod Igoto* first appeared, in serial form, in the excellent *Sbornik* (or Miscellany) published by the Bulgarian Ministry of Public Instruction. The same review issued in 1892 a book by M. Vazoff entitled *The Great Desert of Rilo*, and in 1893 another, called *In the Heart of the Rhodope*. In 1891–92 our author undertook the editorial management of the monthly periodical *Dennitsa* ("The Morning Star "). He is now, without a rival, the leading writer of Bulgaria, and actively engaged in the production of prose and verse.

The poems of Vazoff enjoy a great popularity in his own country, and selections from them have been translated into Russian, Czech, Slovenian, and Servian. The Bohemians may read him in a version by Voracek, published at

Prague in 1891, which is recommended to me as particularly admirable. But alas ! Bohemia is itself remote, and a poet to whom a translation into Czech appears to be an introduction to the Western world seems to us inaccessible indeed. Professor Gueshoff considers that Vazoff will hold in the history of Bulgarian literature a place analogous to that of Chaucer in our own. Having no Bulgarian models to follow, and no native traditions of poetical style, Vazoff has had to invent the very forms of versification that he uses. His success has already led to the creation of a school of young Bulgarian poets, but, though many have imitated Vazoff with talent, not one approaches him in the melody of his metrical effects or in his magical command of the resources of the Bulgarian language.

Written during an epoch of intense national excitement, in a language quite unused before, Vazoff's poems are described to me as reflecting with extraordinary directness and simple passion the woes and burdens, the hopes and the pleasures, of a pastoral people, long held in servitude but at length released. Most of the figures celebrated in his ballads and his odes are the heroes of contemporary patriotism—men, unknown till yesterday, who rose into momentary fame by fighting and dying for their country. They live crystallised in this beautiful verse, already classical, already the food and inspiration of Bulgarian youth—verse written by a son of the new country, one who suffered and struggled with her through her worst years of hope deferred. How tantalising it is that we cannot read such poetry, with the dew of the morning of a nation upon it ! It is almost enough to tempt the busiest of us to turn aside to the study of Bulgarian.

We may regret our wider loss the less, since it is now practicable to read in English what all Bulgarians seem to admit is the leading prose product of their nation. In *Pod Igoto* ("Under the Yoke") Vazoff is understood to have concentrated in riper form than elsewhere the peculiar gifts of his mind and style. The first quality which strikes the critic in reading this very remarkable book is its freshness. It is not difficult to realise that, in its original form, this must be the earliest work of genius written in an unexhausted language. Nor, if Vazoff should live eighty years, and should write with unabated zeal and volume, is it very likely that he will ever recapture this first fine careless rapture. *Under the Yoke* is a historical romance, not constructed by an antiquary or imagined by a poet out of vague and insufficient materials accidentally saved from a distant past, but recorded by one who lived and fought and suffered through the scenes that he sets himself to chronicle. It is like seeing *Old Mortality* written by Morton, or finding the autobiography of Ivanhoe. It is history seen through a powerful telescope, with mediæval figures crossing and recrossing the seventies of our own discoloured nineteenth century.

When the passion which animates it is taken into consideration, the moderate and artistic tone of *Under the Yoke* is worthy of great praise. In an episode out of the epic of an intoxicated nation, great extravagance, great violence might have been expected and excused. But this tale of forlorn Bulgarian patriotism is constructed with delicate consideration, and passes nowhere into bombast. The author writes out of his heart things which he has seen and felt, but the moment of frenzy has gone by, and his pulse as an observer has recovered its precision. The passion is there still, the intense conviction of intolerable wrongs, scarcely to be wiped out with blood. He reverts to the immediate past—

Seeing how with covered face and plumeless wings,
  With unreverted head
  Veiled, as who mourns his dead,
Lay Freedom, couched between the thrones of kings,
  A wearied lion without lair,
And bleeding from base wounds, and vexed with alien air—

but already the image is settled, and has taken the monumental and marmoreal aspect of past history.

The strenuous political fervour of this romance is relieved by a multitude of delicate, touching, and humorous episodes. The scene in the theatre, where, in the presence of the indulgent and indolent Turkish Bey, songs of Bulgarian insurrection are boldly introduced into a sentimental farce, a spurious running translation being supplied to the unsuspecting governor ; the thrilling slaughter of the bandits at the Mill ; the construction of the hollow cherry-tree cannon, which bursts so ignominiously at the moment of trial ; the beautiful and heroic love-scenes between Ognianoff and Rada, cunningly devised and prepared as the very food of patriotism for youthful native readers ; the copious and recurrent, but never needless or wire-drawn, descriptions of the scenery of the Balkan valleys ; the vignettes of life in Bulgarian farmsteads, and cafés, and monasteries, and water-mills—all these are but the embroidery of a noble piece of imaginative texture, unquestionably one of the finest romances that Eastern Europe has sent into the West.

EDMUND GOSSE

TRANSLATOR'S NOTE

Apart from the difficulty of rendering into English a work written in Bulgarian, a language which may be said to be as yet uncultivated and in a state of transition, which possesses no dictionary worthy of the name, and which, at all events in peasant mouths and in certain districts, is a strange jumble, where Turkish words, and sometimes even Greek, predominate —it is no easy task to bring before the English reader a more or less accurate picture of village life in the Balkans, where so much must appear strange and inexplicable. It has been thought best to take the fewest liberties possible with the text, so far as this could be done without giving the translation too un-English an appearance.

Such Turkish words as it has been thought necessary to retain will be found explained in footnotes where they occur. But it may be not amiss to give a somewhat fuller explanation of the term " chorbaji " and the class designated by that name.

The Turkish word chorbaji literally means a soup-man, one who makes, distributes, or otherwise deals with soup. In the hierarchy of the Janissaries the chorbaji was an officer, probably charged with the superintendence of the commissariat, whose rank equalled that of a captain. The term was also applied to the principal resident in Christian villages, who extended his hospitality to such chance strangers as might arrive, there being no inn accommodation then available. So it came to mean any comparatively wealthy and respectable townsman, any one who belonged to " Society." And as, not unnaturally, these were usually men of thoroughly conservative notions, opposed to any upheaval which might endanger their possessions and security, the chorbajis became as a class most unpopular among the ardent and enthusiastic youth who were eager for their country's emancipation. But M. Vazoff defends them from the sweeping imputation, often made against them, that they did nothing but impede and even betray the national movement, and at least two of his insurgents belong to this much-abused class.

CONTENTS

PART I.

PART II.

xvi CONTENTS

PART III.

PART I

CHAPTER I: A VISITOR

On a delightful evening in May, Chorbaji Marko, bareheaded and in dressing gown and slippers, was sitting at supper with his family in the courtyard. As usual, the table was laid at the foot of the vines ; on one side flowed the clear, cold brooklet, which sang night and day like a swallow as it rippled past ; on the other, the high hedge of clustering ivy made an evergreen cover for the wall all the year round. A lantern shone down from an overhanging branch of lilac, which spread its odorous blossoms over the heads of the assembled family. The family was a large one. Round Marko, his old mother and his buxom wife, were crowded a complete circle of children, great and small, all armed with knives and forks, and ready for a terrible on-slaught on their victuals ; they fully personified the Turkish saying : "Saman doushmanlari" (foes to their fodder). From time to time their father cast an approving glance at the execution done by the teeth of these indefatigable, workers, and encouraged them with a smile and a merry "Set to, young 'uns. Fill up the jug again, Pena." And the maid would go to the well, where the great wine jar was cooling, and fill the earthenware jug ; while Marko, handing it to the children, would say, "Drink, you young rascals !" and so the jar would go round the table. Eyes brightened, cheeks sparkled, and lips parted in a smile of satisfaction, and Marko would turn to his wife, and seeing a look of disapproval on her face, would say, "Let them drink in my presence. I won't stint them of wine—for I don't want them to become drunkards when they grow up."

Marko was a thoroughly practical man. His education had been but slight—he was of the old *régime*—but thanks to his natural common sense, he understood human nature well, and knew that people always hanker most after what is forbidden. For the same reason he always entrusted his children with the key of his money-chest, so as to prevent any inclination to theft. "Gocho," he would say, "go and open the cypress-wood chest and bring me the money-bag"; or else, as he went out, "My boy, just count out twenty liras in gold, and give them to me when I come in."

In spite of the then prevailing custom, which required

1

that during meals children should remain standing till their elders had finished, as a mark of respect, Marko's children were always allowed to be seated ; nor was this rule changed when there were guests present. " I want them to get used to company," he would say, " not to run wild, and sink into their shoes when they see a stranger, like Anka Raspopche," who had become proverbial for bashfulness of the most abject description whenever she met a man with cloth trousers on.

As he was engaged with his business all day, Marko only saw his whole family once a day—at supper—and it was then that he carried out his system of education in his own peculiar manner.

Thus : " Dimitr, don't sit down before your grandmother takes her place—you're becoming a regular Freemason ! * Ilia, don't hold your knife like a butcher ; cut your meat, don't hack it. Gocho, what are you about ? Take off your fez when you sit down to supper. Why, your hair is as long as a Toutrakan peasant's ; go and have it cut presently, cossack-style. Vassili, turn in those elbows of yours— you're sprawling all over the table. You can do that in the fields, but not in here. Abraham, what do you mean by getting up from your supper without crossing yourself ? None of these Protestant * ways here, sir ! "

But this was only when Marko was in a good temper ; if he was put out, no one dared to open his mouth.

Being extremely pious and particular, Marko took the greatest pains to inculcate a proper religious spirit in his children. Every evening the older members of the family had to be present while prayers were read. Every Sunday or holiday, all were obliged to go to church—this was a rule which admitted of no exception ; any infringement led to a storm in the household. One Christmas Eve, Kiril had been told to go to confession, as he was to communicate the following morning. Kiril came back from church suspiciously early—in fact, he had not been near the Pope. " Did you confess ? " his father asked, incredulously. " Yes." " To whom ? " " To—to Father Enio," stammered Kiril. That settled it, for Father Enio was a young deacon who could not give absolution. Marko at once

---

* The terms " Freemason " and " Protestant " are almost synonymous in Bulgaria, and are applied to persons who do not comply with the orthodox fasts, &c.

detected the lie, seized his son angrily by the ear, and so
dragged him to the church, where he handed him over to
old Father Stavri, with the words, " Father, just confess this
donkey " ; and, sitting down, he waited there himself, till
the operation was over. He was still more severe in cases
of playing truant from school.

For though he had but little education himself, he loved
learning and the learned. He was one of those numerous
patriots whose eager zeal for the new educational movement
has in so short a time filled Bulgaria with schools. He had
but a dim notion of the practical benefit likely to accrue to
a nation then consisting almost exclusively of farm labourers,
artisans, and merchants. Marko saw with regret that there
was neither work nor bread for the learned when they left
school. But he felt, he understood in his heart that some
secret force lay hidden in learning which would change the
world. He believed in learning as he did in God—without
inquiry : hence he sought to advance it as far as lay in his
power. His only ambition was to be elected a member of
the School Committee, as indeed he invariably was, being
universally respected and esteemed. For this modest social
duty Marko spared neither time nor trouble ; but he
sedulously avoided all other dealings with the authorities,
and especially with the Konak.*

When the table was cleared Marko rose. He was about
fifty years of age, very tall, with a slight stoop, but still hale.
His ruddy face, tanned by sun and wind in his frequent
journeyings to and from shearings and fairs, had a serious
and somewhat stern expression even when he smiled. The
thick eyebrows, which almost met, added to the severity
of his mien. But a certain air of geniality, straightforward-
ness, and sincerity toned this down, and made the whole
sympathetic and worthy of respect.

Marko sat down on the wooden bench among the ivy,
and puffed at his chibouk. The children scattered round
in free play, and the maid brought in the coffee.

That evening Marko was in a good temper. He watched
with pleased interest the gambols of his well-fed, rosy
children as they filled the air with their ringing laughter.
Every moment the scene changed, while the pattering of
their feet and the chorus of chattering, laughter, and

* The Konak is the official residence of the chief executive officer,
and hence comes to be used for " the Turkish authorities."

shouting grew louder and louder. It was like a swarm of sparrows playing in the boughs. But the innocent gladsome game soon assumed a more serious aspect; the shouts became angrier, and little hands were raised in passionate expostulation : the merry concert turned into a quarrelsome brawl—screams were heard and tears began to flow. A rush was made for their parents, the assailants being eager to justify themselves ; the wronged pouring forth their complaints ; one ran to his father for protection, the other to her mother, to win her over as counsel for the defence. Then, from an impartial spectator, Marko suddenly assumed the rôle of judge. In true kadi fashion, and in defiance of all known legal procedure, he would listen to neither plaintiff nor defendant, but simply pronounced and executed his judgment—a slap here and there, as occasion called for it ; but, with the little ones—the pets—a kiss usually met the requirements of the case.

So peace was restored ; but the noise had woke up the youngest, who was asleep in his grandmother's arms. " Hush, darling, hush, or the Turks will come and carry you off," crooned Grandma Ivanitsa, as she gently rocked him. This roused Marko. " Mother," he said, " why do you always terrify them with the Turks ? You'll only make cowards of them." " Well, well, that's my way," said the grandmother. " Why shouldn't I ? Aren't the Turks terrible enough ? I've seen 'em now for over sixty years, and they'll be just the same when I die." " Ah ! grandma," said little Petr, " when I and brother Vassili and brother Ghiorghi grow up, we'll take our scythes and kill all the Turks." " Won't you leave a single one of them, dear ? "

" How is little Asen ? " asked Marko of his wife, as she came out of the house. " He's quieter now—he's fallen asleep," she answered. " There, again, what business had he to be looking at that kind of thing ? " grumbled the grandmother ; " there he is now, ill in bed." Marko frowned, but said nothing. It should be mentioned that Asen had been taken with convulsions through looking out of the school window while they were bringing in the headless corpse of Gencho, the painter's child, from the fields. Marko hurriedly changed the conversation. " That will do, children ; I want your elder brother to tell us a story : after that you shall all sing a song. Come along, Vassili, tell us what the teacher taught you to-day." " A lesson out of the History of the World." " Well, tell us all about it." " The war for the Spanish Succession." "What, them Spanishers ? No, no, my boy, that's no good ; tell us something about Russia." "What ? " asked Vassili. "Why, something about Ivan the Cruel, or Bonaparte when he burned Moscow, or ⌣—" Marko did not finish his sentence. Something rustled at the dark end of the yard ; tiles fell with a clatter from the wall. Hens and chickens woke up in terror, and rushed hither and thither with despairing cluck. The servant who was taking in the washing hung out to dry shrieked " Thieves ! thieves ! "

The courtyard became the scene of the wildest confusion. The women rushed to the house and hid themselves ; the children vanished ; but Marko, who was no coward, rose to his feet, and after peering into the darkness from whence the noise had proceeded, ran into the house, from which he immediately emerged with a pistol in each hand, and hurried towards the stable.

This act—perhaps not the most prudent one possible— was effected so rapidly that his wife had no time to seek to restrain him. All that she did was to raise her voice in entreaty, but even this was drowned by the angry barking of the house dog, who had halted, terrified and enraged, by the fountain.

For there really was a stranger there in the shadow between the stable and the fowl-house, but the darkness was so thick that nothing could be seen, being still more impervious to Marko's eyes owing to the haste with which he had rushed from out of the light of the lantern.

Marko hastened to the stable, caressed the horse so as to pacify him, and peered through the lattices of the window. Whether his eyes had become used to the darkness, or whether it was fancy, he saw in the corner, by the window itself, something upright, like a man, but quite motionless.

Marko cocked his pistol, leant forward, and cried in loud, stern tones, " Don't stir, or else you're a dead man." He waited a moment with his finger on the trigger.

" Gospodin * Marko," whispered a voice.

" Who's there ? " asked Marko in Bulgarian.

* Gospodin is Mr.

"Don't be afraid ; it's a friend." And the stranger approached nearer to the window. Marko could now see his figure clearly.

"Who are you ? " asked Marko suspiciously as he lowered his pistol.

' Ivan, son of old Manola Kralich, of Widdin."

"I don't know you. What are you doing there ? "

"I'll tell you directly, sir," answered the stranger, lowering his voice.

"I can't see you. Where have you come from ? "

"I'll tell you, sir ; from far away."

"Where from ? What do you mean by far away ? "

"From very far away, Marko," whispered the stranger almost inaudibly.

"From where ? "

"From Diarbekir ! " * murmured the stranger.

The word had an electric effect on Marko's memory. He remembered that one of old Manola's sons had been transported to Diarbekir. Manola had long had business dealings with him, and had rendered him many a service.

He went out of the stable, approached his nocturnal visitor in the darkness, took him by the hand, and led him through the stable into the shed.

"What, Ivancho, is that you ? I remember you now, my lad. You can stop here overnight, and we'll look after you in the morning," said Marko, in a low tone.

"Thank you, Marko. You're the only person I know here," whispered Kralich.

"Don't talk of it. Your father has no better friend than me. Make yourself at home here. Did anyone see you ? "

"I don't think so ; there was no one in the street when I came in."

"Came in—yours is a nice way of coming in—over the wall ! Never mind. Old Manola's son is always a welcome guest here, especially when he comes from that distance. Are you hungry, Ivancho ? "

"No—thanks, sir ; I'm not hungry."

"Come, come, you must take a bit of supper. Let me go and quiet my people down first, and then I'll come back and we'll talk things over. God bless you, my boy, I might

* The fortress of Diarbekir, in the heart of Asia Minor, was much used as a place of transportation for political criminals.

have done you a mischief," said Marko, unloading his pistols.

"Forgive me, Marko; I acted very foolishly."

"Stop there till I come." And Marko went out and closed the stable door.

He found his wife and mother fainting from fright, and when they saw him safe and sound they shrieked and threw their arms round him, as if to prevent him from going out again. Marko reassured them laughingly; he had seen no one in the courtyard—probably some cat or dog had knocked one of the tiles down, and that had frightened silly Pena.

"As it is, we've roused the whole neighbourhood," he said, hanging his pistols up again on the wall.

The family calmed down once more.

Old mother Ivanitsa called out to the servant-maid: "Pena, my girl, botheration take you! You've given us a proper fright. Go and put the children to bed at once."

Just then there came a loud knock at the door. Marko went into the court and asked, "Who's there?"

"Open, guv'nor," was the answer in Turkish.

"The on-bashi,"* muttered Marko uneasily. "We must hide him in some other place." And taking no notice of a fresh knock at the door, he hurried to the stable.

"Ivancho!" he called in the shed.

There was no answer.

"He must have fallen asleep. Ivancho!" he repeated, louder.

No one replied.

"Poor fellow! he must have run away," thought Marko. noticing for the first time that the stable door was open. "What will become of the lad now?" he said to himself, anxiously.

To make sure, he called again once or twice, and as no reply came he returned to the door, the knocking at which had become furious, and threatened to break it in.

CHAPTER II: THE STORM

IN truth, at the first knock at the door, and without knowing why or how, Ivan Kralich had clambered hurriedly over the wall and leapt into the street. For a few moments he

* Lit. decurion. a corporal of Zanties (police).

stood bewildered. Then he looked carefully round him,
but there was nothing save impenetrable darkness. Black
storm clouds were already covering the sky ; the cool evening breeze had become a chill blast, which whistled shrilly
through the empty streets. Kralich turned down the first
of these and followed it hurriedly, guiding himself by the
walls. Every door and window was closed and dark. Not
a single light gleamed through the shutters—not a sign of
life anywhere. The hamlet was as still as death, like all
country towns long before midnight. He kept on at random
for some time, hoping to find his way out into the open
country. Suddenly he started and stopped under a broad-
spreading roof. His eye had discerned dark figures moving.
Kralich stood still and turned with precaution to the door
before which he found himself. A growl, followed by an
angry bark, made him start back. He had woke up the
house-dog, who was asleep inside the porch. His movements and the barking betrayed him. The night patrol
stopped, weapons clashed, and "Halt!" was cried in
Turkish. At moments of unavoidable danger a man's
presence of mind deserts him, like a coward, and only a
blind instinct of self-preservation takes the place of all his
moral faculties. One then has, so to speak, no longer a
head, but only one's hands for self-defence and one's legs
for flight. Kralich had only to turn back and the darkness
would at once have put its impenetrable barrier between
him and the patrol. But he rushed straight at it—ran like
the whirlwind right through the police—and fled. The
patrol followed, and the streets rang with shouts and footsteps. Amongst other exclamations was heard the loud
voice of the Bulgarian constable (*pandour*), "Stop, confound you ! we are going to fire !" But Kralich fled without turning back. A few carbines were discharged after
him, but without effect—the darkness saved him. His
flight was not so successful, for he soon felt some one grasp
him by the sleeve. He hurried on, managing to free himself
of his coat, which he left in the hands of his pursuers. Two
more shots were fired after him. Kralich continued to fly,
without knowing whither he was going : he scarcely knew
what he was doing : his legs tottered under him from
weariness. At every step he was ready to fall and remain
on the ground Suddenly a blinding flash of lightning
illuminated the darkness, and Kralich saw that he was in

the fields and no longer pursued. Then he threw himself down, panting, under a walnut tree, to rest for a moment. The mountain blast was blowing hard, the rustling of the leaves mingled with its roar and the dull rumbling of the thunder. Soon the storm came perilously near ; the flashes became more frequent, and more than one bolt fell close by the fugitive. The short rest and cold breeze restored Kralich's strength. He saw it would soon rain, and pressed onward to find some refuge from the storm. The trees round him soughed mournfully, their lofty summits bent under the force of the wind, grass and weeds waved to and fro, and all nature seemed on the alert and quivering with terror. Big drops of rain fell here and there, and struck the ground like bullets. Another flash of lightning lit up the sky behind the Balkan, followed by a deep roll of thunder that seemed to rend the heavens in two. Heavy rain poured from the leaden firmament ; flash after flash cleft the clouds and gave fantastic outlines to the trees and rocks. Those momentary glimpses of scenery, at once swallowed up in deep darkness, resembled some wonderful and fearful panorama. There was a wild beauty in the strife of the elements—in the conflict of the horizons—the infernal illumination of the abysses ; a majestic spectacle, in which the wonderful combination of the boundless with the mysterious was blended in an unearthly demoniacal harmony. In storms nature attains themes of sublimest poetry.

Though dripping with water and blinded by the lightning, while the crashing thunder still rang in his ears, Kralich wandered on at random among the fields, orchards, and gardens, where no refuge was to be had. At last the plashing of a waterfall overcame all other sounds and reached his ears. It was a mill-stream. On a sudden a new flash disclosed to him the roof of the mill, nestling among drooping willows. Kralich stopped under the eaves. He pushed at the door, which opened. He entered. The mill was dark and silent. Outside, the storm had calmed down : the rain was slowly ceasing, and the moon began to appear behind the clefts in the clouds. The night had cleared up. These rapid changes in weather are usual only in May.

Soon steps were heard approaching from outside, and Kralich hastened to hide in a narrow space between the granary and the wall.

" There now—the wind has blown the door open," said a rough voice in the darkness, and a petroleum lamp was at once lighted.

Kralich, hidden in his corner, stooped and saw the miller, a tall gaunt peasant, and with him a barefooted girl in a short blue dress, probably his daughter, who was closing and trying to bolt the door. She was about thirteen or fourteen years old, but still quite a child, and her black eyes peeped out with childish innocence from under her long lashes. Despite her neglected dress, her figure gave promise of future gracefulness. She seemed to have come from some mill close at hand, for they were dry. The miller added :

" It's a good thing we turned off the channel, or this storm would have smashed it. Old Stancho's stories never come to an end. It's a blessing no robber came in." He looked round him. "Now, Marika, you go off to bed. I wonder why your mother sends you here ? Only for me to have the more anxiety," added the miller, hammering down the plank in the channel, and humming a tune to himself. Marika, without waiting any longer, went to the far end of the mill, said her prayers, shook out some blankets and lay down to sleep : in a moment she was slumbering peacefully.

Kralich watched the scene with lively curiosity. The miller's rough but kindly face inspired him with confidence. It was impossible that a traitor's soul could lurk behind that straightforward and honest countenance. He decided to come out and ask him for aid and counsel. But at that very minute the miller stopped humming, drew himself up, and listened to sounds of voices outside. A loud knock was heard at the door.

" Open the door, miller," cried some one in Turkish.

He went to the door, fastened the bolt securely, and returned pale with terror.

The hammering at the door continued, and a fresh summons was made, followed by the bark of a dog.

" Turks out hunting," muttered the miller, whose ear had recognised the bark of a greyhound. " What do the brutes want ? It must be Yemeksiz Pehlivan."

Yemeksiz Pehlivan, the wildest of midday and midnight marauders, was the terror of the neighbourhood. A fortnight before he had murdered the whole family of Gancho

Daghli in the village of Ivanovo. They said—and not without some ground—that it was he who had cut off the child's head which had been brought to the town the day before.

The door shook under the knocking.

The miller remained for a moment plunged in thought, clasping his head with both hands, in doubt as to what course he should follow. A cold sweat broke out on his forehead. Suddenly he moved to a dusty shelf, from under which he took an axe, and then went to the door, which was nearly beaten in by the knocking. But his momentary decision vanished as soon as he glanced at his daughter. A terrible hopelessness, torture, suffering were depicted on his face. The paternal feeling overcame his perturbed conscience. He thought of the Bulgarian proverb: "The sword does not strike the bowed head," and decided, instead of resistance, to beg for mercy—from the merciless. He hurriedly replaced the axe behind the granary, where Kralich was hidden, covered up Marika carefully, and opened the door.

On the threshold stood two armed Turks in hunting costume. One held a greyhound in a leash. The first, who was in truth the bloodthirsty Yemeksiz Pehlivan, cast an inquisitive glance round the mill, and entered. He was tall, lame, cadaverously thin, and beardless. His face was not as terrible as his name and his deeds would imply; but his small, grey, almost colourless eyes twinkled with evil cunning, like a monkey's. His companion was a short, thick-set, muscular man, with a face of bestial expression, in which the lowest animal instincts and ferocity were apparent; this man followed with the greyhound, and stood by the door.

Yemeksiz Pehlivan looked angrily at the miller.

The two men took off their dripping overcoats.

"Why didn't you open, miller?" he asked. The miller muttered some excuse, bowing to the ground, and casting an uneasy glance at the end of the mill where Marika lay sleeping.

"Are you alone here?" and Yemeksiz looked round.

"Quite alone," was the hurried reply; then, thinking a lie was useless, the miller added, "and the child is asleep over there."

Just then Marika moved, and turned her face towards

them. The pale light of the lamp shone on her white throat. The Turks cast eager glances at the sleeping girl. A cold sweat moistened the miller's forehead.

Yemeksiz turned to him with an assumed kindliness. "Guv'nor," he said, "sorry to trouble you. Go and buy us a bottle of raki."

"But, Pehlivan Aga, all the shops are shut now—it's midnight," answered the miller, trembling at the terrible idea of leaving Marika alone in such company.

The cripple answered: "Go along with you; no shop would refuse to serve you if you say it's for me. I want you to treat us—that's the way to make friends."

He said this in jest, being certain of obtaining his end. He did not even seek to hide his intention from the unhappy father.

Yemeksiz glanced at the sleeping child in her careless and innocent attitude. Seeing that the miller did not move, he began to grow impatient, but still retained his assumed gentleness, and said quietly:

"Mashallah! that's a pretty girl of yours, guv'nor. Off you go; we're your guests, you know—you must treat us. You fetch the raki, and we'll look after the mill." Then he added in a threatening tone: "Don't you know Yemeksiz Pehlivan?"

The miller had understood from the first the abominable design screened by that shallow trick. His simple, honest nature revolted at the thought. But he was caught in the trap—he was alone against two armed men. To resist was foolish and useless: his death, which was now a matter of indifference to him, could not save his child. He tried again by prayers to soften his enemies:

"Gentlemen, I'm an old man—take pity on my poor old bones. I'm worn out by my day's work: let me sleep in peace. Don't blacken my face."*

He was addressing deaf ears. The lame Turk exclaimed: "Come, come, man, we're thirsty—you talk too much. Don't you live in the mill? Go for the raki!" And he pushed him to the door.

"I won't leave my mill at this time of night! Let me alone!" said the miller, hoarsely.

The two Turks then threw aside their feigned gentle-

---

* I.e., "Don't bring disgrace upon me"—a common oriental expression.

ness of manner, and their eyes flashed furiously on the miller.

"What! he shows his tusks, the pig!" cried Yemeksiz, drawing his gataghan, while his eyes became bloodshot.

"You may kill me, but I won't leave my child alone," said the miller, humbly but decidedly.

Yemeksiz stood up. "Topal Hassan," he said, "throw the dog out—I don't want to dirty my knife."

The other rushed at the miller, seized him, and forced him to the door, whence he tried to spurn him with his foot. The miller rose to his feet and sprang in again, crying "Mercy! mercy!"

The noise woke Marika, who stood up in terror. When she saw the Turk's drawn sword she shrieked and fled to her father.

"Mercy, mercy, gentlemen!" cried the unfortunate father, clasping his child in his arms.

At a sign from Yemeksiz the powerful Topal Hassan threw himself like a tiger on the miller, seized his hands, and bound them.

"That's it, Topal Hassan; let's tie up the old rat of a miller; since he wants to stop here, let him stay and see the show—that's what a fool like that deserves. He shall remain tied up, and when we set fire to the mill it'll be our turn to look on and enjoy ourselves."

And the two brigands, paying no attention to his cries, forced the miller up to a beam and began to tie him with ropes.

The miller, frenzied with terror at the thought of what he was going to see, roared for help like a wild beast; but no help was to be hoped for in that lonely place.

Marika opened the door and began to shriek and wail. But only the echoes replied.

"Here, miss, you come in. We want you," cried Yemeksiz, as he fetched her in. "Help, help!" cried the miller in despair. "Is there no one? Marika, come, dear," he shouted in his frenzy—calling on his child for help.

Kralich had all the while been watching the scene motionless; his legs trembled unnaturally, his hair stood on end, and the cold dew was on his face.

All that he had seen and undergone that evening, from leaving Marko's house till that moment, was so strange and

fearful that it seemed to him like a dream.   The whistling
of the bullets, the roar of the thunder were still echoing in
his ears.   His thoughts were confused.   At first he had
made sure the Turks had come for him, and that his fate
was sealed.   The conviction of his utter helplessness had
quenched all his energy, and left him only enough to give
himself up to the Turks, so as to save the miller.   But now
that he saw that he was to be a spectator of something far
more terrible, and when he heard the miller call Marika to
his assistance, a blind rage and despair fired his very soul.
He had never looked on blood before, but the Turks
seemed to him like flies.   Fatigue, weakness, doubt—all
disappeared.   He stretched out his hand mechanically and
seized the axe ;   he passed along mechanically, stooping
behind the wheat-sacks ;   rose up, pale as death, rushed at
Yemeksiz, who stood with his back to him, and plunged the
axe into his body.   All this he did as in a dream.

The Turk fell to the ground without a groan.

At sight of this sudden and dangerous foe, Topal Hassan
left the rope with which he was fastening up the miller, drew
his pistol, and fired it at Kralich.   The mill was filled with
smoke, the action of the shot put out the lamp, and all were
plunged in darkness.   Then in the dark began a terrible
struggle, with the hands, nails, feet, teeth.   The combatants,
at first two, but soon three in number, rolled in the dark
with wild cries and groans, mingled with the loud bark of
the dog.   Topal Hassan, as strong as a bullock, resisted
desperately his two antagonists, who on their part knew they
must conquer or meet a fate which was only too certain.

When the lamp shone again, Hassan was writhing in his
death-agony.   Kralich had during the fight managed to get
hold of his knife and plunge it in his breast.   The two
bodies were weltering in blood.

Then the miller rose and looked with wonder at the unknown assistant who had come to his rescue.   Before him
stood a tall young man, deadly pale, thin, with piercing
black eyes, long shaggy hair, covered with dust ; his coat
was torn, stained with mud, and wet ; his waistcoat had lost
its buttons, and showed that he had no shirt ; his trousers
were in rags, and his boots scarcely held together.   In a
word, it was a man either just out of gaol or on his way
thither.   The miller took him as such.   But he cast a look
of sympathy on him, and said earnestly :

" Sir, I don't know who you are or how you come to be here. But as long as I live I can't pay you back for this. You've saved me from death and from worse than death ; you've spared my grey hairs from shame. May God bless and reward you. The whole nation will honour you for what you've done. Do you know who he is ? (pointing to Yemeksiz). He's made mother and daughter weep before now. Now the world's free of the monster. God bless you, my son ! "

Kralich listened with tears in his eyes to these simple and sincere words—then, much moved, he said :

" I haven't done much, father : we have killed two, but there are thousands and thousands more such monsters. The Bulgarian nation can only free itself and live in peace if all seize their axes and cut down the enemy. But tell me, where are we to bury these bodies, so as to leave no trace ? "

" I've got a grave ready for the unbelievers : only help me to carry them out," said the old man.

Then the two men, between whom that night of blood had placed an eternal bond of union, carried the corpses out to an old pit behind the mill, and threw them in, covering them over carefully with earth so as to leave nothing showing. On returning to the door with the pick-axe and shovel, something white bounded round them.

" Ah, the dog ! " cried Kralich ; " it will lurk round here and betray us. I must knock it over the head," and he struck it with the axe. The dog fell yelping by the water. Kralich pushed it into the mill-stream with his axe, and it sank there.

" We ought to have buried it by the other two dogs," said the miller.

They removed the blood-stains from their clothes, and covered the ground over with leaves.

" Why, what's that running from you ? " asked the miller, seeing that Kralich's hand was bleeding.

" Nothing ; only where the brute bit me while I was stabbing him in the heart."

" Let me bind it up for you at once," said the miller, tying it up with a rag. Then, leaving his hand, he looked him straight in the face, and said :

" I beg your pardon, my son, but where do you come from ? " And he cast another look of surprise at the stranger.

" I'll tell you later on, father ; and all I can say is that I'm a Bulgarian, and a good Bulgarian. Have no doubts on my score."

" My God ! I should think you were. You're a real Bulgarian and no mistake, and for such as you I'd give my life."

" Tell me now where can I get clothes and find a shelter for the night ? "

" Let's go to the monastery to Deacon Vikenti. He's a relation of mine. That man has done no end of good. And he's a real Bulgarian too. Come along ; we'll all sleep there. It's a good thing no one saw us." Father Stoyan was mistaken : behind the walnut-tree the moon now showed a tall human figure which had witnessed, motionless, the burial of the two Turks. But neither he nor Kralich had noticed it.

Soon after, the miller, Kralich, and Marika (who during the struggle had hidden herself behind an elm-tree and was sobbing piteously) started towards the monastery, the high walls of which, standing out in the moonlight, shone forth against the dark branches of the walnuts and poplars. Behind them the unknown figure also proceeded towards the monastery.

CHAPTER III : THE MONASTERY

THEY passed through a field, where great boulders of rock were scattered here and there, under the branches of the century-old walnuts, with their trunks worn and rotting away with age : soon the high walls of the monastery came clearly into view. In the mysterious softness of the moonlight it resembled an old Gothic castle, with fantastically carved gables.

Some years before, the old building had rejoiced in a gigantic pine-tree, which sheltered the church with its high-spreading branches—the home of a thousand feathered songsters. But a storm had uprooted the pine and the church tower, and a new tower, which had been erected in its place, with a lofty new-fashioned cupola, made a strange contrast to the dilapidated old remains of a past age : it gave one the same shock that is produced by a piece of fresh white paper stuck on a time-worn parchment. The old church and tower have fallen under the assaults of time and destiny, and henceforth the monastery has become sombre : the eye no longer follows the towering pine to the clouds : the soul no longer draws pious inspirations from the paintings on the walls representing saints, archangels, holy fathers, and martyrs, defiled and with their eyes put out by the Kirjalis and Delibashis.*

Our trio passed behind the monastery and stopped by the back wall : this was easier of access, and nearer to Deacon Vikenti's cell. Moreover, there were no monastery dogs there to bark at them, nor servants to ask unnecessary questions.

The mountain waterfalls plashed hard by and filled the neighbourhood with a wild echo.

Some one had to climb over the wall, so as to fetch the ladder from inside and pass it to the others. This duty naturally fell to Kralich's lot, he having begun that evening by scaling Marko's wall.

The three clambered quickly over the wall, at the risk of a shot from the warlike higoumen,† in case he should happen to see them from his window. They entered the small back-yard, which communicated with the great quadrangle by a door closed on the inside. The deacon's cell, which was on the ground floor, looked on to the back-yard. They stopped under the window, where a light was still burning.

" Vikenti's still reading," said the miller, raising himself on tip-toe and looking in. He knocked at the window. It was opened, and a voice asked :

" What, Stoyan, is that you ? Whatever do you want ? "

" Give me the door-key, deacon, and I'll tell you. Are you alone ? "

" Yes ; everybody's asleep. Here you are."

The miller disappeared in the shadow, and in two or three minutes reappeared and led Kralich and his daughter into the inner quadrangle, locking the door behind him.

The great courtyard, when they entered, was quite still. The silence was broken only by the monotonous and drowsy gurgling of the spring, which resembled the last groan of a dying man. Dark rows of covered verandahs, silent and deserted, rose all round the quadrangle. Black cypress-trees soared high above, like gigantic phantoms. The deacon's cell opened, and his nocturnal visitors entered.

* Brigand bands that infested the Balkans early in the past century.
† The Higoumen (from the Greek ἡγούμενος) is the abbot of a monastery.

B

The deacon, who was quite a lad, with a lively countenance, black intelligent eyes, and a sprouting beard, received
Kralich in a friendly manner, his cousin's hurried explanations having been enough to assure him of the stranger's
quality.   Indeed, he gazed with surprise and respect at the
hero who had accounted for the two ruffians as easily as one
wrings the neck of a couple of chickens, and had saved the
old man and his daughter.   The deacon's honest soul recognised at once in the stranger a nature as noble as it was
heroic.   Old Stoyan had given him a hurried and confused
account of the affair in the mill, and had been loud in his
deliverer's praise.   Vikenti observed his utter exhaustion
and pallor, and proposed to take him to a cell where he
might find shelter for the night.   So they proceeded thither.
The deacon, with a bundle of blankets and clothes under
his arm, led the way through the slumbering courtyard ;
they reached the staircase of the opposite building, consisting of three storeys of covered verandahs, and mounted
it.   They passed through corridors and fresh flights of stairs
to the topmost storey.   Though they stepped with precaution, every stair creaked under their feet, as happens in all
empty wooden houses.   Vikenti lighted a candle, and the
cell into which they had entered was exposed to view.   It
was bare and cheerless enough to look at, containing only a
bed with a straw pallet and a jug of water.   It was more like
a prison cell than a bedroom, but Kralich just then desired
nothing better.   After some conversation as to the events
in the mill, Vikenti prepared to say good-night.

"You are worn out, and need rest as soon as possible ;
so I will not weary you with any questions.   There is no
need.   The deed of heroism which you have accomplished
to-night tells me all.   We shall meet to-morrow, and I will
only say now : don't worry yourself about anything. Deacon
Vikenti is at your entire disposal.   Good-night."   And so
saying he stretched out his hand to take leave.

Kralich seized and held it.

"No," said he, "you have given me your hospitality
blindly, and have exposed yourself to danger for my sake.
You ought to know who I am.   My name is Ivan Kralich ! "

"What, Ivan Kralich, the exile ?   Why, when did they
release you ?" asked the astonished deacon.

"Release me ?   I escaped from the fortress of Diarbekir.
I'm a runaway."

Vikenti pressed his hand, and greeted him :

" Welcome here, Kralich : you are a still dearer guest to me now. Bulgaria requires her good sons. There is much work to be done—much work. The tyranny of the Turks is unbearable and the national dissatisfaction has reached its utmost limit. We must get ready. Stay with us, Gospedin Kralich, no one will know you here. Stay and work with us —will you ? " asked the deacon, much excited.

" With all my heart, Father Vikenti."

" To-morrow we will talk the matter over in detail. Here you are in complete safety. I have hidden Levski * in that cell before now. No one comes here—there is more danger from ghosts than from human beings. Good-night," said the deacon, in jest, as he left the room.

" Good-night, father," answered Kralich, shutting the door.

He undressed quickly, lay down, and blew out the candle ; but he lay tossing on his bed for many an hour before sleep came to his weary eyelids. Fearful memories troubled his spirit. Before his fancy there passed one by one the various scenes and forms of that night, with repulsive and savage accuracy. This torture lasted for a long time. At last nature conquered : his physical and moral strength, exhausted to the utmost, yielded to the imperious necessity of repose. He fell asleep. But on a sudden he started and opened his eyes in the darkness. He heard the slow and heavy tread of some one walking in the passage. Then a sound of singing was heard, which sounded almost like a wail of sorrow. The steps came nearer, and the unfamiliar singing became louder. It was at times like a loud wailing, at others like a mournful dirge. Kralich thought that the sounds came from somewhere else, and that it was the surrounding silence which made them seem so near and ghastly. But no—the steps were hard by, in the corridor. Suddenly a dark figure appeared at the window and peeped in. Kralich, startled, fixed his eyes on the apparition, and with terror saw that it was making wild, weird gestures with its hands, as if beckoning to him. All this was clear in the semi-darkness. Kralich could not withdraw his eyes from the window. He began to think that the figure was that of Yemeksiz Pehlivan, whom he had killed. Then he

* A noted worker in the cause of Bulgarian liberty, who was eventually taken prisoner by the Turks, and hanged at Sofia in 1873.

thought he must be dreaming, and rubbed his eyes. Again he looked—and found the shadow still at the window, peering in.

Kralich was not superstitious, but this deserted building, with its deathlike silence and darkness, had inspired him involuntarily with terror. He thought of the deacon's jesting remark about ghosts, and the place seemed to him doubly uncanny. But suddenly he felt ashamed of himself. Groping for his revolver, he grasped it, rose, opened the door quietly, and went out barefoot into the corridor. The tall mysterious figure was still walking and singing in its strange fashion. Kralich approached it boldly. The singing phantom, instead of disappearing, as in stories, shrieked with terror, because Kralich himself, in his night-shirt, was far more like a ghost.

"Who are you ? " asked the new ghost of the old, seizing him by the garment.

Fear closed the unhappy being's lips. He could only make the sign of the cross, gibbering, and shaking his head like an idiot. Kralich at once understood that such he was, and let him go.

Vikenti had forgotten to warn his guest of the nightly wanderings of the harmless idiot Mouncho, who had for years lived in the monastery. It was he who, unobserved, had witnessed the burial of the Turks.

CHAPTER IV : BACK AT MARKO'S

WHEN Marko opened his door on the previous night, after Kralich's escape, he encountered on the threshold the on-bashi and his zaptiés, who entered with precaution.

"What's up here, Marko Chorbaji ? " asked the on-bashi.

Marko quietly explained that nothing was the matter, but that the servant had somehow taken fright. The on-bashi at once expressed himself satisfied with this meagre explanation, and went out in glee at having got off an unpleasant job.

Just as Marko was shutting his door, his neighbour appeared. "All over, neighbour ? "

"What, Ivancho ! Come in and we'll have a cup of coffee."

"Good evening, Marko. Is little Asen better ? " asked

a tall youth in the middle of the road, who was hurriedly approaching.

"Come in, come in, doctor." And Marko led them into the room, which was at once brightly lit up with two spermaceti candles fixed in shining brass candlesticks.

The guest-chamber into which they entered was a small room, but bright and airy. It was furnished and ornamented in the unassuming and original manner which even now holds sway in some of our provincial towns. The floor was covered with bright carpets, and the two divans with scarlet rugs, all of home make. Against one of the walls stood an iron stove, which was lighted only in winter, but was not taken away in summer, as being one of the ornaments of the room. Opposite it, on the eikonostasis,* where a light burned continually, were nailed eikons, over which hung sacred prints from Mount Athos, a pious gift from pilgrims. The eikons were very old paintings, which made them all the more precious to Grandmother Ivanitsa, as old arms are to collectors. One of them, of great antiquity, enjoyed the most reverential attention of the old lady, who asserted with pride that it had been painted by her great-grandfather, Father Hajji Arseni, who had accomplished the miraculous work of art with his feet—an assertion no one ever ventured to controvert, so confidently did she make it. Behind the eikonostasis was fastened a bunch of dried cornflowers, which had been sprinkled with holy water, and a willow branch from the decorations of last Palm Sunday. The presence of these in a house was an infallible preservative of health and prosperity. Round the walls ran shelves filled with porcelain dishes and cups—the inevitable decoration of every house worthy of respect—and the corners were furnished with triangular brackets on which stood flower-vases. Chibouks, as an article of use, had long since gone out of fashion, but these were ranged against the wall, with their yellow amber mouthpieces and inlaid bowls. Marko, for old tradition's sake, kept one chibouk for his private use. The wall opposite the windows played the important part of picture-gallery. In all, it contained six lithographs, in gilt frames, brought from Wallachia. Their strange selection bore witness to the easy-going taste of the time in matters artistic. Some represented scenes

* The place where the sacred pictures or eikons are placed against the wall.

from the internal wars of Germany—one was a picture of Abd-ul-Mejid on horseback, with his suite. The next portrayed episodes of the Crimean War : the battle of the Alma, of Eupatoria, the raising of the siege of Silistria in 1852. The last picture of all represented the Russian generals in the war, all depicted down to the knees only. Pope Stavri asserted that their legs had been cut off by the English cannon, and on the strength of this Grandmother Ivanitsa always called them " the martyrs." " Who has been touching the martyrs ? " she would ask angrily of the children. By the side of the martyrs stood a large Dutch clock, the chain and weights of which reached down to the back of the divan. This aged timepiece had long since become past work : its springs were worn out, its works distorted, its face obliterated, and its hands broken and twisted. It was like a living ruin. But Marko prolonged its life at the cost of great efforts and much attention. No one but he was allowed to touch it ; he would mend it, take it to pieces, wind it up, and clean it with a feather dipped in oil, thus giving it a new lease of life for a few days, after which it would again come to a standstill. Marko jestingly called it his " consumptive patient," but he and all the family were so accustomed to it that the whole house seemed silent when its creaking pendulum stopped. Whenever Marko took hold of its chains to wind it up, the sufferer vented from its inmost recesses such weird and wrathful sounds that the cat fled in terror.

Two photographs of family groups on the same wall completed the treasures of the picture-gallery, which with the clock constituted a museum.

Doctor Sokoloff was a young man of twenty-eight, lively, with bright ruddy hair and blue eyes, an open, simple expression of countenance, and a somewhat boisterous, easy-going, and eccentric manner. He had served as veterinary surgeon in a Turkish regiment on the Montenegrin frontier, and had acquired a thorough knowledge of the language and customs of the Turks—he drank raki and fraternised with the on-bashi every afternoon, but at night terrified him by firing a revolver up his chimney : at present he was devoting much of his time to the education of a bear. The better-class Bulgarians looked somewhat askance at him, and placed their trust rather in the Greek apothecary Yaneli ; but he was a popular favourite with all the youth of the town on account of his gay, open nature, and his fervent patriotism. He was always the prime mover in social festivities and "Committee"* plots, and, indeed, spent most of his time in these two occupations. He had never gone through a regular course of medicine, but his younger friends had given him the title of Doctor to place him on a higher footing than the Greek chemist, and he had not thought it necessary to protest against the calumny. As for his treatment of his patients, he left them to the care of his two faithful assistants—the healthy Balkan air and nature. Hence he rarely had recourse to his pharmacopœia, which, indeed, being in Latin, was a sealed book to him ; and all his dispensary was contained on a single small shelf. No wonder that he thus managed to take the wind out of the sails of his rival.

Sokoloff was Marko's family doctor, and had come to visit little Asen

The other visitor was Ivancho Yotata. He, like a good neighbour, had come to see what was the matter, and pass the time of day. For a few minutes the conversation was taken up with the event of the evening, and Ivancho eloquently described his impressions and dismay.

"To tell you the truth," he rambled on, " just as our Lala was clearing the table, I heard a most prodigious to-do in your courtyard, Marko. Then the dog was making a tremendous row. I was frightened—at least, I wasn't exactly frightened, but I said to Lala : 'Lala,' says I, ' whatever is the matter next door ? Just look over the wall into their courtyard.' Then it struck me that this was more a man's business than a woman's. So I boldly climbed on to the wall and looked over. Your courtyard was pitch dark. What's all this to-do about ? thinks I, knowingly ; let me give notice to the police. But Lala was standing behind me and catching hold of my coat. ' Where are you going?' says she. ' Not to Marko's, I hope ? ' ' No, no,' says I. ' There's nothing the matter : lock the gate into Marko's yard.' "

"There was no need, Ivancho—there was nothing the matter," said Marko, smiling.

* The Revolutionary Committees, common in Bulgaria from about 1872 to 1876, had made a great impression on the Turks, and all Bulgarian insurgents were by them called " Koumitajis," or simply " Koumita."

"Then," continued Yotata, "I said to myself : 'We must inform the authorities : M. Marko is my neighbour, and mustn't be left in danger.' So I rushed downstairs, with Lala screaming after me. 'Silence,' said I in a manly tone. I went out of the door, and lo and behold ! all was as still as the dead."

"Is little Asen asleep yet, Marko ? " asked the doctor, to stay the flow of Ivancho's oratorical display. But Ivancho hastened to continue :

"When I saw that the street was as still as the dead, I said to myself : 'Don't you trust it, Ivancho'; and I turned back and came out by the back door—that is, I got out into the blind alley, turned out of it past Petko's door, then past the Mahmoud's, past Uncle Gencho's dung-heap, and then straight to the Konak. I went in, looked round, and at once boldly informed the on-bashi that there were robbers in your house, and that the fowls were flying about the yard."

"I tell you there was no one there ; your trouble was quite unnecessary, Ivancho." Meanwhile the storm was raging outside in all its fury.

"By the way, Marko, I had quite forgotten to ask you," said the doctor suddenly ; "did a young man call this evening ? "

"What young man ? "

"A stranger, pretty badly dressed, but fairly intelligent-looking, as far as I could see. He was asking for your house."

"Where did you see him ? No one called," answered Marko, with evident confusion, which, however, his visitors had no reason to observe.

The doctor went on quietly :

"A young man addressed me just at nightfall, near Hajji Pavli's rose-field. He asked me politely, 'Can you tell me, sir, if Marko Ivanoff's house is far ? I want to see him,' says he, 'it's the first time I have been here.' I happened to be going the same way, so I offered to show him your house. On the road I looked at him carefully : the poor fellow was almost in rags—his coat was very thin and all torn, as far as I could see in the dark. He was tired and weak, and could scarcely stand on his feet, and in this awful weather, too ! I didn't dare to ask him where he was coming from or why he was in that state, but I was sorry for the poor fellow. And when I saw his vest was in rags, and, so to speak, falling to pieces, I couldn't resist asking him, ' I hope you won't be angry with me, sir, if I offer you my overcoat—you will forgive me, won't you ? ' He said ' Thank you,' and took it. So we came as far as your house, and then I left him. I wanted to ask you who he was."

" I tell you, no one came to call."

" That's funny," said the doctor.

" Perhaps it was a robber, who climbed on to your roof, Marko ? " asked Ivancho. " That may have caused all this to-do."

" It's impossible that that young man should have been a robber," said the doctor, curtly ; " anyone could see that from his face."

The conversation was assuming an unpleasant tone, and Marko, to change it, turned to Sokoloff.

" Have you read the paper, doctor ? How's the revolt in the Herzegovina getting on ? "

" It's all over, Marko. That heroic nation has achieved miracles, but what can they do against such odds ? "

" Goodness me ! A handful of men like that to hold out so long. Why can't we do something of the kind ? " said Marko.

" We've never tried," said the doctor ; " we're five times as many as the Herzegovinians, but we don't know our own strength yet."

" Don't think of such a thing, doctor," said Marko. " We're one thing and the Herzegovinians are another ; we're in the jaws of hell : we've only to move to be cut down like sheep. There's nowhere we can look to for aid."

" Well, well, I've got a gun, but I haven't cleaned it for twelve years," said Yotata.

" I ask you, have we ever tried ? " repeated the doctor impatiently.

" They kill us and cut us to pieces without our trying : the more submissive we are, the more they ill-use us. What had that poor child of Gancho's done, that was brought in yesterday beheaded ? They threaten us with the gallows if we venture to protest against their tyranny, and the Yemeksiz Pehlivans are allowed to torture us to their heart's content, unpunished. What kind of justice do you call

that ? The mildest would revolt against it. Even a worm
will turn, as the saying is."

Grandmother Ivanitsa entered.

" What do you think ? " said she ; " Pena says before the
rain began she heard guns fired. Dear, dear ! I wonder
what is the matter. Holy Virgin, some poor Christian soul
has perished again, I suppose."

Marko started : his countenance changed. He had a
presentiment that something had happened to Kralich.
His heart overflowed with grief, which he was unable to
conceal.

" Why, Marko, what's the matter ? " said the doctor,
feeling his pulse and scanning his countenance, which
showed only too plainly the signs of intense moral
suffering.

The rain had stopped. The visitors rose to take leave.
The news had disturbed them.

" Nonsense ! the maid must have fancied it all—most
likely some one shutting his shutters. Don't be afraid—
courage ! " said Ivancho Yotata, boldly. " Grandmother,
is your side door open ? " And while Marko was showing
the doctor out, Ivancho hurriedly left by the side door,
opened for him on the other side by his wife.

CHAPTER V : THE REST OF THE NIGHT

Doctor Sokoloff knocked at his door.

It was opened by an old woman, whom he asked, as he
passed by her hurriedly : " How's Cleopatra ? "

" She's been asking for you," replied the old woman with
a smile.

The doctor passed through the long courtyard, and
entered his room. This apartment, which was at the same
time his receiving-room, study, dispensary, and bedroom,
was a broad bare room with cupboards in the walls and a
deep fireplace. On a small shelf were arranged all his
drugs ; on the little table were scattered a small mortar and
pestle, a few medical books, and a revolver ; a double-
barrelled matchlock hung over the bed. The only picture
with which the walls were adorned was a portrait of Prince
Nicolas of Montenegro, beneath which was the photograph
of some actress. Everything showed that the room was that
of an easy-going bachelor : it was dull, bare, and untidy.

In the corner was the half-opened door of the cellar, where three years ago Levski had spent the night.

The doctor flung off his fez and coat carelessly, approached the cellar door, clapped his hands, and cried out : "Cleopatra, Cleopatra ! "

There was no answer.

" Come out, Cleopatra darling ! "

A sound was heard from the cellar.

The doctor sat down on a chair in the middle of the room, and called, " Here, Cleopatra ! "

A bear, or rather a bear-cub, came out.

It approached, dragging its massive paws along the ground, and purring joyfully. Then it sprang up and placed its forepaws on the doctor's knees, opening its capacious jaws and displaying its teeth, sharp and glittering. It fawned on him like a dog, while the doctor gently stroked its head, and gave it his hand to lick.

The beast had been caught, while quite young, on the Sredna Gora, by a peasant, who had given it to Sokoloff for having cured his child of a serious illness. The doctor had become much attached to it, and took the greatest pains to procure proper food for it. Cleopatra flourished exceedingly under this sedulous care, took lessons in gymnastics with the best grace possible, and her devotion to her master increased daily.

Cleopatra now danced a bear's polka, carried the doctor's hat for him, waited on him, and guarded his room like a dog. But it was a real " bear's (*i.e.*, doubtful) service," for her presence in the house kept away the doctor's patients : however, he did not trouble himself about that.

When she got well into her polka, Cleopatra would roar furiously, so that when she danced the whole neighbourhood knew it. On such occasions Sokoloff danced gaily with her.

That evening he was altogether in the mood for dancing. He threw Cleopatra a piece of meat, saying, " Eat it, darling ; they say a hungry bear won't dance, and I want you to dance for me like a princess to-night."

The bear understood, and answered with a growl, which meant " I am ready." The doctor began to sing, beating time on a brass dish :

Dimitra, dear, my fair-haired lass,
Go tell your mother, Dimitra,
You're the only lass I love . . . .

Cleopatra stood up on her hind legs and danced with frenzy, roaring all the time. Suddenly she sprang to the window with an angry growl. The doctor looked out and saw there was some one in the courtyard.

He seized his revolver. " Who's there ? " he asked, forcing the bear to be quiet.

" Doctor, you're wanted at the Konak ! "

" Is that you, Sherif Aga ? What the devil do you want me for now ? Who's ill ? "

" Stop that bear's noise first."

The doctor made a sign to Cleopatra, who retreated unwillingly, and with an ominous growl, into her cellar, the door of which he closed after her.

" My orders are to take you to the Konak. You're a prisoner," said the on-bashi sternly.

" A prisoner ? I ? What for ? "

" You'll find that out soon enough. Come, let's get on." And they went off with the doctor confused and dismayed : he had a presentiment of trouble.

As they went out they heard a heartrending roar from Cleopatra, which sounded almost like human lamentation.

At the Konak all was confusion. They took the doctor to the Bey.

The latter was sitting in his usual place in the corner of the room. By his side sat Kiriak Stefchoff, reading from some paper, at which Necho Pironkoff—the Bulgarian member of the Local Council—was peeping over his shoulder. The Bey, who was about sixty years of age, received the doctor coldly, but offered him a chair. Sokoloff was the Bey's family doctor, and rather a favourite of his. And the Turks usually treated their prisoners with a show of kindness, to induce them to confess.

The doctor, in looking round the room, was astonished to see on the divan the overcoat he had given to Kralich. This discovery redoubled his dismay.

" Doctor, is that coat yours ? " asked the Bey.

The doctor did not dream of denying the fact, which was, indeed, self-apparent. He answered affirmatively.

" Why is it not in your possession ? "

" Because I gave it to a poor man."

" Where ? "

" In the Hajji Shadoff street."

" At what time ? "

" At two o'clock (Turkish time)." *

" Do you know who he was ? "

" No ; but I was sorry for him, because he was in rags."

" How the poor fellow lies ! " said Necho contemptuously.

" Well, that's only natural—a drowning man catches at a straw," replied his neighbour.

The Bey smiled ominously as having detected a manifest lie. He was perfectly certain that the coat had been taken from the doctor's back by the police, as the patrol, indeed, assured him was the case.

" Kiriak Effendi, give me the papers. Do you know these papers ? "

The doctor looked. They were a copy of the newspaper *Nezavisimost* † and a printed revolutionary proclamation. He denied all knowledge of them.

" Then how do they come into the pockets of your coat ? "

" I have already told you that I gave the coat away to some one. Perhaps he put them there."

The Bey shrugged his shoulders. The doctor saw that things were getting serious—at best they made him out to be connected with a revolutionary, as it seems the stranger was. If he had only known that, he would have been more careful, and might have saved them both from trouble.

" Call the wounded Osman," ordered the Bey.

A zaptié came in with his arm bound up above the elbow. It was he who had seized the coat from Kralich's shoulders and at that moment had been wounded by a shot fired by one of his comrades. He was, or pretended to be, fully convinced that it was the fugitive " Koumita " ‡ who had fired at him.

Osman advanced towards the doctor : " That's the man, sir."

" Is that the man from whom you took the coat ? Do you recognise him ? "

" That's the man, and it's he who fired at me."

The doctor looked at him bewildered : he was struck

* *I.e.*, two hours after sunset.

† *Independence*, the organ of the Bulgarian Revolutionary Committee at Bucharest.

‡ The insurgents were by the Turks called " Koumitaji " or simply " Koumita," the nearest approximation to the word " Committee," with which they were supposed to be connected.

dumb by the grave and unfounded charge brought against him.

"The zaptié lies in the most barefaced manner," he said.

"You may go, Osman Aga. Well, sir," added the Bey, in a serious tone, "do you deny all this?"

"The whole thing is a fabrication. I never carry a revolver, and I didn't go through the Petkanchoff Street this evening."

The on-bashi approached the lamp, examined the doctor's revolver which he had taken off his table, and said significantly: "There are four chambers loaded, but one cartridge is missing." The Bey nodded attentively.

"I tell you that's another mistake of yours—I never took my revolver this evening."

" Tell us, doctor, where were you at three o'clock when all this affair happened."

This unexpected question fell like a thunderbolt on Sokoloff. He reddened with confusion, but managed to reply in a confident manner:

"At three o'clock I was at Marko Ivanoff's—his child is ill."

"It was nearly four o'clock when you went in to Marko's —we were just coming out," said the on-bashi, who had met the doctor on his way thither.

The doctor remained silent: appearances against him were too strong. He saw he was in a fix.

"Well, then, tell us where you were from the time you gave away your coat in the Hajji Shadoff Street, until you went to Marko's house," said the Bey, thus skilfully putting a simple question which could only be met with a simple answer. But Dr. Sokoloff did not reply. His face gave signs of a sharp internal struggle, accompanied by moral suffering.

His confusion and silence were clearer than a confession. They completed the other proofs. The Bey was convinced he had the real culprit before him; however, he asked yet once more:

"Tell us where you were at that time, doctor."

"I cannot tell you," said the doctor, in quiet but decisive tones. This answer struck everybody. Necho, the member of Council, winked ironically at Stefchoff, as if to say, "The poor fellow is done for."

" Come, doctor, tell us where were you ? "

" I can't possibly tell you that ; it's a secret which my honour, both as a man and a doctor, forbids me to reveal. But I was not in the Petkanchoff Street," said the doctor, firmly and resolutely.

The Bey pressed him to answer the question, pointing out the dangerous consequences if he should continue to refuse to speak. But the doctor seemed quite calm, like a man who has said all he has to say.

" Won't you say ? "

" I have no more to say."

" Then, sir, you will be my guest to-night. Take the doctor down to the cells," said the Bey, sternly. The doctor went out, bewildered by the crushing accusations which he was not in a position to refute ; for, as he said himself, he could by no possibility reveal the place where he was at three o'clock that evening.

CHAPTER VI : THE LETTER

MARKO slept badly that night. The events of the evening had disturbed his peace of mind. He got up earlier than usual, and when he went to Ganko's for his morning cup of coffee the proprietor had only just taken down his shutters and was lighting his fire. Marko was his first customer.

Café-keepers are great chatterboxes, and Ganko, after the usual obligatory jokes, which he always produced with Marko's morning coffee, at once proceeded to give him an account of the doctor's adventure in the Petkanchoff Street and its consequences, interlarding his story with a number of coarse and silly jests. Ganko told his tale with much excitement. In general the misfortunes of others invariably produce a threefold impression on small minds : first, surprise ; next, an internal satisfaction that the misfortune has happened to some one else ; and thirdly, a secret and malicious joy. Such are the hidden instincts which human nature conceals. As for Ganko, he had even greater cause for wishing evil to the doctor, the latter having once deducted twelve cups of coffee from his score as payment for one professional visit. Ganko had never forgiven him this exorbitant and unheard-of charge.

Marko could not contain himself for surprise. He had conversed with the doctor on the previous evening, and neither his countenance nor his conversation had led him to suspect anything extraordinary. Besides, why should the doctor have concealed such a thing from him ?

The entry of the on-bashi into the café afforded Marko an opportunity for further enlightenment. He saw that the doctor was the victim of some strange blunder on the part of the police, as also that Kralich had escaped from their grasp ; this latter thought gave him much satisfaction. He turned on to the on-bashi : " I will stake my life on the doctor's innocence," said he.

" God grant it," answered the on-bashi ; " but I don't see how he's to prove it."

" He'll prove it, only they may ruin him first. At what time does the Bey come to the Konack ? "

" In about an hour ; he comes early."

" You must release the doctor ; I'll go bail for him : I'll stake my house and my children on it, that he's innocent."

The on-bashi cast a glance of surprise at him.

" There's no need of bail—they've sent him away already."

" When ? Where to ? " cried Marko.

" We sent him off to K. last night, with a police escort."

Marco was unable to conceal his disappointment.

The on-bashi, who had a regard for him, said in a confidential tone : " Marko Chorbaji, if I were you I wouldn't interfere in an ugly business like this. What is it to do with you ? These are times when every one keeps himself to himself."

The on-bashi drank his coffee, and said :

" I must go in half an hour, to take a letter from the Bey inclosing the doctor's revolutionary papers. If you want to know, they're the only proofs against him, and quite enough too. As for the other thing—Osman's wound—that's all a mistake, he didn't fire at him—it was one of us—it's a wound from a rifle-bullet. Well, the bigwigs will see to it. Ganko, give me an old bit of paper to wrap the letter in or it'll get dirty."

So saying, he took from his sash a large envelope with a red seal which he wrapped up in the paper the café-keeper gave him. Then, lighting another cigarette, the on-bashi saluted Marko and went out.

Marko remained for a moment deep in thought. The café-keeper (who was at the same time the town-barber) was already lathering Petko Buzzouniak's head. Marko rose and went out.

"Good-day to you, Marko. You're off very early," cried the barber, dashing the lather about in soapy waves on his victim's head, "so you want to go bail for the doctor! As a man sows, so shall he reap. Why don't they come and haul off Petko Buzzouniak to prison? Eh, Petko, what do you say?"

An inarticulate murmur was heard from among the lather, but it was unintelligible. In a few minutes the barber had shampooed his customer, wiped his head and face dry with a towel of very doubtful cleanliness, handed him the looking-glass, and said, "There you are."

As he was ushering his customer out, Ganko met Marko on the threshold.

"I forgot my tobacco-pouch," said he, and went hurriedly to the seat where he had left it.

Buzzouniak laid his piastre on the looking-glass, and went out. Ganko turned back.

"By-the-by, Ganko, tell me what my account is. I settle up at the end of the month, you know," said Marko.

Ganko pointed to the ceiling which was covered with hieroglyphics in chalk. "There's the ledger," said he; "you've only to reckon it up and pay."

"I don't see my name there."

"That's the way I put 'em down, à la franga." *

"You'll soon have the brokers in, if that's the way you keep your accounts, Ganko," said Marko, chaffingly, as he took out his purse. "Well, if that fellow hasn't left his letter behind!" he added, pointing to the shelf.

"My eyes! the on-bashi's letter," cried Ganko, surprised, and casting a glance of interrogation at Marko, as if to ask what was to be done.

"Send it him—send it him at once," said Marko, hastily —"there you are, twenty-eight piastres and thirty paras— you've taken my last farthing, you rogue." Ganko went out, dumbfounded, thinking "what a curious man Marko is. He's ready to go bail with his house for that bear-trainer and yet he won't throw the letter in the fire—it might have been done in a minute and no one the wiser."

Meanwhile new customers were arriving, and clouds of smoke soon filled the café, whilst conversation was busy with the doctor's mishap.

* *I.e.*, in "Frank" or European fashion.

c

CHAPTER VII : HEROISM

THE sun was already high in the heavens, and its rays lighted up the green vines at the foot of the courtyard of the monastery. The courtyard was now as bright and gay as it had been dark and dreary at night, when every object assumed a ghostly appearance. The merry chirp of birds filled it with joyous sounds : the transparent ripples of the stream murmured pleasantly on their way down the hill ; the leafy cypresses and elms rustled softly to the morning mountain breeze. Everything was clear and peaceful. Even the surrounding verandahs with their dark cells had a more welcome aspect, and rang with the twittering of the swallows as they flew in and out of their nests.

In the courtyard by the vines was a majestic-looking old man, with long white beard reaching to his waist dressed in a long blue gown. This was Father Yeroté, an old man of eighty-five, the relic of a former century, almost a wreck, yet a hale and honourable wreck. He was living out, quietly and simply, the last years of his protracted life. Every morning he would walk there, breathing in the fresh mountain air, and enjoying like a child the sun and the heavens, towards which he was already far on the road.

Close by, against one of the vine-props, as a contrast to this relic of the past, stood Deacon Vikenti, book in hand (he was preparing for his admission to a Russian seminary). His juvenile face beamed with youth and hope : strength and life shone in his eager gaze. He represented the future, towards which he looked with the same confidence as did the old man towards eternity.

It is only the untroubled life of the cloister that can give this restful quiet to the soul.

On the stone steps leading to the Church sat the rotund Father Gedeon, a deeply learned man : he was gazing attentively at the peacocks as they walked about the yard with tails outspread, fan-like. He compared them to the self-satisfied Pharisee in the Gospel, and their screams reminded him of wise King Solomon, who understood the language of birds. Plunged in these pious reflections Father Gedeon was quietly awaiting the grateful sound of the summons to breakfast, as he sniffed the savoury odours proceeding from the refectory kitchen which announced the preparation of the meal.

Mouncho's colleague, the cross-eyed idiot of the monastery, was standing on the threshold in the sun. He was examining with an attention no less profoundly philosophical the domestic habits of the peacocks—indeed, to say this scarcely gives the true state of the case, for the glance of the idiot embraced not only the peacocks, but also the entire horizon ; since while one eye pointed due west, the other took in at the same time the east.

Erect beside him, Mouncho was clasping his hands, while with head upturned he anxiously scanned the windows on the top-story, for reasons known only to himself.

If we add the higoumen, who was out, and some few lay-assistants, we have before us the whole population of the monastery.

Just then the higoumen trotted up on his horse, dismounted, and handed the reins to the cross-eyed brother, saying as he did so to Vikenti : " I have come from town, and bring bad news."

Thereupon he told them the story of Sokoloff's mishap : ' Poor Sokoloff, poor Sokoloff ! " he sighed.

The higoumen Natanael was a tall, powerful man, with a virile face and a bold, dashing manner. Remove his monk's garb, and little of the monk remained in him. The walls of his cell were hung with guns ; he was a first-rate shot, swore like a trooper, and was as skilled in healing wounds as he was in dealing them. Chance had made him the higoumen of a monastery instead of a voivode in the Balkans. Moreover, rumour had it that he had once been the latter, but was now repentant.

" Where is Father Gedeon," asked the higoumen, looking round.

" Here am I," answered Father Gedeon, in a shrill voice, emerging from the monastery whither he had gone to see if breakfast would soon be ready.

" In the kitchen again, Father Gedeon : don't you know that gluttony is a deadly sin ? " So saying, the abbot enjoined him to fasten the saddle-bags on the donkey, and proceed to the village of Voinyagovo, to inspect the hay makers who were mowing the monastery's fields.

Father Gedeon was round, bloated, and puffy as a sheep's bladder when blown out. The slight movement he had made in coming to the door had brought the dew of suffering to his forehead.

" Father Higoumen," he murmured in tones of agonised entreaty, clasping his hands before him, and appalled at the idea of a journey in this sinful world ; " Father Higoumen, were it not better to remove this bitter cup from the lips of your lowly brother ? "

" What bitter cup, man ? Do you mean my sending you to the mowers ? Why, you're going to ride the donkey, and as for the labour, all you've to do is to hold the reins with one hand and give your benediction with the other," said the higoumen, smiling.

" Father Natanael, it isn't for the labour ; we come into the world for a life of labour and suffering. But the times are evil."

" Evil ? In May ? Why, the trip will do you good."

" The times, father, the times," murmured Father Gedeon. " You see they have taken the doctor, and may send the Christian to destruction. The race of Hagar is merciless. God forbid, if they accuse me of stirring up the people to revolt, the whole monastery may suffer. The peril is imminent."

The higoumen burst out laughing.

" Ha ! ha ! ha ! " he cried, in uncontrollable mirth, with arms akimbo, as he looked at the rotund form of Father Gedeon. " And do you think the Turks will suspect *you !* Father Gedeon a political emissary ! Ha ! ha ! is it not written, ' thou shalt make the sluggard to work, that he may learn wisdom.' Your besetting sin of idleness has made me laugh when I was but little disposed to do so. Deacon Vikenti ! Deacon Vikenti ! Come and listen to Father Gedeon. Mouncho, go and call Vikenti ; I want to make him laugh."

In truth, the boisterous merriment of the higoumen made the walls ring again.

When he heard the order, Mouncho shook his head still more strangely, his eyes staring with terror.

" The Russian ! " he cried, trembling, and pointed to the staircase up which the deacon had gone. And to avoid the errand, he fled hurriedly to the opposite side of the quadrangle.

" Russian ! What does he mean by that ? "

" He means the ghost, your reverence," said Father Gedeon.

" And how long is it since Mouncho has become such a

coward ? Why, he used to live all alone, like an owl in the wilderness."

" Of a truth, father, a spirit walks nightly on the verandah. Last night Mouncho came to my cell in a paroxysm of terror. He had seen a ghost in white garments coming out of the cell with the windows. He also told me of other things, from which may the Lord deliver us. We must sprinkle the top story with holy water."

Mouncho had stopped some distance off, and was staring terrified, at the top story.

"What can he have seen ? Come, father, let's inspect the premises," said the higoumen, who fancied that perhaps a thief might have concealed himself there.

" The Lord forbid," said Gedeon, crossing himself. The higoumen went upstairs alone.

In truth, when the higoumen called the deacon, the latter had gone to Kralich's cell.

" What's the news, father ? "asked the latter, seeing his disturbed countenance.

" There's no danger," said the deacon at once reassuringly, " but the higoumen has brought very bad news. Last night Sokoloff was arrested and carried off to K."

" Who is this Sokoloff ? "

" He's a doctor in the town—a very decent youth. It seems they found revolutionary books or papers on him. I know him to be a fervent patriot," said the deacon, sorrowfully ; then, after a moment's pause, he added, " When the police were pursuing him last night he fired and wounded a zaptié, who had laid hold of his overcoat. Poor doctor ! I'm afraid he's done for. Thank God, you got off safe, and nothing seems to have been heard of you in town."

As the deacon stopped talking, he observed with surprise that Kralich had taken his head between his hands, and was pacing up and down the room like a madman, sighing deeply. These signs of a despair, as inexplicable as it was sudden, greatly astonished the deacon.

" Why, what's the matter, man ? Thank God, you're all right," cried Vikenti.

Kralich stopped in front of him, with a face distorted by moral suffering, and exclaimed almost angrily :

" All right ! all right, am I ? That's easily said ! " and he struck his forehead. " What are you thinking of,

Vikenti ?   Don't you understand ?   My God !   I forgot to
tell you that the overcoat was mine.   Last night, at the
outskirts of the town, some kind young man, who showed
me Marko's house—evidently this Dr. Sokoloff—gave it to
me, seeing what a state I was in, and that's the coat I left
in the zaptié's hands.   I took some papers out of an inner
pocket and put them in the pocket of the coat : they were a
copy of the *Nezavisimost* and a proclamation which they
gave me in a hut at Troyan, where I spent the night.   That's
not enough, but they must go and say he fired at a zaptié,
when I never touched the revolver !   Ah ! the scoundrels !
Now do you see ?   that man has sacrificed himself for me !
It is my accursed fate to bring misfortune on all those who do
good to me ! "

"It's a great misfortune," said Vikenti, pityingly ;
" especially since you can't help him, as matters stand."

Kralich turned on him with a burning countenance.

" What do you mean, I can't help him ?   Am I to leave
a generous benefactor, and, as you say, a fervent patriot,
to perish on my account ?   That would be baseness
indeed ! "

The deacon looked at him bewildered.

" No, I shall rescue him from this mishap, even if it
costs me my life ? "

" How ! what's to be done ?   tell me : I am ready to do
anything," cried Vikenti.

' I alone will save him ! "

" You ! "

" Yes, I ; I'll rescue him.   I am the only one who is
able and bound to rescue him," cried Kralich, excitedly, as
he paced up and down the cell, with an expression of
utmost decision and courage.

" Are we to make an assault on the prison ? " asked
Vikenti, who was lost in astonishment and half afraid lest
Kralich had taken leave of his senses.

" Mr. Kralich," he continued, " how do you mean to save
him ? "

" What !   don't you understand ?   I shall give myself
up ! "

" You—give yourself up ?—alone ? "

" Do you think I should entreat them to release him ?
Listen, Father Vikenti !   I'm an honest man, and I won't
owe my life to the sufferings of others.   I haven't come

1500 miles to commit an act of baseness. If I can't sacrifice my life nobly, at least I can do so honourably. Do you understand ? Unless I give myself up to the Turks this very day, and say ' this man is innocent—I have never had any dealings with him—the coat was taken from my back— the papers are mine—I'm the culprit—I'm guilty—if you like, I fired at the zaptié—do what you please to me '— unless I do this, Dr. Sokoloff is lost—especially as he was unable or unwilling to say where he was ? Tell me, can I do otherwise ? "

The deacon was silent. In his heart he recognised, as an honest man, that Kralich was right. This self-sacrifice was imposed on him by feelings of justice and humanity, and he could not wait for others to point out to him the course he should take. The man seemed to him to become greater and more dignified in his eyes. His figure assumed that calm, noble, heavenly brightness with which only a great and sudden flash of valour can inspire the human countenance. Kralich's earnest, simple, and ringing words echoed in his ears with a soft and majestic sound. He would have liked to be in his place, to say such words— ay, and carry them out. His eyes filled with tears.

" Show me the way to K.," said Kralich. Suddenly the great bearded head of the higoumen appeared at the window; they had not heard his footsteps in the heat of their discussion. Kralich started, and glanced inquiringly at the deacon.

Vikenti hurriedly pointed to the door, took the higoumen aside to the corridor, and whispered to him long and passionately, with excited gestures, and side-glances at the cell where Kralich was waiting impatiently. When the door opened and Vikenti and Natanael returned, Kralich advanced towards the higoumen and sought to kiss his hand.

" No, no, I'm not worthy that you should kiss my hand," cried the higoumen, in tears ; and placing both arms round his neck, he kissed his lips affectionately, as a father kisses a beloved and long-absent son.

CHAPTER VIII : AT CHORBAJI YORDAN'S

There was a great family gathering that day at Chorbaji Yordan's, given in accordance with the old Bulgarian custom, in honour of a recent wedding in the family. All his relations and the friends of the family had been invited.

Yordan Diamandieff was now an old man, somewhat feeble, of a morose and nervous disposition : he belonged to that section of the Bulgarian *bourgeoisie*—the Chorbajis— who have done so much to make the whole class odious. His wealth went on increasing, his numerous family flourished, and he was universally feared, but no one liked him. Certain old stories of iniquitous acts of oppression and wrong, in which the poor had suffered and the conniv- ance of the Turks been obtained by fawning, flattery, or still worse means, kept up his unpopularity, even now that he was unable or unwilling to injure any one. He belonged entirely to the past generation.

The only acts of oppression he now permitted himself to carry on were exercised at the cost of the school- teachers—or of such as refused to bow before his will. The wolf may change his skin, but not his teeth, says the proverb.

In spite of Yordan's surly disposition, the meal was a merry one. Mother Ghinka, his married daughter still fairly good-looking, loquacious, quick at repartee, and very lively, who did not scruple to box the ears of her thoroughly subdued husband whenever necessary, kept the guests in fits of laughter by the jests and stories which her indefatig- able tongue scattered hither and thither. Those who enjoyed her wit most were the three nuns. One of these, Sister Hajji * Rovoama, Yordan's sister, who was lame, malicious, and a thorough mischief-maker, was no less talkative than Ghinka, and had many a bitter jest at the ex- pense of absent friends. Hajji Simeon, the host's son-in-law, laughed loudly with his mouth full ; Hajji Pavli, the lately married bridegroom, carried away by his mirth, was eating with the spoon of Alafranga Mikhalaki, who, annoyed at this inadvertence, cast reproving glances round him Mikhalaki bore the well-deserved nickname of " Alafranga," because thirty years ago he had been the first in the town to wear European trousers and stammer a few words of French. Unfortunately his efforts had stopped short there. The coat he wore to-day was of the fashion prevailing at the time of the Crimean War, and his slender French vocabu- lary had not received a single addition. But his renown

* The word " Hajji " implies that the person to whose name it is prefixed, whether Christian or Mussulman, has performed the pilgrimage to Jerusalem or Mecca respectively,

as a man of learning, and with it his flattering nickname, had come down to the present day. Mikhalaki fully realised his own importance, and was very proud of it ; he was stiff in manner, spoke with a pompous air, and would allow no one to call him simply Mikhal, so as to avoid being taken for the policeman, who also rejoiced in that name. Indeed, Mikalaki was very susceptible with respect to names. He had had a feud of many years' standing with his neighbour, Ivancho Yotata, because the latter had twice in one evening mispronounced his name, in his usual blundering fashion.

Opposite Alafranga sat Damiancho Grigoroff, a man of fifty years of age, of moderate height, thin, dark, with a look of intense cunning, and thin mobile lips of ironical expression, but with an extremely serious countenance ; he also had a reputation for wisdom, but of an entirely different kind from Alafranga's. He was a loquacious and fluent story-teller, of inexhaustible resource, as deep as a well, and with a very powerful imagination, rich as the treasury of Halim Aga : with him a drop became an ocean, and a molehill a mountain—indeed, he would often begin by inventing the molehill. The most remarkable feature was that he believed his own stories—the surest means of making others believe them. In other respects, Damiancho was one of the principal tradesmen, a patriot, and a man of sage counsels.

Mother Ghinka's husband was eating his dinner in a subdued manner, for he knew that if he ventured to say anything his wife would at once transfix him with a look of piercing severity, so that he dared not open his mouth before her. He was a weak man of no character, and was of so little account that instead of his wife being called Ghinka Ghenkova, after him, he was known as Ghinka's Ghenko. By his side Necho Pironkoff, the member of Council, sat whispering with an air of importance to Kiriak Stefchoff, who was dressed in the height of fashion, and nodded now and then absently in response without noticing what his neighbour was saying, his attention being taken up by Yordan's daughter, Lalka, on whom he kept casting admiring glances. But his inattention did not go unpunished, for Necho raised his glass to clink it against his, and meeting no response the wine was spilt over Stefchoff's white trousers.

This youth, whom we have already met at the Bey's, and who will reappear in the course of our story, belonged by birth and breeding to the Chorbaji class : he was the son of a man of the same stamp as Yordan Diamandieff. He was young, but his ideas were old-fashioned : the new and absorbing current of liberal thought had left him untouched. It was, perhaps, for this reason that the Turks viewed him with favour—this, however, made him unpopular with the younger men, who considered him as a Turkish spy. And his unpopularity was heightened by his haughty, spiteful character, and his deceitful and cowardly nature. In spite of this, however—or, perhaps, on that very account—Chorbaji Yordan had a weakness for Stefchoff which he did not seek to conceal. Hence rumour had, rightly or wrongly, fixed on him as Yordan's future son-in-law.

Dinner was over and coffee was served by a tall, slender, dark-eyed girl, dressed in black, to whom no one paid any attention. The conversation went on briskly, for Ghinka was anxious to amuse the guests with her inexhaustible verbosity and wit. Soon the topic of the day—Sokoloff's arrest—came on the *tapis*. This subject at once attracted the general notice, and gave a new and agreeable impulse to the after-dinner chat.

" I wonder what's become of the doctoress ? " sneered Mother Seraphina.

" What doctoress ? " asked the bride.

" Why, Cleopatra, of course."

" We must go and call on her, and get her to write to him —he must be fretting after her," said Mother Ghinka.

" Mikhalaki," asked the bride, turning to Alafranga, " what kind of a word is Cleopatra ? Mother Kouna can't pronounce it at all."

Mikhalaki frowned, remained for a moment deep in thought, and then delivered himself pompously : " Cleopatra is a Hellenic—that is to say, Greek word. It comes from ελαίω, I weep for, and . . . I weep for . . ."

" I weep for the doctor," laughed Hajji Simeon, fumbling in his pockets.

" Well, well, what signifies a name ? " said Sister Hajji Kovoama ; " there's some one else, though, weeping for the doctor as well." So saying, she bent towards Mrs. Hajji Simeon and another lady, and whispered something. The three laughed slily. The laughter spread to all the guests.

" What do you mean, Ghinka ?   The Bey's wife ? " asked Machovitsa, astounded.

" Mind your own business—the wolf eats the heifer in the stall sometimes," said Mother Ghinka.

And they all laughed at this sally.

" Kiriak, what were the papers they found on Sokoloff ? " asked Yordan, who did not understand what they were all laughing at.

" Rank treason from beginning to end.   The Bey sent for me at midnight to translate them for him.   Such wild, insensate rubbish, as only lunatics can invent.   Another of these proclamations from the Bucharest Committee, calling on us to rise and put the country to fire and sword, so that it may be freed."

" Get yourselves massacred, all of you, so that we may be freed," sneered Necho Pironkoff.

" These scoundrels are ready enough to put the place to fire and sword—why not ?   It's not their property they want to destroy.   They haven't a foot of ground, or a stick, in the place.   It's easy for them to talk—a set of ruffians ! " said Chorbaji Yordan, angrily.

" Thieves, the whole lot of them ! " muttered Hajji Simeon.

Damiancho Grigoroff, who had been impatiently awaiting his opportunity for introducing one of his stories, caught at Simeon's last words, and began :

" You say they're thieves, Hajji : that reminds me of a story—but there are thieves and thieves.   I was once going to Ishtip in Macedonia—it was in 1863, in this very month of May, on the 22nd, at three o'clock, after sunset on a Saturday, and a cloudy night."   With which Damiancho proceeded to relate an interminable story of an encounter with brigands, in which there figured the Ishtip innkeeper, two Pashas, a Greek captain, and the sister of Prince Couza of Wallachia.

Everybody listened with the utmost attention, if not with perfect faith, to the absorbing story told by Damiancho, while they sipped their coffee with much satisfaction.

" Dear, dear—they talk of fire and sword—they'll be burning our convent down next," said Sister Serafima.

" May the fire of heaven consume them," murmured Sister Hajji Rovoama.

" Just think of it," said Stefchoff, " the very dissemination of such stuff is high treason. It's that which perverts the minds of the youngsters, and either makes idle dreamers of them or else brings them to the gallows ! Look at Sokoloff —there's a sad case ! "

" Ay—a sad case ! " acquiesced Hajji Simeon.

Mikhalaki Alafranga added :

" Only yesterday I had a conversation with the doctor, and it was easy to see what his ideas are. He was regretting that we hadn't got a Lioubobratich ! " *

: " What did you answer ? "

" I answered that there might be no Lioubobratiches, but that gallows were plentiful enough."

" And a very good answer too," said Yordan.

" Whoever are them Lioubobratiches ? " asked the inquisitive bride.

Ghenko Ghinkin, who was a regular reader of the *Pravo* and well-posted in politics, was just going to answer, when he was quelled by a glance from his wife, who replied :

" He's the leader of the rebels in Herzegovina, Dona dear. Ah ! if we had a man like him, I'd volunteer to be his standard-bearer myself—and then we'd go and cut cabbages ! " †

" Ah ! if we had a man like him—that would be another matter altogether—I'd join under his command too," said Hajji Simeon.

Yordan cast a stern glance at them. " What's that you're saying ? such things are not even to be jested about. As for you, Hajji, you're talking nonsense." Then turning to Alafranga, " What will become of the doctor ? "

" The law," answered Stefchoff, with a look of triumph, " punishes an assault on a servant of the State by death, or Diarbekir for life."

" Serve him right," grunted Hajji Rovoama ; " what harm has the convent done to him that he should want to set fire to it ? "

" Well, he's brought it on himself," said Necho, the member. " Last night's thunderstorm struck some one, anyhow."

" Talking of thunderstorms reminds me that about the

* Lioubobratich was the heroic leader of the Herzegovinian revolt of 1875.

† An allusion to the green turbans worn by Turks claiming descent from Mohammed,

time of the Crimean War, Ivan Boshnakoff and I were on our way to Bosnia. I can call it to mind as if it was yesterday : it wanted only a day or two to the feast of St. Nikola. We were snowed up at Pirot, when there was the most tremendous thunderstorm I ever saw." And Grigoroff began to explain how the bolts had fallen round them, set fire to a walnut tree, killed fifty sheep, and cut off his horse's tail, which he had to sell afterwards at a very low figure in consequence.

Grigoroff told his story with such sincerity and eloquence that his audience listened with unflagging attention to the very end. Stefchoff and Necho, the member, smiled at one another. Mikhalaki sat stiff and pompous as ever, and Hajji Simeon was struck dumb by the extraordinary fierceness of Damiancho's thunderstorm in mid-winter.

While Damiancho was still busy with his story, Mother Ghinka began looking round for Lalka. "Rada, what has become of Lalka ? Go and call her at once," said Hajji Rovoama in an authoritative tone to the young girl in black.

Lalka, on hearing Stefchoff's words as to the probable fate of the doctor, spoken with such ferocious calmness, had quietly withdrawn to her own room : there she had flung herself on the divan, and lay sobbing piteously. A flood of tears, long pent up, poured from her eyes. As she lay, the poor girl shook with the violence of her sobs and was powerless to restrain herself. Her face reflected her passionate grief and the torture she was undergoing. Her whole soul revolted at the cruelty with which these people gloated over the doctor's misfortune. " My God—my God—have they no pity ? " she thought.

But tears can soften even the most desperate sorrow ; and the doctor's fate being yet unknown, there was at least still ground for hope.

Lalka rose, dried her pretty pale face, and sat by the open window for the fresh air to remove the traces of her tears. She looked out listlessly on the unheeding passers-by in the street, but all was a blank to her. For her this cruel world did not exist : she wished to see only one face, to hear only one voice—they were all the world to her.

Suddenly the rapid trot of a horse attracted her attention. She looked up and could not believe her eyes. There was

Doctor Sokoloff galloping gaily back on a white horse. He bowed politely to her as he passed under her window. In her delight, she never thought of answering his bow, but rushed, as if impelled by an irresistible force, into the guest-chamber, and cried joyfully :

" Doctor Sokoloff is back again ! "

A feeling of astonishment and displeasure was depicted on the faces of most of those present. Hajji Rovoama clenched her teeth viciously, and Stefchoff grew pale, as he said with an air of indifference :

" They've probably remanded him for further inquiry. He won't escape Diarbekir, or else the gallows so easily."

At that moment he encountered the contemptuous glance of Rada, which wounded him so deeply that his face flamed with mortification and anger.

"No, no, Kiriak. I hope the poor fellow will get off, when I think how young he is," said Ghinka, feelingly.

Her previous jests at the doctor had been from the lips merely ; but her heart was sound. The bright spark of humanity can always be struck from the heart by the blows of suffering, if only it be there to begin with.

To Hajji Simeon's honour, also, be it said, that he was equally delighted at the doctor's escape, but dared not say so before Yordan.

CHAPTER IX : EXPLANATIONS

THE doctor was no sooner at home than he went out again, passed rapidly by Ganko's café, where many greeted him with a " Glad to see you back, doctor "—the heartiest welcome being Ganko's—and proceeded straight to Marko's house. On his way he espied Stefchoff on the other side of the road, coming out of Yordan's house.

" My best respects, Terjuman * Effendi," cried the doctor with a contemptuous smile.

Marko, who had finished dinner, was taking his coffee on the bench beneath the ivy.

He was overjoyed at seeing the doctor. After various greetings, Sokoloff said : " Listen, Marko, while I tell you something that will make you laugh."

" How did it all go, my lad ? "

" That's what I can't make out myself. It seems to me

* Dragoman, or Interpreter.

like a fairy tale—I can't believe it all. Here am I arrested at night, the moment I had got home after leaving you, and taken off to the Konak. You've heard all about my examination and the charges they brought against me. Who would have thought my poor old coat would raise such a bother. Well, I was locked up. An hour afterwards, in come two zaptiés. 'Doctor, up you get!' 'What for?' 'You're to be taken to K——; it's the Bey's orders.' 'Very well.' So we start, one zaptié in front of me, another behind, with loaded rifles. We got to K—— at dawn. There they locked me up again, as it was too early for the Court to sit. Four mortal hours I waited in prison—they seemed to me like four years. Finally I was taken before the Court. There were several Members of the Council and other notables, and they read out a protocol of some kind, of which I didn't understand one single word. More silly questions about my unfortunate coat, which was lying on a green table and seemed to be eyeing me piteously. The judge opened a letter—evidently from our Bey—took some papers out of it, and asked me, 'Are these your papers?' 'I know nothing about them.' 'Then how did they get into your pocket?' 'They were not put there by me.' He went on reading the letter. The Bulgarian member, Tinko Balta Oghlou, takes up the newspaper and examines it. 'Beg pardon, your worship,' says he to the judge; 'there's nothing wrong in this newspaper, it's printed at Constantinople.' And he cast a smile at me as he said it. I couldn't understand what he meant, and stood like a log of wood. The Kadi asks, 'Isn't that the newspaper issued by the Revolutionary Committee in Roumania?' 'No, your worship,' answers Balta Oghlou; 'this paper doesn't treat of politics—it's a religious * paper, published by the Protestant missionaries.' I couldn't trust my own eyes! It was the *Zornitsa*. Tinko Balta Oghlou takes the proclamation, glances at it, looks at me, and smiles again. 'There's nothing seditious in this either, your worship; it's a prospectus!'—and he began to read aloud: 'Try Doctor Ivan Bogoroff's patent medicines.' The Kadi looked at him in astonishment; every one began to laugh; even the Kadi smiled; as for me I roared—who could have helped laughing? How in the world did this miraculous transfor-

* The *Zornitsa*, the Bulgarian organ of the American Missionaries, published at Constantinople since 1858.

mation takes place ? That's more than I can tell. Anyhow after a short discussion with the Court the Kadi turned
to me and said, ' Doctor, there's some mistake. I am
sorry you've been put to inconvenience ' (he calls several
hours spent in prison and being dragged at night from
one Konak to another an inconvenience !) ; ' if you can
find bail I'll let you go at once.' There I stood utterly
bewildered."

" But how about the wounded zaptié ? "

" They didn't say a word about him. As far as I can
make out our Bey, either by himself or at some one else's
suggestion, has found out there was some mistake, and
must have put in his letter that he didn't consider I was
guilty of that. Perhaps the zaptié himself admitted he was
lying."

Marko beamed with satisfaction. He thought that old
Manola's son really had fired, and was anxious about the
consequences.

" Well, thank God, you're free now."

" Yes, as you see. But wait a bit—there's something
yet stranger to come," said the doctor, looking carefully
round to assure himself that none of the family were within
hearing. ' Chorbaji Nikolcho lent me his horse to come
home with ; he also went bail for me. Well, as I was coming
out of the town, just by the Jewish cemetery, I noticed two
people coming towards me from the Balkan. One of them
was Deacon Vikenti, and he called out to me to stop.
' Where are you bound for, doctor ? ' he cried, surprised at
seeing me at liberty. ' I'm going home,' I said ; ' there was
nothing the matter.' You should have seen him open his
eyes ! I told him the whole story. Suddenly he throws his
arms round my neck, and begins to kiss and hug me. ' Why,
what's all this, deacon ? ' says I. ' I must introduce
you to—to Mr. Boicho Ognianoff,' says he, taking me to
his companion. I looked at him. What do you think ?
It was the man to whom I had given my coat the night
before ! "

" What—old Manola's son ? " cried Marko involuntarily.

" Why—do you know him too ? " asked the doctor
astounded.

Marko shrank back. " Go on—we'll see," said he.

" Well, we shook hands and made friends. He thanked
me for my coat and begged my pardon most humbly.

' Don't mention it, Mr. Ognianoff,' I said, ' I never like to talk about any little thing I may do for anybody. But where are you going to, if I may ask ? ' ' Mr. Ognianoff was going to look for you,' answered Vikenti. ' For me ? ' ' Yes, he wanted to rescue you ! ' ' To rescue me ? ' ' Yes,' by giving himself up to the authorities and confessing that he alone was guilty.' ' Do you mean to say that that's why you came here ? Ah, Mr. Ognianoff, what were you intending to do ? ' I asked, almost angrily. ' My duty,' he replied simply. Well, I couldn't help it. I burst out crying and put my arms round his neck, as if he had been my brother, there, in the middle of the road. There's a noble nature for you, Marko—there's real chivalry. That's the kind of man Bulgaria requires."

Marko made no reply. Two tears flowed slowly down his cheeks. He was proud for old Manola's sake.

The doctor remained silent a moment, then went on again. " We separated—they struck back across the fields, and I came straight on ; but I am still upset by the meeting, and especially by the changing of the papers. I tell you I saw with my own eyes the *Nezavisimost*, and the proclamation. How can they turn into the *Zornitsa* and Bogoroff's prospectus ? Who changed them ? Was it a mistake of the Bey's ? I've been puzzling over it for hours. What do you think of it, Marko ? "

And the doctor clasped his hands and awaited the reply.

Marko puffed at his chibouk thoughtfully, and then said, with an uncontrollable smile on his lips :

" Don't you understand that some friend must have done it ? How can it be a mistake ? Do you suppose the *Zornitsa* and Bogoroff's advertisements are likely to be found at the Bey's ? "

" But who is the unknown benefactor who has saved me from peril, and Ognianoff from certain death ? Help me to find him—I must thank him—I must kiss his hands and his feet."

Marko turned to the doctor, and said to him, in a low tone :

" Doctor—listen. You must never breathe a word of what I am going to tell you as long as you live."

" I give you my word of honour."

" It was I who changed the papers."

" You, Marko," exclaimed the doctor, with a start.

D

" Sit down, and listen quietly. This morning, very early, I went to Ganko's café, and it was from him that I heard you were arrested : this astonished and grieved me very much. As luck would have it, in came the on-bashi and told me you had been sent during the night to K——, and that he was just going there too with the Bey's letter in which the fatal papers were enclosed. I didn't know what was to be done. The on-bashi stayed for some time, and then went out. Well, to my surprise, I noticed he'd left his letter behind. Ganko was busy shaving some one. It came into my head to take the letter and destroy it, but that wouldn't have helped you much—the suspicion would always have remained. What was to be done ? There was no time to think. Well, something occurred to me which I'd never even thought of all my life. See here, doctor ; I've grown grey in business, but I never yet opened a letter belonging to any one else before : I've always considered it the most dishonourable thing a man can do. God forgive me, but I did it this morning, for the first and last time. I rushed home, locked myself in the office, unfastened the red seal on the letter carefully, and put in the first two papers that came to hand—you know the Turks are not over sharp in these matters. Then I brought back the letter and left it in the place where I'd found it, without the café-keeper noticing me. Thank God, the thing came off all right—my conscience is easier now."

The doctor listened, gasping, and then said with emotion :

" Marko, my gratitude to you is eternal. What you call dishonourable is noble—it's glorious. You have saved two lives from destruction at the risk of your own. There are few fathers who would do as much for their children."

The doctor's emotion would not let him continue.

Marko added : " Last night old Manola's son did come to see me, but he climbed over the wall, and that made all the noise and brought the police."

" What, Boïcho Ognianoff ? "

" Is that what you call him ? Yes, yes, that's the man. His father's a great friend of mine ; and he, poor fellow, not knowing any one else, came to me for shelter : it was you who directed him here. I didn't want to tell you this before Ivancho ; but he ran away the moment the police came."

"Where was he coming from ? " asked the doctor completely overcome by these successive revelations.

" Didn't he tell you ?   From Diarbekir."

" From Diarbekir ! "

" Not so loud—and where is he now ? "

" He's at the monastery, where the deacon has undertaken to keep him hidden. I'm to go and see him there. Will you let me tell him—only him—what you've just told me ? He ought to know who it is to whom he owes his life, for he would certainly have given himself up if they hadn't released me."

" No, no ; you've given me your word ; you're never to reveal it—on the contrary, try to forget it. I only told you as a kind of confession, to relieve my own conscience. As for old Manola's son, you can give him my best wishes, and say I shall be glad to see him here—only let him come in by the front door next time."

CHAPTER X : THE NUNNERY

THE women's convent at Bela Cherkva * (white church) was the complete antithesis of the monastery already described as being entombed in the rocks of the Balkan and eternally silent and deserted.

Here, on the contrary, were sixty or seventy sisters, young and old, gadding about all day in the quadrangle and galleries, and filling with mirthful sounds the broad enclosure which was the barrier between them and the vanities of this sinful world. They were perpetually on the move from morning till night.

The convent had the reputation of being the most fertile hotbed of scandal in the whole city. It was the cradle of every bit of tittle-tattle which made the round of and scandalised the hearths of the erring laity of the town : it was there that betrothals were whispered of and prepared ; and, sometimes, impending marriages broken off too. From thence innocent little tales would set out on their way round the town, and return, well and hearty, but magnified a hundredfold, or else completely metamorphosed ; naturally such a centre of gossip attracted troops of lay-friends, especially on feast-days, when these were regaled by the holy Sisters with stories of the town and morella-cherry preserves.

* Better known under the name of Sopot, a little town about two miles from Karlovo, which is probably the town alluded to as " K " throughout the work.

Sister Hajji Rovoama, whose acquaintance we have already made at her brother Yordan's, was renowned as the most skilful pryer into all the secrets of the town, and the most inveterate scandal-monger in it. She had at one time been the abbess—but a revolution in the little state had deposed her—none the less was she still, morally, the moving spirit of the community. Her advice was appealed to in every matter. She vouched for the accuracy of truthful rumours and exposed the incorrect : she had the prerogative of starting fresh tales, which afforded mental pabulum for the little republic for some days, after which they spread beyond the confines of the cloister.

Sister Hajji Rovoama had been for some days enraged at the liberation of Dr. Sokoloff, the sworn foe of the convent. She cherished her malice in secret, asking herself who could possibly have come to his assistance ? Who could it have been who had robbed her of the satisfaction of listening to and inventing every day new stories as to his fate ? The thing was disgraceful. Indeed, so much did she fret about it that for the last four or five nights she had not had a wink of sleep. She was continually cudgelling her brains to discover firstly, why the Doctor had refused to tell the Bey where he had been at three o'clock on the eventful night of his arrest ; and, secondly, who had changed the papers. At last a brilliant idea flashed across her mind at the very moment when she was saying her prayers before going to bed. She clapped her hands for joy, like Archimedes when he discovered his great law of physics. She went straight to Sister Serafima, whom she found already undressed, and said in a voice that shook with excitement :

"Sister, do you know where the doctor was that night, when he refused to tell the Bey ? "

Sister Serafima pricked up her ears.

"He was with the Bey's wife, my dear."

"Do you think so, Hajji ? "

"Of course, Serafima—else why shouldn't he say so ? Is he mad ? Holy Virgin ! and to think that I've only just found it out ! " said Hajji Rovoama, crossing herself before the eikonostasis. "And do you know who released the doctor ? "

"Who, Sister ? " asked Serafima.

"Why, she did, of course—the Bey's wife."

"Really—you don't mean it ! "

" My God ! Holy Virgin ! what *can* I have been thinking about all this time ? " And, having relieved her excited feelings, Sister Hajji Rovoama went off, finished her prayers, and slept with the clear conscience of one who has done her duty.

Next morning the whole convent was acquainted with the secret. The history of the doctor and the Bey's wife grew and assumed alarming proportions.

Each Sister, as she heard it, asked :

" Who told you so ? "

" Why, Sister Hajji Rovoama."

The name disarmed the most sceptical : every one rushed to Hajji Rovoama for a detailed account.

In two hours the story had spread all over the town.

But every scandal, however interesting, grows stale in three days. Society was beginning to yawn and to clamour for more gossip. The appearance in the town of Kralich, whom hardly any one knew, was a godsend to the convent, which was at once busy with him. Who is he ? Where does he come from ? What is his business ? No one could answer these questions, though the most curious tales were current respecting him : but the only point in which these agreed was his name ; in all other particulars they were of the most contradictory nature.

Sister Sofia alleged that he had come there for his health.

Sister Ripsimia averred that he was a dealer in attar of roses.*

Sister Nimfidora was sure he had come after an engagement as schoolmaster.

Sister Solomona and Sister Parashkeva asserted that neither of these reports was correct ; that he had come there to look out for a wife ; and that, as a matter of fact, they knew on whom his choice had fallen.

Sister Apraxia was ready to swear that he was a Russian prince in disguise, who had come to inspect the old fortress and distribute funds for their church. But less faith was attached to what Sister Apraxia said, because she was not on visiting terms with the best houses, but drew her information from the wife of Petko Buzzouniak or Fachko Dobiche's family.

Sister Hajji Rovoama listened to all these confident

* The scene where the story is laid is in the heart of the " Valley of Roses," where the famous attar is produced.

assertions, and smiled behind her moustachios (of which Nature had been very prodigal to her). She knew all about it, but wanted to enjoy the efforts of the Sisters to find out the truth. The oracle declared itself only late at night.

The next morning the whole convent knew that the stranger Ognianoff was a Turkish spy.

One of the chief reasons—perhaps the only one—why Hajji Rovoama launched this unflattering rumour touching Ognianoff was the fact that he had not yet paid his respects to her : this was a mortal affront to her vanity, which gained for Ognianoff a relentless enemy.

It was Sunday. Service was nearly over in the convent chapel, which was thronged with worshippers. Crowds stood outside under the chapel windows, beneath the spreading branches of the great pear tree. Most of these were young girls or married women from the town, all decked with flowers and arrayed in their brightest Sunday frocks, like dolls. They prattled merrily together, turning from time to time to the door to inspect the Sunday dresses of the other representatives of the fair sex who were continually flocking into the convent. The rest were nuns, mostly young, who were engaged, with no less merriment, in looking about them, giggling and laughing perpetually. From time to time they would rush forward in swarms to pick up the ripe golden pears as they fell from the tree, and occasionally a battle royal would ensue for the possession of the fruit, after which they would return heated and flushed to the rest of the worshippers, crossing themselves.

Service was over. A stream of people emerged from the chapel and flowed into the cells.

Hajji Rovoama's cell, though somewhat richly furnished, was small and could scarcely contain her guests. The nun received them with a gratified smile, whilst Rada, in a clean black frock and hood, went round serving preserves and coffee on a red tray. After an hour the stream began to decrease. Hajji Rovoama rose frequently to look from the window, as if she expected some special visitor. Soon a fresh batch came in, among whom was Alafranga, Stefchoff, Pope Stavri, Necho Pironkoff, and a young schoolmaster. Evidently it was these whom she was expecting. She gave a friendly greeting to her new visitors, who all shook hands also with Rada ; Stefchoff, indeed, gave her hand a prolonged pressure, accompanied with a wink ; this threw the girl into a state of confusion, and she blushed rosy-red.

" Kiriak, I want to ask you again about that business of the doctor's," the nun inquired after the usual greetings ; " there are all sorts of stories about it."

" What stories ? " asked Stefchoff.

" They say that you purposely tried to make the Bey believe the papers were treasonable, so as to injure Sokoloff."

Stefchoff flamed up. " Whoever says that is a fool and a liar. The papers taken from his pocket were a copy of the *Nezavisimost*—No. 30—and a proclamation. Necho was there ; he can tell you if I am speaking the truth."

Necho promptly assented.

" We don't require to ask Necho. What can Necho tell us ? " declared Pope Stavri. " We know the whole business. Wherever the doctor goes he carries the gallows with him. I said so only last night to Selamsiz. I went to his house to taste his new raki—he knows just how much aniseed to put in. But how are you, Sister ; are you all right? "

" As you see, Father. I feel as young as they oungest of them," said the nun, who at once turned again to Stefchoff. " But don't you really know who changed the papers ? "

Hajji Rovoama could scarcely keep her tongue from revealing her discovery.

" The police will find out."

" I wouldn't give a farthing for your police. Shall I tell you who it is—shall I ? " she grinned ; then bending over to his ear, she whispered a name. But the secret was in so loud a whisper that the whole party heard it. Necho, the member, tossed his rosary up to the ceiling in glee ; the little schoolmaster looked meaningly, first at one, then at another ; and Pope Stavri interposed a pious ' Good Lord, lead us not into temptation ! "

Rada fled in shame to the cellar.

" There he is—there he is ! " cried Stefchoff, noticing Sokoloff as he passed through the courtyard with two friends. One was Vikenti and the other Kralich. All crowded to the window.

This gave the nun an opportunity of disclosing her second discovery. " Do you know who he is ? "

" What the stranger ? He's a certain Boïcho Ognianoff," answered Stefchoff ; " but he looks to me as if he had something to do with the Committee too."

Hajji Rovoama shook her head in sign of dissent.

" Don't you think so ? " asked Stefchoff.

" No, no ; he's another sort altogether."

" He's a revolutionary, I'll be bound."

" Not he—a spy," answered the nun authoritatively.

Stefchoff glanced at her in amazement.

" Everybody knows it but you."

" Anathema upon him," cried Pope Stavri.

Hajji Rovoama watched jealously to see where they would go in.

" They've gone in to Sister Christina's cell," she cried.

Sister Christina had an evil reputation. She passed for a patriot, and was connected with the Committees. Levski had once spent the night in her cell.

" It's curious how fond the deacons are of Sister Christina," added Hajji Rovoama with a bitter smile. " Do you know that Vikenti's going to throw up the frock ? And quite right too, poor boy—he became a monk too young."

" He did right—you must either marry early or else become a monk early," affirmed Pope Stavri.

" Well, I agree with you as to the first."

" Hush ! hush ! for shame ! "

" He's going to send an offer of marriage to Orlianko's daughter. If she accepts him, he'll throw up the frock and they'll be married in Roumania. But I think she'll have nothing to say to him," and the nun cast an attentive and protecting glance at the little schoolmaster, for whom she was preparing the girl just alluded to. The schoolmaster blushed with confusion.

Just then fresh visitors arrived.

" Ah ! there's brother ! " cried Rovoama, running to meet Yordan Diamandieff.

The visitors rose and followed her out. Stefchoff remained a little behind the rest, seized Rada's hand to say goodbye and pinched her blushing cheek. She slapped him on the face and recoiled from him.

" Aren't you ashamed of yourself ? " she murmured, choking, and fled with tears in her eyes to her own cell.

Stefchoff, who was as unmannerly with women as he was conceited and pompous with men, adjusted the tassel of his fez which had been disarranged by the blow, gazed menacingly after Rada, and left the house looking vexed.

CHAPTER XI : RADA'S TRIALS

RADA GOSPOJINA, as she was called to show that she be-longed to the " Gospoja " (Sister) Hajji Rovoama, was a tall, slender, and pretty girl, with regular features, and a frank and simple countenance ; her face looked still whiter and prettier from under the black hood she wore.

Rada had been an orphan from her earliest years, and had lived nearly all her life under the roof of Hajji Rovo-ama, who had taken charge of her while yet a baby. Her protectress had made a " probationer " of her—that is to say, a girl who is preparing to become a nun, and obliged her to wear the regulation black. At present Rada acted as teacher in the lowest class at the girl's school, for which she received a salary of ten pounds a year.

The lot of all orphan girls is a hard one. Too soon bereft of a father's love and protection, as well as the tender care of a mother, exposed to the kindness or cruelty of the world, they grow up without ever an affectionate encouraging smile being bestowed on them, surrounded by the indifferent faces of strangers. They are like plants which have sprouted and bloomed in some dark cellar, joyless and unscented. Let but a gladdening ray of kindly light fall upon them, and their hidden perfume scents the air.

Rada had grown up in the pernicious and suffocating atmosphere of convent life, under the severe unsympathetic supervision of the old mischief-maker, and in the power of that stony-hearted woman, who had never experienced the holy feelings of maternal love : her young soul had pined in the foul and marshy soil of conventual malice and tale-bearing. It never for a moment occurred to Hajji Rovoama that she might have behaved more humanely to the orphan ; she was too busy with her intrigues to see that her despotism was daily becoming more felt and more insupportable to Rada, in proportion as the girl's nature developed and her self-respect increased. That is how Rada, though a school-mistress, was to be seen waiting at table at the house of Hajji Rovoama's brother Yordan.

For some days Rada had been very busy, because the annual examination-day was approaching. The eventful morning arrived. The girls began to flock into school quite early, all decked out and arrayed in their best by their mothers. They flitted about like a swarm of bees, conning their lessons over yet once more before the examination.

Church was over and people began to crowd into the schoolhouse, according to the custom, to be present at the examination. The doors, windows, and platform, were tastefully decorated with flowers, and the picture of Saints Kiril and Metod * was half hidden by a gorgeous frame of roses festooned with garlands of ivy. The front benches were soon filled up by the pupils, and the rest of the floor was occupied by the spectators, the most important being in front, and some of these were even provided with chairs, amongst the latter being several of our acquaintances. But a few empty seats still remained for such distinguished visitors as might yet come. Meanwhile, Rada was busily marshalling her pupils along the benches, and whispering to them a few last instructions. Her sweet face was flushed with excitement on this momentous day, and her great moist eyes made her look prettier than ever. Transparent rosy clouds flitted across her cheeks and showed the agitation of her simple soul. Rada felt that a hundred curious looks were directed towards her, and the thought made her shy and uncomfortable. But when the head schoolmistress began her speech, and everybody's attention was fixed on her, Rada felt a great relief, and began to pluck up her courage. She even ventured to look round her ; with delight she noticed the absence of Kiriak Stefchoff. The speech ended in solemn silence, the custom of applauding not having yet been introduced. The examination began as appointed in the programme, with the little ones in the lowest class. The kind pleasant face of the head teacher and her encouraging speech had inspired the children with confidence. Rada followed the children's replies with the closest attention, and every little blunder they made was reflected by a painful contraction of her features. But their clear, ringing little voices, their tiny red lips which seem to attract kisses, decided their fate. She caressed them with her glance, encouraged them with a heavenly smile, and tried to instil her whole soul into their faltering little lips.

At that moment the crowd standing at the door divided and made way for two belated guests, who passed along

* The pioneers of Slavonic civilisation, who introduced Christianity into Bulgaria, in the tenth century, and were the authors of the Cyrillic alphabet.

quietly and sat down in the empty seats. Rada looked up and saw them. The elder of the two was the chairman of the School Committee—Chorbaji Micho—the other was Kiriak Stefchoff. Involuntarily she grew pale with dismay. But she tried hard not to see his face, which filled her with aversion and terror.

Kiriak Stefchoff exchanged a few nods of recognition, without, however, greeting his neighbour, Sokoloff, who did not look at him : he crossed his legs and assumed a haughty and defiant air. He listened carelessly, glancing every now and then towards a corner where Lalka, Yordan's daughter, was standing with her friends. Once or twice only he scanned Rada from head to foot, sternly and contemptuously. His face expressed only self-conceit and ferocity. From time to time he sniffed at a carnation which he held in his hand. The teacher, Clement, handed the book to Alafranga Mikhalaki, who, however, waved it away, saying he would examine the children in French. The teacher turned to the right and offered the book this time to Stefchoff, who took it and moved his chair forward.

A dull murmur arose from the crowd. Everybody stared at Kiriak. The subject for examination was the abridged history of Bulgaria. Stefchoff laid the book on the table, passed his hands through his hair as if to refresh his memory, and propounded a question aloud. The child remained silent. The cold, repellent look of the examiner froze her very soul to ice ; she became confused, and did not even remember the question, but glanced piteously at Rada, as if to implore her aid. Stefchoff repeated his question, but only a fresh silence followed.

" Let the child go and call another," he said coldly to the teacher.

Another child appeared, and the question was put to her. She heard it without understanding a word, and remained speechless. Silence reigned also among the spectators, who began to experience a painful sensation. The little girl stood as if transfixed, but her eyes filled with tears of mortification, which she was even too frightened to shed. She tried to speak, but the effort was too much for her.

" The subject appears to have been very carelessly taught indeed. Please call another pupil."

Rada sadly uttered the name of a pupil.

The third child answered quite at random ; she had not understood the question. Seeing a look of disapproval on Stefchoff's face she lost her self-control, and began to look round her in despair. Stefchoff put another question. This time the child did not answer at all. Her confusion was apparent ; her lips quivered, bloodless ; suddenly she burst into tears, and ran to hide herself where her mother was sitting. Everybody seemed to feel oppressed. The mothers whose daughters had not yet been called up looked on in doubt and fear, each one trembling lest she should hear her daughter's name.

Rada stood like one thunderstruck. Not a drop of blood remained in her face ; her cheeks quivered and her bosom heaved with agitation. She did not dare to raise her eyes. She seemed to herself to be sinking into the ground ; a feeling of intense oppression seized her, and it was all she could do to restrain her tears.

The audience was unable to endure this extreme tension any longer, and murmurs of disapproval were heard. People looked at each other astounded, as if to ask, What does all this mean ? Everybody was anxious to put an end to this impossible state of things. Only Stefchoff's triumphant countenance expressed satisfaction. The murmuring grew louder. Suddenly an ominous silence reigned ; everybody turned to Boïcho Ognianoff, who had risen and walked up to Stefchoff.

"Excuse me, sir," he said firmly. "I have not the pleasure of your acquaintance, but your questions are so abstract and so obscure that they would puzzle fifth-form pupils. It is not fair to these poor children."

Then turning to Rada, he asked :

"Will you allow me, miss ?" Then, as he stood, he begged her to call up one of the children who had failed.

A general feeling of relief followed. A murmur of sympathy and approval greeted Ognianoff's proceeding. In a moment he had drawn all eyes to himself and gained the good wishes of all. The calumny launched by Hajji Rovoama fell to the ground. His open countenance, pale with suffering and illuminated by a manly and energetic look, won over all hearts irresistibly. The faces of the spectators brightened ; they breathed again. Every one saw with satisfaction that Ognianoff was master of the situation.

Ognianoff asked the child, in simple words, the very same question which Stefchoff had put to her. This time she answered correctly. The mothers revived, and cast grateful glances at the stranger. His name, which was new and strange, passed from mouth to mouth, and remained engraved on their hearts.

Another child was called up. She, too, answered as satisfactorily as could be expected from a child of her age.

Then all these children, who a moment ago had been in a state of wild terror, began to cast friendly glances at Ognianoft. Their spirits rose ; each was anxious to be called first so as to go and talk with that kind man, whom they all liked now.

Rada passed from one emotion to another. Dumfounded, despairing, moved to tears but a moment ago, she now looked gratefully at the kind and courageous stranger who had come to her assistance at so critical a moment. It was the first time she had ever met with such warm and brotherly sympathy—and from a stranger too. He a spy ! As he stood there he seemed to her a guardian angel. He had crushed Stefchoff like a worm. She was triumphant ; she breathed freely, and looked proudly and happily on every side : on every side she met sympathetic glances. Her heart melted with a grateful emotion, and her eyes filled with tears.

Ognianoff addressed the third child in these words :

" Raïna, my dear, can you tell me what Bulgarian Tsar introduced Christianity among us—made us Christians ? "

And he looked kindly and gently into the innocent little eyes turned up to him, which still bore traces of tears.

The little girl hesitated for a minute, faltered with her lips, and then in a clear ringing treble, like the morning-note of the lark, she answered :

" King Boris introduced Christianity among the Bulgarians."

" Bravo, Raïna ; quite right. Now can you tell me who invented the Bulgarian alphabet ? "

The question puzzled the child a little. She tried to bring herself to speak, but her timidity overcame her and she nearly broke down.

Ognianoff came to her assistance. " I mean our A B C, dear—who found it out ? "

The child's countenance lighted up. Raïna stretched out

her little arm, bare to the elbow, without uttering a word, and pointed to SS. Kiril and Metod, who were looking down on her approvingly.

"That's right, darling ; SS. Kiril and Metod," exclaimed several of the spectators in the front row.

"Well done, Raïna. May SS. Kiril and Metod protect you and grant you to become a queen," cried Pope Stavri, much moved.

"Bravo, Raïna ; you may go," said Ognianoff kindly.

Raïna, proud and triumphant, ran to her mother, who took her in her arms, pressed her to her heart, and covered her with fond and foolish caresses and tears.

Ognianoff turned to the teacher Kliment and handed back the book to him.

"Won't you examine my Subka, sir ? " asked Chorbaji Micho of Ognianoff.

A bright-looking, fair-haired little girl was already in front of him, watching him with an air of pleased expectation. Ognianoff thought for a moment, and asked :

"Subka, can you tell me what Tsar it was that freed the Bulgarians from the Greek yoke ? "

"The Bulgarians were freed from the Turkish yoke by . . . " the child began erroneously.

"No, no, Subka," cried her father. "You're to tell us by what Tsar they were freed from the Greek yoke. We all know what Tsar is to free us from the Turkish yoke."

"What God has decreed no man can prevent," said Pope Stavri.

Chorbaji Micho's simple remark caused much laughter in the audience.

Subka cried eagerly : "The Bulgarians were freed from the Greek yoke by Tsar Asen, but they will be freed from the Turkish yoke by Tsar Alexander of Russia."

She had misunderstood her father's words.

The schoolroom rang with the child's words.

But annoyance and disapproval were depicted on many faces. All glanced mechanically at Rada, who blushed and hung her head. Some of the glances cast on her were of reproof, others of approbation. But every one felt uncomfortable. Stefchoff had recovered from his temporary downfall ; he raised his head and looked round triumphantly. Every one knew of his intimate relations with the Bey, and his habit of fawning to the Turks ; and they tried to read from his face what he thought. Public feeling, which but a moment before had been warmly in favour of Rada and Ognianoff, cooled down and was replaced by a dull sense of dismay. Stefchoff's connections began to murmur their disapproval in audible tones, and those who were well-disposed to the poor teacher remained silent. Poor old Pope Stavri was overwhelmed with confusion. He was afraid for what he had said, and in his heart uttered a fervent " Good Lord, have mercy upon us." But the two camps were more sharply defined on the women's side. Hajji Rovoama, especially, enraged at Stefchoff's previous discomfiture, looked daggers at Rada and Ognianoff and blamed them aloud. She even called the latter a rebel, forgetting that only a few days before she had proclaimed him to be a spy. But there were others who were just as loud in their defence. Mother Ghinka cried so that all could hear her :

" What's everybody making such a fuss about ? The child hasn't blasphemed, has she ? She's only said the plain truth. There, I don't mind saying so myself, that Tsar Alexandri will liberate us, and no one else."

" Be quiet, you stupid," whispered her mother.

As for Subka, she was quite bewildered. She had only said what she had heard her father or his visitors say every day, and she could not conceive why her words should have caused such a commotion.

Stefchoff got up and turned to the spectators in the front rows :

" Gentlemen," he said, " revolutionary ideas are being expressed against the Government of H.I.M. the Sultan. I cannot stop here and listen to such language."

He went out, followed by Necho Pironkoff and three or four others. But his example found no other imitators.

After a minute's excitement people began to see that the incident did not deserve special attention. A child had in her innocence spoken a few misplaced words—but what of that ? Calm was restored, and with it the previous feeling of sympathy towards Ognianoff, who from every side of the room received friendly glances. He was the hero of the day ; he had on his side all the honest-minded and all the mothers.

The examination proceeded and came to an end in perfect quiet.

The pupils sang a song and the people dispersed satisfied. When Ognianoff approached Rada to take leave of her, she said to him earnestly, " Mr. Ognianoff, I thank you heartily both for myself and my little girls. I shall never forget your kindness " ; so saying she gave him a look in which deep gratitude was expressed.

" My dear young lady, I have been a teacher myself, and felt for you—that's all. I congratulate you on the success of your pupils," said Ognianoff, with a warm and friendly grasp of the hand. After he had gone, Rada noticed no one of all the visitors who came to congratulate and shake hands with her.

CHAPTER XII : BOÏCHO OGNIANOFF

THE appearance in the town of Boïcho Ognianoff (for Kralich had definitely assumed the name by which Vikenti had introduced him to Sokoloff at their first meeting in the cemetery at K——) naturally enough drew upon him general attention. There had been a long discussion as to what he should do, in which his three friends Vikenti, Dr. Sokoloff and the Higoumen had taken part. At first they were of opinion that he ought not to show himself in public ; but Ognianoff was able to disarm their apprehensions with ease. He assured them that he was from distant Widdin, where nobody from Bela Cherkva, except Marko Ivanoff, had ever been—that he had been so long absent that no one, even from there, would recognise him, the sufferings of eight years' exile in Asia, coupled with the climate, having aged him so much and changed him so completely.

But so far from his enthusiasm for the ideas for which he had suffered having been calmed down by exile and suffering, they had made him a still more fervent idealist— bold to madness, frienzied in his love for his country, and chivalrous to the degree of self-sacrifice. Fateful occasions have already shown him to us at work. Aye, he had come to Bulgaria to work for its liberation. Such a man, who had escaped from exile and was living under an assumed name, who was bound by no family or social ties, exposed at every minute to be betrayed or discovered, without any future or purpose in life, could have been brought to Bulgaria, or have been kept there after the double deed of blood he had committed, only by some such great purpose as this.

How could he work so as to bring about some result ? What was the field afforded for his labours ? What could he do ? Was his aim possible of attainment ? He could not tell. All that he knew was that he would encounter great difficulties and dangers, which indeed began to beset him at the very beginning of his labours.

But, for such chivalrous natures as his, difficulty and danger are but the anvil against which their strength is hardened and welded. They are strengthened by opposition, attracted by persecution, nourished by danger ; for these constitute a struggle, and every struggle fortifies and ennobles. It is beautiful in the worm which raises its head to bite the foot about to crush it ; it is heroical when undertaken by a man for self-preservation ; it is divine when it is on behalf of humanity.

In the first few days Hajji Rovoama's calumny had averted from him many with whom his friends wished him to become acquainted. But his triumph at the examinations, occasioned by Stefchoff's baseness, had in a moment closed the mouths of his traducers, and opened to him all doors and all hearts. Ognianoff became the favourite guest of the whole hamlet. He gladly accepted the offer by Marko Ivanoff and Micho Beyzadé of a situation as teacher, so as to have some ostensible grounds for remaining there. His colleagues were : Climent Belcheff, the head teacher ; Frangoff ; the pupil-teacher Popoff ; and the chorister Stefan Merdivenjieff, who was the teacher of the Turkish language. The first named was a Russian seminarist, and as such an agreeable, unpractical visionary ; when the superintendents called on him he recited to them lines from Khomiakoff and Derjavin's " God." Chorbaji Marko would have preferred stories on the greatness of Russia, or about Bonaparte. The third was a hot and excitable youth, a former friend of Levski's, who dreamt only of committees, revolutions, and insurgents. He hailed with delight his new colleague, to whom he at once became passionately devoted. The only uncongenial person was Merdivenjieff, with his devotion to the psalter and his love for the Turkish language. The first showed a mind gone to rust ; the second, one who bows beneath the lash. For a Bulgarian who likes the Turkish language must either love the Turks themselves or expect some reward from them. Naturally this coincidence of tastes united him with Stefchoff.

E

In accordance with the duties he had undertaken, Ognianoff taught both in the boys' and in the girls' school; consequently he met Rada every day. Every time he saw her he discovered fresh charms in the young girl, and one fine morning he awoke to find himself deeply in love with her. Need it be said that she already loved him in secret? From the day when he had so chivalrously come to her assistance she had been filled with that potent feeling of warm gratitude which in a moment gives way to love. 'Her poor little heart, thirsting after sympathy and affection, was at once seized with an ardent, pure, and boundless love for Ognianoff. In him she saw realised the dim ideal of her dreams and her hopes, and under the beneficent influence of this new emotion Rada bloomed and flourished like a rose in May.

Two such pure and honest natures were fated to understand each other without need of a lengthy acquaintance, or much preliminary intercourse. Every day Ognianoff found a greater joy and relief in her conversation. His love for her grew and flourished in his heart by the side of that other great love he had for his country. The one was a giant pine, ready to withstand the furious storm-blast, the other, a lowly flower, thirsting for sun and dew; both grew on the same soil, but the rays which the sun shed on the one did not reach the other.

Yet his heart was often oppressed by sad thoughts which fell on it like lead. What would become of this innocent creature, whose fate was becoming entwined with his own uncertain destiny? Whither was he leading her? What would be their end? He, the combatant, the man of perils and adversity, was he to draw towards his terrible path this pure, loving child, whose life was only now beginning to expand under the kindly fostering of love? She sought for and awaited from him a secure and happy future, joyful and untroubled bliss beneath the new heavens his love had created for her. Why was this poor girl to share the cruel blows fate was preparing for him alone?

No, it was his duty to disclose all to her, to pluck from her eyes the veil of blindness, and to show her with what manner of man she was uniting her lot. These thoughts weighed heavily on his mind, and he determined to seek relief in a full and open confession of the truth.

He sought out Rada.

She had now left the convent and was living in one of the rooms of the school, modestly and even poorly furnished. The only ornament the room boasted was its occupant.

Ognianoff knocked at the door and went in.

Rada received him with a smile on her tearful face.

"Rada, you've been crying ? What is it, darling ? " and he tenderly clasped her head and caressed her blushing cheeks.

She drew back, wiping her eyes.

"What's the matter, dear ? " asked Ognianoff surprised.

"Sister Hajji Rovoama has just been here," answered Rada in a broken voice.

"Has she been vexing and ill-treating you again ? Tell me all about it. Why, some one has been trampling on my songs ! "

"You see, Boïcho, the Sister threw them down, and trampled on them—she found them on the table—' Revolutionary songs,' she called them, and then she abused you in such terrible words. How can I help crying ? "

Ognianoff became serious.

"What terrible things did she say of me ? "

"What didn't she say ? She called you a rebel, a bandit, a murderer ! My God, how can she be so merciless ! "

Ognianoff looked thoughtfully at Rada, and said :

"Listen to me, Rada, you and I are friends, but we don't know each other yet ; or rather you don't know me. The fault is mine. Do you think you could love me if I really was the kind of man they say I am ? "

"No, dear ; I know very well you're the most honourable man in the world—that's why I love you " ; so saying she clung to his neck like a child, and looked lovingly into his eyes.

He smiled bitterly, moved by her simple faith.

"And don't you know me well enough ? Else how could we have fallen in love with each other ? " whispered Rada, still clinging to him.

Ognianoff kissed her affectionately, and said :

"Rada, my darling, if I am to be an honourable man, as you call me, I must tell you things you know nothing about. My love for you has kept me back till now, for fear of paining you, but my conscience impels me to speak. You *must* know to whom you are binding yourself. I have no right to remain silent any longer."

" Tell me all—you'll always be the same to me," she said, with emotion.

Ognianoff made her sit down, and seated himself beside her.

" Rada, Hajji Rovoama says that I am a rebel. She doesn't know what she means—she calls every decent youth a rebel."

" Yes, dear, she's a very wicked woman."

" But I really am a rebel, Rada."

Rada looked at him astounded.

" Yes, Rada, and a real rebel, too, busy preparing an insurrection."

She sat motionless without uttering a word.

" We intend to begin the insurrection next spring. That's why I came here." Rada remained silent.

" That is my future—a future full of uncertainty and danger."

Rada looked at him in dumb surprise, but said nothing.

Ognianoff saw his fate in her cold silence. At every word he said the girl's devotion to him was dissolving into air. He made an effort to keep calm, and proceeded with his confession.

" That is my future ; now I must tell you my past life."

Rada fixed her troubled glance on him.

" It is still darker, if not more terrible, Rada. Do you know that for eight years I was imprisoned in Asia for a political offence, and that I am a fugitive from Diarbekir, Rada ! "

Rada made no reply.

" Tell me, Rada, did the Sister say anything of all this ? "

" No ; she knows nothing of it," answered Rada faintly.

Ognianoff remained deep in thought for a moment, and added :

" She called me a murderer and an assassin. She knows nothing of that either, Rada ! She called me a spy only a few days ago—but listen."

This time Rada felt something terrible was coming. She grew deadly pale.

" Listen ! I killed two men—and not very long ago."

Rada recoiled from him involuntarily.

Ognianoff did not dare to look at her ; he was addressing the wall ; his heart seemed as if being crushed in an iron vice.

" Yes, I killed two Turks—I, who had never harmed a
fly before in my life.   I was bound to kill them, or they
would have violated a girl before my eyes—before me and
her father, whom they had bound.   Yes, I'm a murderer,
and Diarbekir again awaits me, if not indeed the gallows ! "

Rada turned and looked strangely at him.

" Go on—go on," she murmured wildly.

" I've told you all ; you know who I am now," answered
Ognianoff in a quivering voice.   He waited to hear the
terrible sentence he could already read in her face.

Rada flung herself into his arms.

" You're mine ! " she cried.   " You're the noblest man
living—you're my hero, my beloved, beautiful hero ! "

And the two young lovers clasped each other in a fond
and passionate embrace, frenzied with love and happiness.

CHAPTER XIII : THE ROAD TO SILISTRIA

SUCH was the name given to a delightful grassy meadow in
the valley of the monastery, surrounded by branching
willows and tall walnuts and elms.   Though it was already
late autumn, this sweet and shady spot still preserved intact
all its greenness and freshness, like Calypso's isle where
eternal spring reigned.   Through the spreading branches
could be seen, north of this happy valley, two peaks of the
Stara Planina—the Crooks and the Point.   Between these
stretched the main ridge of the Balkans, with its sharp
precipices and jagged rocks, below which murmured and
sparkled the rill.   The cool mountain breeze softly fanned
the leaves, and brought the scent of the Balkans as well as
the murmur of the mills nearer.   On the other side gleamed
the dry, bleached beds of the torrents which the winter
floods had scooped and hollowed out.   The sun was at its
highest, and its rays, darting through the trees, rained on
the grass a shower of quivering flakes, round and golden.
A marvellous coolness and quiet reigned in that poetic spot,
which bore nevertheless so prosaic and inaccurate a name.
For no road, either to Silistria or anywhere else, had ever
passed through the lonely meadow, which nestled so grace-
fully beneath the hereabouts inaccessible Stara Planina.   It
owed its designation not to its geographical situation, but to
a totally different and, so to speak, historical circumstance.
The pleasant coolness of this retired spot had made it for

many years past the favourite rendezvous for all picnics, merrymakings, and orgies. It was in this Capua that many a merry tradesman of Bela Cherkva, many a spendthrift heir had made their money fly in a too prodigal conviviality : when all was spent the *decave*, as a matter of course, took the road to Silistria, where, thanks to the fertility of the country and the backwardness of its inhabitants, an easily earned livelihood—sometimes even a fortune—was to be found : and the success of the first emigrants from Bela Cherkva had attracted others to the promised land—the Plains of Silistria.

In this manner Silistria and its surrounding villages had received quite a number of the roysterers of Bela Cherkva, who acted as the pioneers of civilisation in that benighted country ; for, amongst others, they had supplied it with a round dozen of popes and upwards of twenty school-teachers. So that for the inhabitants of our hamlet it was the most direct road to Silistria.

In spite of its fatal significance, the glory of the " Road to Silistria " continued to flourish and to attract all who had a taste for jaunts and merrymaking ; nor were these few in number, for with all its hardships bondage has yet this one advantage : it makes a nation merry. Where the arena of political and scientific activity is closely barred, where the desire of rapid enrichment finds no stimulant, and far-reaching ambition has no scope for its development, the community squanders its energy on the trivial and personal cares of its daily life, and seeks relief and recreation in simple and easily obtainable material enjoyment. A flask of wine sipped beneath the cool shade of the willows by some clear murmuring rivulet will make one forget one's slavery; the native guvech (stew) with its purple egg-plants, fragrant parsley, and sharp pepper-pods, enjoyed on the grass under the spreading branches overhead, through which peeps the blue distant sky, constitutes a kingdom, and if only there be a gipsy piper present, is the height of earthly bliss. An enslaved nation has a philosophy of its own which reconciles it to its lot. When a man is irretrievably ruined, he often puts a bullet through his head or ends his life in some equally rapid and decisive manner. But a nation, however hopeless its bondage, never ends its own existence ; it eats, drinks, begets children. It enjoys itself. If one but look at the poetry of a nation, one finds clearly expressed the national spirit, the nation's life, and its views of existence. There, amid cruel torments, heavy chains, dark dungeons, and festering wounds, is yet interwoven the mention of fat, roasted lambs, jars of red wine, potent raki, interminable marriage feasts, and mazy dances on the green sward beneath the shade ; these form the subject of a whole anthology of national songs.

By the time that Sokoloff and Ognianoff arrived, the " Road to Silistria " was already echoing with the shouts of the gay company. There were present, amongst others, Nikolai Netkovitch, an educated and enlightened youth ; Kandoff, a student at a Russian university, who had come to the Balkan for the benefit of his health, a man of wide reading but a thorough idealist, imbued with all the utopias of Socialism ; Fratio-Frangoff, the teacher, a hot-headed youth ; Popoff, an exalted patriot ; Pope Dimcho, also a patriot, and at the same time a drunkard ; and Blind Kolcho. The latter, who was completely blind, was a shrivelled-up little fellow with a thin and wizened but intelligent face ; he played the flute with much skill, and was accustomed to wander over the length and breadth of Bulgaria, his powers as a wit and story-teller rendering him an indispensable guest at all festivities.

The meal was already laid out on a bright rug on the grass. Two great demi-johns—one of red wine, the other of white—were cooling in the mill-stream which flowed below the meadow. A party of gipsies were merrily fiddling away and singing Turkish love songs lustily. A clarionet and two cymbals completed the noisy orchestra. The meal was a merry one. Toasts followed fast, being drunk sitting, as was then the custom.

The first toast was proposed by Ilicho the Inquisitive.

" Here's a health to all of us, boys ! To all of us God grant whatever most we want. May He His fear instil in those who wish us ill, and send His wrath on those who fain would be our foes."

Glasses clashed gaily.

" Long live all of us ! " cried Frangoff.

" I drink to the ' road to Silistria ' and its pilgrims ! " declared Pope Dimcho.

Popoff raised his glass, and cried :

" Brothers, to the Lion of the Balkans ! "

The music, which had ceased, now struck up again and

interrupted the toasts : but Fratio, who had not yet proposed his, beckoned to the gipsies to stop, rose to his feet,
and said enthusiastically, glass in hand :

"Gentlemen, I propose the health of Bulgarian *liberté*.
Vivat ! " And he emptied his glass. But the company,
who did not quite understand what he meant, kept their
glasses full, thinking from his excited air that he meant to
make a speech. Fratio was astonished at meeting with no
response, became confused, and sat down again.

"What is it you mean, sir ? " asked Kandoff coldly,
turning to Fratio. Fratio frowned.

"I thought I had made myself quite intelligible, sir," he
said : "I drank to Bulgarian Liberty ! " The last word he
spoke low, with a look of suspicion at the gipsies.

"But what do you understand by liberty ? " insisted the
student.

Sokoloff turned to them.

"I think we ought rather to drink to Bulgarian bondage.
Bulgarian Liberty does not exist."

"Not yet, but we will get it."

"How will you get it ? "

"By drinking its health," said some one ironically.

"No, by fighting for it," cried Fratio, in excitement.

"All right, Fratio, you try, then—an ox is bound by the
horns, but a man by his word."

"The sword, gentlemen, the sword ! " and Fratio shook
his fist frenziedly.

"Then I drink to the sword, the God of slaves," said
Ognianoff, raising his glass.

This electrified the assemblage.

"Agoush," cried some one, "play ' Proud Nikifor* determined,' " which was then the Bulgarian Marseillaise.

The music struck up and the whole party began to sing ;
when they came to the line "Strike, slay, until the land be
freed ! " the excitement became intense, and knives and
forks were brandished in frenzy.

Fratio had seized a huge knife, with which he was slashing
the atmosphere. With one wild gesticulation he struck a
large glass of red wine that the boy was taking to some one.
The wine was spilt, and Fratio's light summer coat and
trousers were drenched.

* An allusion to the defeat of the Byzantine Emperor Nikifor (Nice-
phorus) by the Bulgarians in A.D. 811.

" Fool ! " cried Fratio.

" Don't be angry, Gospodin Fratio," said Pope Dimcho ; " don't you know that where there is striking and slaying blood will be spilt ? "

At this stage every one was shouting his loudest, and each was inaudible to the other, for the musicians were playing a Turkish march, with a deafening accompaniment of cymbals.

Ognianoff and Kandoff had separated from the others and were carrying on a discussion under a tree. Nikolai Netkovitch had also joined them.

" You tell me that we must prepare for the struggle," said Kandoff, continuing the discussion, " because its object is freedom. But what is this freedom ? We are to have a prince—that is to say, a petty Sultan—of our own ; we're to be oppressed by officials ; monks and priests are to fatten on our toil ; and the army will sap the very life-springs of the nation. Is this your freedom ? I would not sacrifice a drop of blood from my little finger for it."

" But listen to me, Mr. Kandoff," answered Netkovitch. " No one respects your principles more than I do, but they have no place here. What we want is political freedom—that is, to be masters of our own land and our own destinies."

Kandoff shook his head in dissent.

" Well, then, explain this to me. You will appoint new masters in place of the old ; you don't want the Sheikh-ul-Islam, but you will set up another, whom you call the Exarch—that is to say, you replace one tyrant by another. You impose rulers on the nation, and annihilate every idea of equality ; you consecrate the right of the strong to despoil the poor, of capital to oppress labour. Give to your contest a more humanitarian, a more modern object ; make it a struggle not only against the Turkish yoke, but also for the triumph of modern principles—that is, the destruction of those foolish distinctions, consecrated by the prejudices of centuries, such as the throne, religion, the right of property and of the stronger, of which human brutality has constituted unassailable principles. Read Herzen, Bakounin, Lassalle. Leave this narrow, animal patriotism, and raise the standard of rational modern humanity and sober science. Then I am with you."

" The ideas you express," answered Ognianoff sharply, " show your erudition, it is true, but prove only too clearly how ignorant you are of the Bulgarian question. Under the standard you speak of you would find yourself alone—the nation would not understand it. You must bear in mind, Mr. Kandoff, that through the nation we can attain only one rational and possible object—that is, the destruction of the Turkish rule. We see before us only one enemy —the Turk ; and it is against that enemy that we will rise. As for the principles of Socialism to which you have treated us, we cannot stomach them. Bulgarian common sense rejects them, and they will never find a field in Bulgaria, either now or at any other time. Your high-sounding principles and standards of ' modern thinking humanity and the sober science of reason ' only serve to confuse the subject. What we have to do is to protect our homes, our honour, our lives from the lowest zaptié who may choose to assail them. Before solving general problems of social science—or, more correctly, obscure theories—we must free ourselves from our chains. Those writers whose teachings you have mastered neither know nor care about us and our sufferings. We can rely only upon the nation, in which we cannot but include the Chorbaji class and the clergy : they represent forces which we must make use of. Abolish the zaptié, and the nation attains its ideal. You may have another ideal, but it is not that of the nation."

Just then the music stopped and the noise ceased. The blind boy was playing on his flute, from which issued sounds of astonishing sweetness.

" Come here, you fellows. What are you philosophising about there ? " cried some to the three disputants.

These, however, did not even turn round ; the discussion continued to rage hotly.

Blind Kolcho continued to play for some time amid solemn silence, the whole party, though some were more or less excited by their potations, enjoying the soothing melody of his flute. Suddenly he stopped and said :

" What do you think I can see ? "

There was a general laugh.

" Will you guess ? " asked Kolcho.

" What will you give us if we guess right ? " asked some.

" My astronomical telescope."

" Where is it ? "

" In the moon."

" You can see the rosy cheeks of Todorich's daughter Milka," said Pope Dimcho.

" Not I ! I'd rather kiss them than see them—it's more in my line."

" Well, you can see Mr. Fratio," said Popoff, for Fratio was standing in front of the blind man and waving his arms about.

" How can one see the wind ? "

" The sun, then ! "

" No, you're wrong again—the sun and I fell out long ago, and I've sworn I'll never look at him as long as I live."

" Well, you see the night," said the doctor.

" No, no ; what I see is the glass of wine you're going to give me—confound it, you've forgotten me."

At once a number of glasses were poured out and brought to him.

" Your health, everybody," he said, and emptied his glass.

" But what am I to have, as you couldn't guess ? "

" The other glasses we poured out for you."

" How many of them are there ? "

" Seven—the same number as the deadly sins."

" Well, I'd rather have the forty holy martyrs, if I were in his place," remarked Pope Dimcho.

" Well said—here's luck ! "

" Vive la Bulgarie, vive la République des Balkans," cried Fratio in French.

Dusk, however, broke up the revels, and a move was made towards the town.

" Boys, don't forget the rehearsal at the school to-morrow," cried Ognianoff.

" What are you going to act ? " asked the student.

" ' Geneviève.' "

" Why did you choose that old piece ? "

" For two reasons—first because it's not of a seditious character—the Chorbajis insisted on that ; and, secondly, because every one has read it and wants it. We had to consult their tastes ; what we want is large takings ; we have to buy newspapers and books for our reading room, as well as ' other things.' "

The band, merry and boisterous, made for the town, and was soon lost among the gardens which the evening twilight was already enveloping. In a quarter of an hour they made their victorious entry in the already dark streets of the town, lustily singing revolutionary songs. This seditious demonstration brought the women and children in crowds to their thresholds.

Ognianoff, however, was not among them. While yet in the fields a little boy had brought him hurriedly some message, and he had left his companions without being noticed.

CHAPTER XIV : AN UNFORESEEN MEETING

OGNIANOFF struck towards the north, and made his way in the direction of the ridge of the Balkans. It was already dark. The sun had set peacefully and majestically. Its last rays that gilded the lofty summits of the Stara Planina were vanishing. Only a few clouds, with golden fringes to the westward, still smiled at the sun from their height in the pure, ethereal atmosphere. The valley was now quite wrapped in gloom. The white torrent-beds in the west were plunged in the dim shade which was stealing, darker and darker, over the monastery meadows, the rocks, and the walnuts, willows, and pear trees, whose outlines were gradually becoming faint and blurred. Not a single flutter or chirp from that world of birds that all day long had made the valley gay—they were silent in their nests, securely perched on the branches or hidden under the eaves of the monastery. Jointly with the darkness reigned the weird and melancholy quiet of the night ; the only sound that broke the utter solitude was the roar of the mountain torrents. Now and again the wind would carry the distant tinklings of some belated herd scampering home to the town. Soon the moonlight shone forth and enhanced the charm of that idyllic hour. A golden flood poured over plain and trees, which cast marvellous shadows on the ground. The dry water-courses showed out more clearly against the dark background of the old ruins ; the new cupola towered white and tall above the.gables and poplars of the monastery, and behind it, high in the heavens, soared the summits of the Stara Planina till they were lost in the dark blue depths above.

Ognianoff passed behind the monastery and followed up the mill-stream, which issued from beneath a dark copse of thick-branching walnuts ; he passed under this rustling

roof, crossed the stream on the huge blocks of stone that
sprawled across its course, and soon appeared on the ridge
of the Balkan whence the stream flowed.

There the scene changed; it became wilder and more
majestic. On either side of the stream the rocks rose steep
and bare, broken here and again by the torrents, and above
the jagged crags peered down in fantastic shapes. The
moonlight reached only the topmost peaks of the rocks; all
the rest was plunged in gloom. Here the noise of the waterfalls became deafening, and reverberated with the echoes
of the wall of rock on either side. The wind sighed and
sobbed out its autumnal plaint through the bushes : the
valley became gradually wilder and more desolate.

Ognianoff pushed his way perilously along the storm-
worn path, which was indeed only used by day, being too
treacherous to venture along by night. He remembered
that some six months before he had passed there when he
had come down from the mountain and made his entry over
the wall into Marko's yard. Soon the path was quite
hidden from view in the increasing darkness. He could
scarcely pick his footing through the sharp-pointed rocks
that strewed the way before him. Had any one seen him
at that moment and in that wild place, now crawling, now
leaping from crag to crag, he would have taken him for a
wild beast rather than a human being. Suddenly a new
sound struck his ear : it was the rumbling of the mill. He
advanced bolder and more confidently towards it. Soon
in the dark depths of the valley he discerned the roof of
Father Stoyan's mill, and in a moment he had reached it.

Father Stoyan met him outside the door.

" What is it ? " asked Ognianoff hurriedly and anxiously.

" Nothing, thank God ! "

This answer relieved Ognianoff at once. He had begun
to fear that something had been found out concerning the
adventure with the two Turks, and that this was the reason
why old Stoyan had sent for him.

" What did you want me for ? " asked Boïcho again.

" Nothing. Forgive me, Master, for having given you
the trouble of coming here, but as it was——"

And old Stoyan, lowering his voice, added :

" I'd have sent for our Vikenti, only he's down with fever
just now ; and as our Christo told me he'd seen you near
the monastery, thinks I, ' Let's send for the Master,

that'll be better still.' But you'll forgive me, won't you,
Master ? "

Boïcho began to grow impatient.

" Well, but what is it ? "

" What, didn't you ask the boy ? "

" No."

" Well, that's odd. Bother the boy ! I told him that if
you asked him he was to whisper it in your ear. This is
what's happened, master "—and he lowered his voice still
more—" a friend's come."

" What friend ? "

" Why, one of us."

" One of us ? "

" Why, yes, a Nationalist."

" Who is he ? "

" I don't know. He came down from the mountain last
night, and made straight for me. He frightened me at first;
I thought he was a brigand. You'll see what a state he's in ;
his legs are like broomsticks. But he turned out all right."

" Did he say who he was or where he was coming from ? "
asked Ognianoff, deeply interested.

" I asked him, but all he answered was that he was flying
from the Turks and had come down the mountain."

" Didn't he ask for anything ? "

" Yes ; he asked for a piece of bread—hadn't eaten for
four days, he said. And he asked me to send for some good
friend—some Nationalist—to come and have a talk with
him. First, I thought of the deacon, but this confounded
fever of his hasn't left him ; so then I sent for you."

" Quite right, Father Stoyan."

" Forgive me, Master, for the trouble I've given you."

" Not I ; I'm glad of it. Where's your guest ? "

" I've got him carefully stowed away. Come with me."
And Father Stoyan led him into the mill.

It was in complete darkness.

He lighted a petroleum lamp, guided Boïcho between the
wall and the mill-stones, past two corn-bins, and stopped
before a little door, over which were still hanging great
cobwebs half torn away, showing it had long been kept
closed.

" What, is he in there ? "

" Rather ! The cat doesn't steal the milk that's put
away—isn't that so, Master ? "

And Father Stoyan knocked at the door, and called out : " Now, sir, come out, if you please."

The door opened, and a young man appeared, glancing cautiously around him. He was short and weakly in appearance, with a very diminutive face, long unshaven : his countenance wore a bright, eager look, and his movements were lithe and active ; but what struck Ognianoff was his utter weakness and emaciation. He was dressed in the coarse white clothes usually worn by Macedonian peasants, and trimmed with the traditional braiding, knobs, and tassels on the back, breast, and knees, but completely worn out, so that the naked skin showed through many a rent.

At the first glance both he and Ognianoff exclaimed with surprise :

"Mouratliski ! "

" Kralich ! "

And they rushed into each other's arms and embraced warmly.

"What ? You ? Where have you come from ? " asked Ognianoff, who recognised in Mouratliski a comrade from the band of insurgents to which he had belonged.

"Never mind me. Where have you been all this time ? Is it really you, Kralich ? "

Kralich turned back with a start, pointed to the mill, and addressed Stoyan, who stood motionless in front of them holding the lamp :

" Father Stoyan, put out the light and shut the door—or rather never mind—we'll go out. There's too much noise here to talk."

Father Stoyan led the way with the lamp, and shut the door behind them, saying :

"There, you have a good talk together. I'm going to bed. When you feel sleepy come in and lie down."

The valley was completely obscure, but the opposite side of the rocks was brightly lit up by the moon. Ognianoff and his companion went into the darkest part of the valley, and seated themselves on a broad ledge of rock, by the side of which the torrent foamed past.

" Let's shake hands again, brother," said Ognianoff, feelingly.

" Why, Kralich, whatever brought you here ? I last heard of you in the paradise of Diarbekir."

" And you, Dobri ?   Haven't you gone to the gallows yet ? " asked Boïcho in jest.

They were very old and intimate acquaintances.   A common fate and common sufferings will unite the most divergent of characters : how much more then two such as Boïcho and Mouratliski, who were brothers in arms and in ideas.

" Well, tell us all about it," added Mouratliski," your story dates further back, so you take precedence.   When did you come back from Diarbekir ? "

" You mean, when did I escape ? "

" What ? did you escape ? "

" Yes, last May."

" And you managed to get here unmolested ?   What road did you take ? "

" I went on foot from Diarbekir to Russian Armenia : from there through the Caucasus to Odessa, thanks to the assistance of the Russians.   At Odessa, I got a steamer to Varna, and from there over the mountains to the shepherd's huts near Troyan, then over the Stara Planina to Bela Cherkva."

" But what made you pick out Bela Cherkva ? "

" I was afraid to go anywhere where I didn't know any one ; on the other hand, I fought shy of former friends, not knowing what might be their views now.   I remembered that my father's best friend, a very worthy man, lived at Bela Cherkva : no one else could possible know me there ; indeed, he wouldn't have known me if I hadn't told him who I was."

" Well, I recognised you at once.   So you stayed on ? "

" Yes, that friend of my father's got me a situation as a schoolmaster, and till now, thank God, everything has gone well."

" So now you've become a schoolmaster, Kralich ? "

" Ostensibly—a schoolmaster ; but, in reality, the same old trade."

" What—preaching ? "

" Yes, revolution."

" Well, how are you getting on ?   We made a mess of our business."

" For the present things are going well.   The people's minds are much excited, the soil is volcanic : Bela Cherkva was one of Levski's nests."

" And what's your plan ? "

" As yet we haven't any. We're preparing the rebellion theoretically, so to speak, and waiting for something to turn up. But the movement grows stronger every day, not only here but round about, and we shall have a rebellion sooner or later."

" Bravo, Kralich ! Well done ! You're a marvellous fellow."

" Come, let me hear about your trials, now."

" Oh, you know all about that business. We made such a mess of it at Stara Zagora that we daren't look any one in the face."

" No, no ; begin from the beginning, from where our band was routed and we all separated. Remember, I've had eight years of Diarbekir, and I've heard nothing of you or any of my friends all the time."

Mouratliski stretched himself out at full length on the rock, placed his hands under his head, and in that position of repose told his story in detail. He had taken part in the Sofia conspiracy under Dimitr Obshti,* and in the attack on the Orkhanié mail. He had been betrayed, arrested, and flung into prison, and had only by some miracle escaped the gallows or Diarbekir. Later he had gone to Roumania, where he had wandered for a year and a half, struggling against famine and misery ; from thence he had returned to Bulgaria on a mission, to fight against the terrors and perils which encompass an agitator. That spring he had appeared at Stara Zagora, and had laboured with enthusiasm to prepare the insurrection.† After the lamentable failure of the movement, during which he had been slightly wounded by the Turks at the short engagement at Elkhovo, he had made for the Stara Planina, pursued by the Turkish patrols and even by the Bulgarian shepherds to whom he had applied for a piece of bread or a change of clothes.

For ten days he had wandered over the Balkan, exposed to a thousand dangers and sufferings. His terrible hunger had forced him to come down from the mountains and beg, revolver in hand, for a piece of bread from the first living man he should meet. Fortunately, he had come upon

* In 1873.

† This abortive movement (the chief leader of which was M. Stamboloff, later the Bulgarian Prime Minister) broke out on the 16th (28th) September 1875, and was at once suppressed by the Turks.

F

Father Stoyan. He related with gratitude how kindly the miller had received him ; he was, he said, the first man who had treated him with humanity since he had been wandering on the Stara Planina.

Mouratliski stopped. The river rippled past their feet. Around all was still. The moonlit rocks opposite them were soundless. Only on the peaks of the hills the night breeze rustled among the wild lilac and other low shrubs.

Ognianoff had followed eagerly Mouratliski's recital of his adventures and dangers. He seemed himself to be passing through all those emotions and sufferings, to feel the same bitter disenchantment and shame at the baseness and cowardice of the people, by which the repression of a revolution is usually followed. Now, with a brother's interest, he was pondering how to assist Mouratliski.

" Well, what do you think of doing now ? " asked Boïcho.

" I shall go back to Roumania, if you can only get me clothes and a passport."

Ognianoff became thoughtful.

" What are you going to do there ? "

" I shall bide my time, and when the revolution breaks out I shall be there—I can't help it—what's born in the flesh, you know."

" That's no good ; you're not fit to travel till you've recovered a little. Stay here ! "

" What, and hide ? No, I can't do that. I don't want a voluntary imprisonment."

" Yes, but you won't want to hide," cried Ognianoff, after half a minute's reflection.

" Why not ? "

" You'll go about the town as freely as I do, and we shall work together."

" With all my heart. But are you mad, Kralich ? I should be caught the very first day. They're looking for me behind every tree."

" They're looking for insurgents and Bulgarians."

" Well, and what do you think I am ? " he said laughingly.

" You will be a respectable and peaceful photographer, and, what's more, an Austrian."

" I don't understand you."

Ognianoff smiled and continued, trying to see Mouratliski's face in the dark ;

" Your hair and beard are as long as a dervish's. To-morrow night I shall take you to my rooms, and we'll get rid of this thatch. We'll leave you only your whiskers. You won't mind ? "

" All right ; what next ? "

" Next, we shall shave off your moustache."

" Well, I suppose that must go too," said Mouratliski, smiling.

" After that, we'll Europeanise you a little. A friend of mine, who arrived yesterday from Roumania, will give us an old velvet suit. I've got a railway guard's cap with a gold band ; and then ' Goot morgen, main Kherr.' "

" Very well. I shall become an Austrian ; but how am I going to make out that I'm a photographer ? "

" You'll have a photographic apparatus. Three years ago the photographer Christoff lived at Bela Cherkva as an agitator. When he went away he left behind his apparatus, which was out of order, with a very good friend of mine, called Netkovitch. We'll have the camera mended as best we may, and buy you all the plates, acids, and cards you want, and then you can start off photographing our worthy townspeople."

" But I've never even dreamt about photography."

" Oh, you'll learn it fast enough. You'll twist their eyes, knock off their noses, distort their mouths, and mutilate their faces a little at first, but you'll soon be a master in the art."

" Well, you shall be my first victim."

" All right."

" And I'm not to talk Bulgarian ? "

" Not a word, you're to avoid it carefully. All that you'll talk is German or Bohemian. Czech is very similar to our language, and people will understand one word in ten ; then as time goes by you may begin with a little broken Bulgarian. I suppose you haven't forgotten your Czech ? "

" I was only in Pisek for a year, after your time, but I remember enough to ask for bread, water, and so forth."

" So much the better, because the passport I have is made out in Czech for a certain Yaroslav Brzobegounek."

" What ? Yaroslav Brzobegounek ? "

" Yes, a glorious Czech name, and not unfitting for you ;

you're a real Brzobegounek ;* haven't you gone over half the Balkan Peninsula on foot ? So, then, Dobri Mouratliski, from to-morrow you will be Pan Yaroslav Brzobegounek, an Austrian Czech, born with a photographic apparatus on his back ! "

And Ognianoff took off his hat with mock solemnity.

" Good morning, Pan Yaroslav, will you take my photograph ? " he asked, in Czech.

" With pleasure, Pan Yane," answered Mouratliski, in the same language.

" Stop, I'm no longer Ivan Kralich ; here I'm known as Boïcho Ognianoff, don't forget."

" Well, you have the advantage of me, you haven't to get into a completely foreign skin—ah, Pan Yane, Pan Yane."

" Pan Boïcho, didn't I tell you," cried Ognianoff, " you're quite likely to betray me through your carelessness. You must remember your part well, Pan Yaroslav."

Half an hour later they went back to the mill, locked the door carefully, and stretched themselves out to sleep on the sacks of grain, to the deafening and monotonous sound of the mill.

CHAPTER XV : A VOICE FROM THE GRAVE

In the morning Ognianoff started for the town. He crossed the ridge of the Balkan and emerged at the monastery. In the field by the monastery, under the great walnut-trees, the Higoumen was pacing up and down, bareheaded. He was enjoying the morning beauty of that romantic spot, and was breathing in deep draughts of the sweet health-giving mountain air. The autumnal nature had a new charm in the russet leaves of the trees, the yellow, velvety summits of the Balkan, and the general tokens of melancholy and decay.

Ognianoff and the higoumen greeted one another.

" These are charming spots, father," said Ognianoff ; " you're lucky in being able to live in the midst of Nature, and to enjoy, peacefully, her divine charms. If I ever feel a vocation to take up your calling it will be out of love for Nature and her eternal beauty."

" Take care, Ognianoff ; you would be coming down in the world if you became a monk after being an apostle. No, no ; stay as you are. Besides, I wouldn't have you in

* I.e., Swift in flight.

my monastery; you'd pervert even Father Yeroté, you're such a godless atheist," said the higoumen in jest.

"What kind of an old boy is he?" asked Boïcho irreverently.

"A very respected and honourable brother, whose only failing is that he's too fond of his money; I think he plants it in the ground so that it may grow. Whenever we ask him for any, for common expenses, he grumbles so much that we've made a proverb out of him—he grumbles like Father Yeroté, we say. But where are you coming from so early?"

"I spent the night at Father Stoyan's mill."

"Why? did you have a scare?" and the higoumen looked at him with some surprise.

"No, no—but a friend has turned up."

Upon which Ognianoff related to him briefly his meeting with Mouratliski.

"Why ever didn't you bring him to the monastery?" said the higoumen, reproachfully. "You must have slept on the sacks of corn!"

"We 'Koumitajis' * can put up with a good deal."

"Well—well—God bless you. What did you say you had christened him?"

"Yaroslav Brzobegounek."

Father Natanaïl laughed.

"You apostles are a funny lot; but take care your waterpot isn't upset for the third time."

"Never you fear; there's a God for us Koumitajis as well as for brigands," said Boïcho, smiling significantly. "Why, you've brought your rifle with you," noticing Father Natanaïl's rifle leaning against a willow-tree.

"Yes; I thought I'd try it this morning. It's a long time since I had it in my hand. You fellows have excited the whole population, and we have music now every day in front of the monastery—nothing but shooting: enough noise to stir up the dead, let alone an old sinner like me."

"Well, it's a good thing to try your hand again, Father Higoumen."

As they walked on the two came to the mill of the terrible night. The mere sight of it brought deep furrows to Ognianoff's brow.

* All insurgents or suspected insurgents were supposed by the Turks to be connected with the Revolutionary Committees at Bucharest or Belgrade, and were hence called "Koumitajis" or Committee-men.

The mill was now closed. Stoyan the miller had left it and taken another, situate, as we have already seen, on the monastery stream.

The mill, deserted and covered with moss, resembled a grave in that beautiful spot.

At that moment Mouncho had stealthily approached ; he stopped and fixed his eyes on Ognianoff. A strange smile played over his idiot's countenance. In that look, bereft of reason, could be read the mingled affection, fear, and surprise which Boïcho had awakened in his mind. Years before he had cursed Mohammad before an on-bashi, who had beaten him till he lay senseless on the ground. From that time his obscured conscience had retained only one feeling, one thought—a terrible, demoniacal hatred of the Turks. He happened to witness the slaughter of the two ruffians in the mill and their burial afterwards, and had conceived an unbounded admiration and reverence for Ognianoff. This feeling amounted almost to worship. He called him the Russian for some inexplicable reason. The first night he had been terribly scared by confronting him on the verandah, but he had since become accustomed to Ognianoff's frequent visits to the monastery. He seemed fascinated by him—could not take his eyes off him, and regarded him as his protector. Whenever the servants teased him he would threaten them with the Russian. " I shall tell the Russian to kill you too," drawing his fingers across his throat. But nobody understood what he meant by these words, fortunately, for he would repeat them in the town when he went there. The higoumen and Boïcho paid no heed to Mouncho, who continued shaking his head and smiling amiably.

" Look ! there's the on-bashi coming this way," said the higoumen.

In truth, the on-bashi was approaching with his gun on his shoulder and a knapsack slung round his back. He was going out shooting.

The on-bashi was about thirty-five years of age, with a yellow, bloated face, a high projecting forehead, small grey eyes, and an inert, sleepy look. He was evidently an opium-eater. After a few words of greeting and a little talk on the prospects of sport that year, the on-bashi took the higoumen's rifle, examined it carefully, as every sportsman does, and said :

" That's a good rifle, your worship—what are you going to fire at ? "

" Well, I was just thinking, Sherif Aga. I haven't had it in my hand for a year, and I thought I'd have a shot this morning."

" What's to be the mark ? " asked the on-bashi, eagerly taking his Martini from his shoulder and evidently desirous of showing his skill.

" Well, that great thistle on the bank, near the clay-pit there," said the higoumen.

The on-bashi looked surprised.

" That's a very long way off," he said : however, he walked to a rock in the field, steadied his rifle on it, aimed for about ten seconds, and fired. The bullet struck some paces distant from the mark.

Sherif Aga reddened and showed some uneasiness.

" Let's have another shot," he said, again leaning against the stone and aiming for nearly a minute. When the gun went off he rose and ran towards the bank, but the thistle was still towering above it.

" Confound the thing," he said angrily, " it's no good aiming at a mark so far off. You fire now, Higoumen Effendi, only I warn you that you're wasting your cartridge. However, try and hit the thistle ! " he added ironically.

The higoumen raised his gun to his shoulder, ran his eye along the barrel, and fired.

The weed had disappeared.

" The good old gun hasn't played me false," said the higoumen.

" It's a fluke," cried the on-bashi, " try again."

The higoumen now aimed at the next thistle and fired. The bullet again struck the mark. The on-bashi grew pale with rage :

" Your eye's wonderfully true, Higoumen Effendi, but I'd lay a wager it's not a year since you fired that rifle. Well, you might give a few lessons to these youngsters of yours who're here firing all day long." Then he added maliciously, " They seem very excited about something. But in the end they'll get a devilish good hiding—mark my words." And the on-bashi's look became fiercer and more ominous, as he turned to Ognianoff.

All this time Mouncho had stood at a respectful distance, but his features were distorted out of all shape with abject terror accompanied at the same time by bestial hatred. He now cast a threatening look at the on-bashi, gnashing his teeth and clenching his fists like a man about to attack some one. The on-bashi mechanically turned towards him and glanced at him contemptuously. The idiot thereupon became still more fierce of aspect, and cried, foaming with rage :

" The Russian'll kill you, too ! " cursing him and his mother. The on-bashi understood a little Bulgarian, but could make nothing of Mouncho's gibberish.

" What's the matter with the fool ? " he asked of the higoumen.

" He means no harm, poor fellow ! "

" What's Mouncho so excited about now when he's here ? In town he's always quiet enough."

" Why, every cock grows on his own dunghill ! "

Just then a huge greyhound, with a leather collar round its neck, from which hung the fragments of a leash, ran towards them across the field.

They all turned to look at the dog.

" The dog's run away from somewhere," said the higoumen. " There must be some sportsmen near."

Ognianoff trembled involuntarily.

The hound had run to the mill and sniffed at the door, after which it wandered round the house, whining piteously.

" Why, that's poor Yemeksiz Pehlivan's dog ! " cried the on-bashi.

The dog, which Ognianoff recognised only too well, was wandering round and round the mill, sniffing suspiciously, and every now and then scratching with its paws. Finally, it raised its head in the air and began to howl piteously. The sound struck on Ognianoff's ear like a knell. He glanced anxiously at the higoumen. The on-bashi watched the scene with surprise, and his face was expressive of doubt and suspicion.

Suddenly the dog rushed at Ognianoff. He recoiled, growing deadly pale. The dog made a wild spring at him, growling desperately.

He drew his knife mechanically to defend himself against the infuriated animal, which the higoumen was unsuccessfully trying to frighten away.

The on-bashi watched the scene in silence, casting suspicious and evil glances at Ognianoff and his glittering knife. But seeing that Ognianoff would perhaps in self-defence wound the dog, he interposed and drove it away. Then he turned to Ognianoff, who was red and heated by his efforts and anxiety.

"That's odd ! How comes this dog to be so furious against you ? "

" I think I must have hit it with a stone once," replied Ognianoff with assumed unconcern.

The on-bashi looked at him incredulously and inquisitively. He was evidently not satisfied with the reply. An undefined suspicion formed in his mind. But he determined to look into the matter, and, in order to show that he thought Ognianoff's answer quite satisfactory, added : " That breed of dog is very vindictive." He saluted the higoumen and proceeded on his way, soon disappearing in the Balkan ridge.

The greyhound was already beyond the field on its way to rejoin its new master.

" Didn't you kill the brute ? " asked the higoumen.

" I threw it half dead into the stream to drown, but here it is alive again, worse luck," muttered Ognianoff, angrily. " Old Stoyan was quite right in saying we ought to have buried it with the other two dogs. Just my luck for that lout of a Sherif to come to this very spot, too. Trouble comes when you least expect it."

" Are you sure you killed them thoroughly, and that they won't rise again like the dog ? " asked the higoumen severely. " When a man undertakes a business of this kind he ought to carry it out to the bitter end, and leave nothing undone. You're a novice at the trade as yet, Boïcho. However, there's no cause for dismay. The rumour we spread at the time calmed people down. But I shall keep my eyes open."

Meanwhile Ognianoff was carefully inspecting the place where the two Turks were buried. To his surprise he saw that a considerable heap of stones was now on it. Neither he nor the miller Stoyan had put the stones there. He expressed his astonishment to the higoumen, who tried to calm him by suggesting that they had probably been put there by chance. They did not know that Mouncho went there every day, stone in hand, to fling at the grave of the Turks, so much so that quite a heap had by this time been raised there.

Ognianoff stretched out his hand. "Where are you going ? "

" Good-bye, I'm in a hurry ; I've a lot to do for these theatricals—that infernal dog has driven my part clean out of my head."

" What part are you taking ? "

" The Count."

" The Count—and what are you Count of, I should like to know ? " asked the higoumen in jest.

" The Castle of Diarbekir—which I'm ready to make a present of to any one who likes."

And Ognianoff went on his way.

CHAPTER XVI : THE THEATRICALS

THE drama " Suffering Geneviève," which was to be given that evening at the boys' school, is probably unknown to the youth of the present generation. But thirty years ago it had acquired the most extensive popularity and enchanted the whole population of the day ; its only rivals in the public favour were " Alexandra," " Berthold the Wily," and " Michaela." The plot is, in a few words, as follows : A certain German count, Siegfried, goes to the wars against the Moors in Spain, and leaves his wife, the youthful Countess Geneviève, inconsolable in her grief. No sooner has he gone than his steward, Golos, appears before the Countess with insulting proposals, which she rejects with scorn. The vindictive Golos then slays her faithful attendant, Drako, and throws her into a dungeon : at the same time he informs the Count that he has surprised the Countess in a guilty intrigue with Drako. The Count's anger knows no bounds : he sends orders to put his faithless spouse to death. But the ruffians whom Golos has charged with this duty take pity on the Countess and leave her to her fate, with her child, in a mountain cave, falsely assuring Golos that his orders have been carried out. Seven years elapse. The Count returns from the wars, heart-broken : in his castle he finds a letter left for him by Geneviève, establishing clearly her innocence : he can but weep over her untimely death. Golos is loaded with chains, and loses his reason under the stings of conscience. Soon the Count proceeds to the chase for recreation, and by chance comes upon the Countess in her cave, together with her child and a doe who has nourished them with her milk. All become reconciled and return joyfully to the castle. This naïve and moving conception has at various times brought tears to the cheeks of every old woman and young bride in Bulgaria. At the time the scene of this story is laid, every one knew the plot, and many had the whole play by heart.

This is why the forthcoming representation had caused such excitement among the townspeople. It was impatiently awaited as a great event, which would be a pleasant change in the monotonous life of Bela Cherkva. Everybody was looking forward to it. The richer housewives had got out their best finery, the poorer had sold their yarn in the market and at once invested the proceeds in tickets, instead of making their usual purchases of salt or soap. Nothing but the theatricals was talked of at family and social gatherings. Old women asked each other at church, " Ghena, are you going to ' Geneviève ' to-night ? " and prepared to weep over the long-suffering Countess. At home the conversation ran on the names of the actors who had taken the various parts—universal satisfaction was expressed when Ognianoff was cast for the Count. The wily Golos, who eventually goes mad, was to be played by Fratio, who was fond of emotional parts (in order to increase the effect Fratio had let his hair grow for a month). Ilia the Inquisitive was the servant, Drako, and rehearsed twenty times a day how he should fall when Golos pierces him with his sword. He was also to bark later on in the piece as the Count's dog : and practised this part with equal assiduity. For Geneviève Deacon Vikenti had at first been suggested, on account of his good looks and long hair ; but it was thought unsuitable for a person in holy orders to take part in the piece, and the rôle was given to another, together with a pot of white pomatum to cover his moustache. The secondary parts were also distributed.

A greater difficulty was presented by the decorations, which had to be provided as economically as possible. The only outlay was for a curtain : for this a piece of red stuff was purchased, and to make it look more artistic a housepainter from Debra was commissioned to paint a lyre on it : he, however, produced something which looked more like a haymaker's fork than anything else. For the decorations of the Count's castle all the best furniture in the town was laid under contribution. Hajji Ghiouro supplied his lace curtains for the windows ; Karaghieuz Oghlou lent two Persian rugs ; Micho Beyzadé his handsome glass vases ; Micho Saranoff a large carpet ; Nikola Netkovitch prints of the Franco-Prussian war ; Bencho Oghlou a worn-out old sofa—the only one in the place ; Marko Ivanoff a large mirror and the picture of the " Martyrs " ; the convent lent its embroidered cushions ; the school a map of Australia and the globe ; the church its small chandelier, which sufficed to illuminate the stage, spectators and all. Even the prison of the Konak supplied the fetters for Golos. As for the costumes, they were the same that had been worn three years before when " Princess Raïna " had been given. Thus the Count wore Svatoslav's clothes, and Geneviève Raïna's. Golos added a few extra ornaments, such as epaulets and high patent leather boots. Gancho Popoff, who acted Huns (one of the two ruffians), carried the long knife he had prepared against the rebellion. Drako proudly donned Mikhalaki Alafranga's tall silk hat, somewhat battered though it was. In vain Boïcho protested against this as an anachronism. Most of the actors insisted that the scene would be more effective, and it was allowed to pass in spite of his objections.

The theatre began to fill at sunset. The front rows were reserved for the notabilities, including the Bey, who had been specially invited. At his side sat Damiancho Grigoroff, who had been put there to amuse him. The general public filled the rest of the room, and soon began to clamour eagerly for the curtain to rise. The noisiest of all was Mother Ghinka, who knew the play by heart, and was telling her neighbours right and left all about it, and what were the first words the Count had to say. Hajji Simeon, in the next row, was explaining how much larger the Bucharest theatre was, and what was the meaning of the pitchfork on the curtain. The orchestra consisted of the local gipsy musicians, who played chiefly the Austrian National Anthem, doubtless in honour of the German Countess.

At last the solemn moment arrived. The Austrian hymn ceased, and the curtain rose amid murmurs of admiration. The first to appear was the Count. Perfect silence ensued. One would have thought the theatre was empty. The Count began to speak, and Mother Ghinka prompted him from in front. Whenever the Count left out or altered a word, she cried, "That's wrong!" A trumpet sounds, and the envoys of Charlemagne enter and summon him to the Moorish wars. The Count takes an affectionate farewell of Geneviève, who falls fainting, and goes out. When she recovers her consciousness and finds the Count gone, she weeps. The weeping aroused general hilarity. Mother Ghinka screamed, "Cry, you booby, can't you?" The Countess groaned still louder, and the audience answered with loud laughter. Mother Ghinka cries, "Let me come there, and I'll cry for you something like!" Hajji Simeon remarks to the audience that crying is a special art, and that in Roumania women are hired specially to cry at funerals. Some one shouts to him to be still, and he motions in turn to his listeners to be silent. But the appearance of Golos changes the situation. He tries to tempt Geneviève's chastity, but she replies to his offers with disdain, and calls for Drako to send him with a letter to the Count. Drako appears, and there is a general roar of laughter at his tall hat, which confuses him. Mother Ghinka calls out, "Drako, take off Alafranga's saucepan—off with it, man!" He takes off the chimney-pot—more laughter. But the scene assumes a tragical character. The enraged Golos draws his sword to run Drako through, but before he stabs him Drako falls like a log to the ground, and remains motionless. The audience is dissatisfied with this foolish kind of death, and some clamour for Drako to get up and go through it again. Servants come in and drag him away by the feet, bumping his head along the ground. But Drako bears his pain heroically, and remains true to his part as a corpse. The Countess is flung into a dungeon.

The act ends, and the Austrian hymn begins afresh. The room resounds with laughter and criticisms. The old women are dissatisfied with Geneviève, whose acting is not pathetic enough; on the contrary, Golos had acted his ungrateful part fairly well, and had reaped the deserved hatred of several old grandmothers. One of them called to his mother, "My word, Tana, fine doings your Fratio's been up to! Whatever has that poor girl done to him?"

In the front row Damiancho Grigoroff was explaining quietly to the Bey the plot of the first act. He surpassed himself in eloquence, telling a long story of some French Consul whom he had once known, and who had repudiated his wife through a similar intrigue. The Bey listened attentively, and the upshot was that he became convinced that the Count was the French Consul, and considered him as such ever after.

" This consul seems to me to be a great fool," he said sternly, " or else why does he order his wife to be killed without even cross-examining her ? Why, I never have a street drunkard put in gaol without making Maikhl the constable smell his breath first."

" But it's written like that on purpose, Bey Effendi, to make it more interesting," said Damiancho.

" Well, sir, the author's a fool, and the consul a still greater one."

Close by Stefchoff was also criticising the Count.

" It's pretty plain," said he pompously and authoritatively, " that Ognianoff never saw a theatre before in his life."

" Why not ? He acts well enough," ventured Hajji Simeon.

" Acts well !—he acts like a monkey ; doesn't pay the slightest respect to the audience."

" No ; that's true enough, he doesn't. Did you see how he sat down on that sofa of Bencho Oghlou's ? One would think he was own brother to Prince Couza," said Hajji Simeon severely.

" We must hiss him," said Stefchoff, spitefully.

" Yes, we must," concurred Hajji Simeon.

" Who's going to hiss ? " asked some one in the same row. Both turned round. It was Kableshkoff.

Kableshkoff had not yet become an " apostle." He happened to be on a visit to a relative at Bela Cherkva.

Hajji Simeon was dismayed by the fiery look of the future " apostle " ; he recoiled a little, so as to allow the real culprit, Stefchoff, to appear.

" I am," answered Kiriak, boldly.

" You're at liberty to do so, sir, but you'll go out into the street first."

" And who asked your leave, I should like to know ? "

" This performance is given for a charitable purpose, and the actors are amateurs. If you can do it any better go on the stage and try," said Kableshkoff, warmly.

" I've paid for my seat, and don't require any advice from you," replied Stefchoff.

Kableshkoff flamed up. The quarrel was taking an unpleasant turn, when Micho Beyzadé hurriedly intervened.

"Come, come, Kiriak, don't be a fool. That'll do, Todor."

Just then the Austrian hymn stopped, and the curtain rose.

This time the scene represented a dungeon lighted by a single candle. Geneviève, with her child in her arms, bewails her fate piteously, and weeps. She now acts more naturally. The midnight hour, the gloomy cell, the sighs of an unhappy and powerless mother have a powerful effect on the spectators. Tears trickle down many of the women's faces. Tears are contagious, like laughter. The number of those weeping increases—even some of the men shed tears when she writes to the Count. Kableshkoff, much moved, claps his hands at a pathetic passage. His applause, however, dies out in the complete silence and finds no echo. Indeed many an indignant look is levelled at him for his noisy interruption at the best place. Ivan Selamsiz, who was sobbing loudly, gives him the angriest glance. Geneviève is carried off to the forest for execution. The curtain falls. Kableshkoff again applauds, and again his example remains unimitated. The custom of clapping one's hands had not yet been introduced at Bela Cherkva.

"They seem a thorough-paced set of scoundrels in that country," remarked the Bey to Damiancho. "Where did you say all this took place?"

"In Austria."

"Austria? I don't think I've ever seen any of those Ghiaours yet?"

"Oh, yes, your Excellency, you must have. Why, there's an Austrian living in the town now."

"What, do you mean a little fellow, with double whiskers, and blue spectacles?"

"Yes, sir, the photographer."

"Oh, he's a good little Ghiaour enough. He always takes off his hat to me, *à la franga*, in the street. I thought he was a Frenchman."

"No, sir, he's an Austrian from Drandaburg."

The third act followed. The scene again represented the castle. The Count has returned from the wars, careworn and gloomy now Geneviève is no longer there. A servant gives him Geneviève's letter written in the dungeon at the hour of death. In it she tells him that she is the victim of Golos' baseness, that she died innocent, and that she forgives him. The Count reads this letter aloud—he bursts into despairing sobs. The spectators share his sufferings : they also weep, some of them sobbing loudly ; amongst these is the Bey, who requires no Damiancho to explain the scene to him. The general effect on the audience is heightened still more when the Count orders the treacherous Golos—the author of all his misfortune—to be brought in. Golos appears, ragged, repulsive, tortured by remorse, and loaded with chains, from the Konak prison. A hostile murmur from the spectators greets him. Fierce glances are cast upon him. The Count reads to him the letter in which the Countess forgives him too. The Count groans, tears his hair, beats his breast ; the audience cannot restrain its emotion ; even Mother Ghinka is in tears, but she tries to console the others by exclaiming :

" Don't cry, good people, Geneviève's safe in the forest."

Some old ladies who don't know the piece show eager surprise.

" Is she really safe, Ghinka ? Then, for pity's sake, tell the poor fellow to stop crying," said grandmother Netkovitsa ; and mother Hajji Pavlovitsa cannot restrain herself, but calls out amid her tears to the Count :

" Don't cry, my lad, don't cry, the girl's not dead."

Meanwhile, Golos goes mad. He looks round him strangely, with staring eyes and dishevelled hair, beckons wildly and gnashes his teeth in despair. His conscience has driven him out of his senses : but his sufferings are a relief to the spectators. A malicious satisfaction appears on many faces. " Serve him right," cry the women. They are even angry with Geneviève for forgiving him in her letter. Fratio's mother, seeing her son in that desperate state, crushed simultaneously by the weight of his fetters and of public detestation, lost her own self-control :

" They've destroyed my son," she cried, " they've driven him out of his senses." And she was on the point of rushing on to the stage, but her neighbours held her back.

The act was a brilliant success. Shakespeare's Ophelia never called forth so many tears in one evening.

The last act is in the forest. A cave is seen. At its mouth appears Geneviève, dressed in the skins of animals, with her child. A goat, for whom dried leaves had been provided so that it should not run away, represented the doe who was supposed to feed them with her milk. Geneviève sadly talks to her child of its father, but hearing the bay of a hound retires hurriedly into the cave, dragging in by the horns the goat, which resists vigorously. The barking grows louder, and the audience is of opinion that Ilia the Inquisitive is more successful in that part. He barks so energetically that he arouses a reply from some of the street-dogs √ outside. Upon this the Count appears in hunting costume, with his train of huntsmen. The spectators hold their breath : they are eagerly waiting to see his meeting with Geneviève. Mother Ivanitsa begins to be afraid lest he should pass by the cave and suggests that he should be told that his wife is in there. But the Count has seen it. He stoops at the mouth of the cave, and exclaims :

"Come forth, I charge ye, be ye man or beast ! "

The reply came, however, not from the cave, but from the audience, in the shape of a loud hiss.

Every one turned in surprise towards Stefchoff, who had become very red.

"Who's that hissing ? " asked Selamsiz, angrily. The audience murmured dissatisfied.

Ognianoff was trying to see who it was who had hissed. When he saw Stefchoff, who met his glance without flinching, he whispered to him :

"I'll pull your long ears for you presently."

Then came a fresh hiss, still louder. The audience was becoming excited ; the dissatisfaction increased every minute.

"Let's catch hold of this fellow, and I'll throw him out of the window," roared Anghel Yovkoff, a giant seven feet in height. And shouts were heard : "Turn him out ! Go out, Stefchoff."

"We haven't come here to listen to clappings and hissings," cried Selamsiz, who had misunderstood Kableshkoff's applause just before.

"Kiriak, be quiet," cried even Mother Ghinka angrily, as Rada sat by her side in tears.

Hajji Simeon whispered to Stefchoff :

"Kiriak, didn't I tell you just now not to hiss ; don't you see they're common people and don't understand ? "

"What's the gentleman hissing for ? " asked the Bey of Damiancho.

Damiancho shrugged his shoulders ; the Bey whispered to a zaptié, who went straight to Stefchoff : "Kiriak," he said quietly, "the Bey thinks as you don't seem comfortable, you'd better go and smoke a cigarette outside."

Stefchoff rose and went out with a bitter smile, delighted at having spoilt the effect of Ognianoff's act.

The tumult at once ceased. The play proceeds. The Count discovers his long-lost Countess ; they embrace—more sobs and tears. The spectators recover their spirits. Virtue's triumph over wickedness is complete. The Count and the Countess relate to one another their past sorrows and their present joys. Mother Petkovitska advises them : "Go home, dears, and be happy together, and don't trust these confounded Goloses——"

"Confound you yourself," cried Fratio's mother to her, infuriated at this abuse of her son.

The Bey gave the same advice as Mother Petkovitsa, only in a lower tone. The general feeling was one of pleasure and satisfaction. The piece terminated with a song, in which the Count, Countess and their suite take part— "Count Siegfried, now rejoice in peace."

But after the first two stanzas of the song had been gone through, suddenly on the stage broke out the revolutionary song : *

> *Blaze forth, fond love of fatherland,*
> *Till 'gainst the Turk arrayed we stand !*

The sound fell like a thunderbolt upon the audience.

At first only one voice had begun, one by one the whole troupe joined in, and it spread gradually till the entire audience took it up. A sudden and patriotic enthusiasm filled all those present. The bold and stirring air spread like some unseen wave, filled the hall, passed the threshold, and was wafted abroad into the night : it overcame every other sound, and sent a hot and fiery emotion through the blood. Its powerful notes awoke a new chord in the audience. Every one who knew the song sang it in chorus —men and women. It drew all hearts with it, united the actors and the audience, and rose to heaven like a prayer.

"Sing out, boys. God bless you ! Sing out !" cried Micho.

* In this and succeeding metrical versions, the metre of the original has been followed as closely as possible, and wherever the Bulgarian lines are in rhyme, an attempt has been made to imitate them in the English rendering.

But some of the older people present murmured, considering this foolish excitement misplaced.

Even the Bey, who did not understand a word of the song, listened to it delightedly. He asked Damiancho Grigoroff to interpret it to him one line after another. Any one else would have lost his head. But Damiancho was not a man to be puzzled by a difficult question. Besides, this was an opportunity for him to exhibit his powers. He explained it all to the Bey with an air of the greatest simplicity and veracity. The song, he said, expressed the ardent love the Count and Countess felt for one another. The Count says to her, " I love you a hundred times more than before " ; to which she replies, " And I love you a thousand times more." He says he will build a church on the spot where the cave is ; and she vows to sell all her diamonds and dispose of the proceeds by building a hundred marble fountains.

" That seems a great many fountains," said the Bey. " I should think a few bridges would have been more useful."

" You see, sir, water is scarce in Austria ; that's why people drink so much beer there," answered Grigoroff.

The Bey nodded approvingly at this reply.

" But where is Golos ? " asked the Bey, as he looked in vain for Fratio among the actors.

" He doesn't come on any more, sir."

" Quite right ; they ought to hang the scoundrel. If they ever act this piece again, you tell the Consul not to leave him alive—that'll serve him right."

And in truth Fratio was not among his colleagues. He had discreetly withdrawn when the seditious song began, not being desirous of the applause of the public.

The song came to an end, and the curtain fell amid cries of " Bravo ! " The Austrian hymn began again, and played the spectators out. The room was soon empty.

The actors changed their clothes behind the scenes, and conversed gaily with the friends who had come to congratulate them.

" Deuce take you, Kableshkoff ! What a fellow you are ! What made you do it ? You suddenly appeared behind my back, and began to roar the song out like a bull. You're as reckless as a gipsy ! " said Ognianoff, taking off Prince Svatoslav's boots.

" I couldn't restrain myself, my boy. I was sick of all

this sobbing and all the women's wailing over your 'long-suffering' wife. Something stirring was needed, and I think I gave it them ! "

" I was expecting every moment to be tapped on the shoulder by a zaptié," laughed Ognianoff.

" Don't be afraid ; Stefchoff went off long before," said Sokoloff.

" The Bey turned him out," said the teacher Frangoff.

" But the Bey was there himself," said others. " I saw him listening very attentively. There'll be the devil to pay to-morrow."

" Don't you bother about him. Wasn't Damiancho Grigoroff sitting next to him ? He'll have made things all right, or I'll never call him a diplomat again."

" I had him put next the Bey on purpose to tell him stories. Don't you bother about him," remarked Nikolai Netkovitch, as he took off Pope Dimcho's gown, in which he had played the part of Geneviève's father.

But he had not reckoned on treachery. Next morning Ognianoff was summoned to the Konak.

He found the Bey in an angry mood.

" Konsoloss Effendi," said he, " did you or did you not sing a seditious song last night ? "

Ognianoff protested his innocence.

" But the on-bashi assures me you did."

" He is misinformed, sir ; you were there yourself."

The Bey sent for the on-bashi.

" Sherif Aga, when was this song sung—in my presence or after I had gone ? "

" The revolutionary song was sung in your presence, Bey Effendi. Kiriak Effendi isn't likely to have told a lie about it."

The Bey looked at him angrily : his vanity was wounded.

" What rubbish you talk, Sherif Aga ! Was I there or Kiriak ? Didn't I hear it with my own ears ? Damiancho translated the song to me word for word, and I talked about it afterwards to Marko Chorbaji, who said the singing was first-rate. Don't let this kind of thing occur again," said the Bey, sternly. Then turning to Ognianoff, " Consul, I'm sorry to have troubled you ; it was all a mistake. Ah ! wait a moment. What do you call that fellow—the one in chains, I mean ? "

" Golos."

" Ah, yes ! Golos. You'd have done better to have given
orders to hang him. That's what I'd have done. Never
listen to women's advice. But the play was very good
indeed, and the song was the best part of it," said the Bey,
still sore on the point.

Ognianoff saluted and went out.

" You'll be hearing another kind of song one of these
days," he thought to himself as he went out of the room ;
" and you won't want Damiancho to translate it for you."

But he did not notice the ominous glance cast at him by
the on-bashi as he passed out.

CHAPTER XVII : TWO STROKES OF LUCK

THE next day was a saint's day. The higoumen Natanaïl
was standing on one side of the chancel, near the pulpit,
chanting the canticle. Suddenly he felt some one plucking
his sleeve ; he turned round and saw Mouncho standing by
him.

The higoumen gave him a severe look.

" What do you want, Mouncho ? Be off with you," he
said angrily and resumed the canticle.

But Mouncho again pulled at his sleeve vigorously and
would not let go. He turned round once more, and saw to
his surprise that Mouncho was in a state of great excitement : his eyes were staring with a look of terror and he
was trembling from head to foot.

" Well—what is it, Mouncho ? " the higoumen asked
sternly.

Mouncho nodded frantically, opened his eyes still wider,
drew himself up, and exclaimed wildly :

" The Russian—at the mill—Turks ! " and instead of
continuing he moved his arms to imitate the action of
digging.

The higoumen stared at him in bewilderment : suddenly
the truth flashed upon him with lightning rapidity. Mouncho must have had some inkling of what there was buried
near the mill : indeed, as he mentioned the " Russian," it
seemed that he knew the whole secret. How ? The
higoumen could not even guess : it was enough for him to
know that the secret was known to the authorities.

" Boïcho is done for ! " muttered Natanaïl in despair,
forgetting the canticle and the whole service, and not seeing

the desperate signs Father Gedeon was making to him from the opposite pulpit to tell him that it was his turn to go on. Natanaïl cast a glance at the altar where Vikenti was busy with the liturgy, signed to Father Gedeon to finish the canticle as best he could, and hurried from the church. In one moment he was in the stable, in another he was galloping like wildfire to the town.

It was a bitterly cold morning. There had been a sharp white frost during the night, and grass and trees sparkled with rime. The higoumen spurred on his fat little black horse mercilessly; he was hurrying to save Ognianoff if there was yet time. He knew that the rumours which had been spread at the time had allayed all suspicion as to the disappearance of the two Turks. Who, therefore, could now have stimulated to action the apathetic chief of the police ? Undoubtedly some traitor. But who could it have been ? He did not believe it could have been Mouncho, even if Mouncho knew the secret. He knew how the idiot idolised Ognianoff—he might have betrayed him unwittingly ; but there must have been treachery. And the consequences to Ognianoff would be terrible.

In four minutes he had covered the distance which usually took a quarter of an hour, from the monastery to the town. His horse was white with foam. He left him on the way at his brother's house and hurried on foot to Ognianoff's lodgings.

" Is Boïcho here ? " he asked, anxiously.

" No, he's gone out. Three zaptiés have just been here to look for him and searched every corner of the house. What do the brutes want of him ?—one would think he'd committed a murder," grumbled the landlord.

" Where's he gone ? "

" I don't know."

" A bad job, but there's still some hope," thought the higoumen, and hastened to Dr. Sokoloff's house. He knew that Ognianoff was not a regular church-goer, and did not even think of searching for him in church. As he passed by Ganko's café he looked in, but Boïcho was not there. " At least I can learn from Sokoloff where he is, if they haven't caught him already," thought Natanaïl, as he hurried into the courtyard.

" Is there anybody at home, old lady ? " he asked of the housekeeper.

"No, your worship," she replied, throwing down her broom and hastening to kiss the higoumen's hand.

"Where's the doctor ? " he asked, with annoyance.

"I don't know, your Reverence," answered the woman with an air of confusion, looking about her aimlessly.

"Dear me ! dear me ! " muttered the higoumen, making for the door.

The old woman followed him. "Wait a moment, your Reverence."

"What is it ? " he asked, impatiently.

She assumed a look of mystery, and whispered :

"He's here, right enough, but he's hiding ; the Turks have just been to look for him. I beg your pardon, Father."

"He's not hiding from me. Why didn't you tell me at once ? " cried the higoumen, as he passed rapidly through the courtyard and knocked at the door, which the doctor opened at once.

"Where's Boïcho ? " were the higoumen's first words.

"With Rada—what is it ? " The doctor guessed that something very serious must have happened, and grew deadly pale.

"They're at this moment digging at the mill. There's been treachery at work."

"Oh ! Boïcho's ruined," cried the doctor in despair. "He must be warned at once."

"They've been to his house to look for him, but he wasn't there," continued the higoumen excitedly. "I came at full gallop on horseback to warn him. My God ! what will become of the lad ? they've found out all. Where are you going to ? " he asked with surprise.

"I'll run round to Boïcho—we must save him, if it's not too late," said the doctor, opening the door.

The higoumen looked at him in increasing bewilderment.

"Well ? and how about you ? They're looking for you too. I'd better go."

The doctor made a movement of dissent.

"Not to be thought of—your appearance at Rada's rooms or in church would be noticed at once ; it would create a scandal."

"Yes, but you'll fall into their hands."

"Perhaps ; but by hook or by crook I must give him warning. The real danger is for Boïcho. I'll go through the back streets."

And the doctor disappeared through the door.

The higoumen blessed him with tears in his eyes.

The doctor knew that Ognianoff had an appointment for that morning at the girls' school, where he was to meet an emissary from the Pazarjik Revolutionary Committee. A few hurried steps brought him to the church unnoticed by the police, and he rushed upstairs to the girls' school where Rada was now living : he burst into the room like a hurricane ; his sudden appearance in so precipitate a manner threw the girl into a state of confusion.

" Has Boïcho been here ? " he cried, panting, without a word of greeting.

" He's just gone out," replied Rada. " But why are you so pale ? "

" Where has he gone ! "

" To church ; what's the matter ? My God ! who's looking for him ? "

" To church ? " cried Sokoloff without further explanation, and opened the door to go out. But he drew back at once, dismayed. He saw that the on-bashi was placing a guard round the church doors.

" Whatever is it, doctor ? " asked the poor schoolmistress, with a presentiment of trouble.

Sokoloff drew her to the window, and pointed to the zaptiés.

" Do you see ?—they're on the watch for Boïcho. He's been betrayed, Rada. They're looking for me, too. Ah, what misery ! " he cried, clasping his head with both hands.

Rada sank powerless on the divan. Her round face, pale with terror, seemed still whiter beneath her black hood : she was like marble.

Sokoloff stared from the window. He dared not show himself to the zaptiés, and was trying to find some trusty friend whom he could ask to warn Ognianoff of the fearful danger he was in.

Suddenly he caught sight of Fratio passing under the window on his way to church.

" Fratio, Fratio ! " he called in low tones, " come nearer."

Fratio stopped.

" Fratio, you're going to the men's church, aren't you ? "

" Yes—as usual," replied Fratio.

" Boïcho's there ; tell him—there's a good fellow !—to look out for himself. The zaptiés are waiting for him outside."

Fratio cast an anxious glance at the church, and saw that the three exits were guarded by zaptiés. His diminutive face blanched with terror.

" Will you tell him ? " asked the doctor, impatiently.

" What—I ? Ye—e—s—I'll tell him," replied the prudent Fratio, with evident hesitation. Then he added suspiciously :

" Why don't you tell him yourself, doctor ? "

" They're on the look-out for me, too," whispered the doctor.

Fratio's face fell still more. He hastened away from so perilous a conversation, and moved on.

" At once, Fratio—do you hear ? " repeated Sokoloff for the last time.

Fratio nodded affirmatively, went on a few steps, and then turned off and entered the nuns' convent.

When the doctor saw this he tore his hair in desperation. He was no longer thinking of himself but of his friend. He saw that even if he could be warned now it would be too late—that only a miracle could save him from the hands of the police. There was only a faint ray of hope left.

For there really had been treachery. Stefchoff had proceeded early that morning to the Konak, and had disclosed to the Bey certain suspicions he had long entertained with regard to Ognianoff. At the same moment a terrible thought flashed upon him. He remembered the affair with Yemeksiz's greyhound, which the on-bashi had related to him the day before. Neither he nor the on-bashi had at the time been able to understand the dog's fury against Ognianoff, nor why it persisted in digging up the ground round the mill. What was the animal looking for ? Why had it flown at Ognianoff ? Was there in all this a clue to the mysterious disappearance of the two Turks, which, moreover, had coincided in point of time with Ognianoff's arrival in the town? Undoubtedly Ognianoff had a finger in it. Stefchoff's malignant mind drew all these conclusions with lightning rapidity, and they gave irresistible force to the terrible suspicions he had long cherished.

Stefchoff at once suggested that they should dig round Stoyan's mill. The Bey immediately gave orders to this effect. His plan was to arrest Ognianoff as early and as quietly as possible, so as to avoid any unnecessary disturbance. By nine o'clock the bodies of the two Turks were found, and Ognianoff's fate was sealed. He was now tracked like a wild beast. The on-bashi preferred to arrest him outside the church : the entry of the police would have disturbed the whole congregation, and have stimulated Ognianoff to a desperate resistance. It would be better to take him unawares. While Sokoloff was bewailing his fate on one side, and Rada lay fainting on the other, suddenly a heavy footstep was heard on the stairs. The doctor started and listened attentively. The steps slowly approached : the new arrival, who was evidently leaning heavily on a stick, stopped outside the door. And a voice was heard chanting, in imitation of the church choir :

"Be pleased to bless, good Lord, the followers of Thy word : Holy Serafima and gentle Cherubima."

"It's Kolcho," cried the doctor, opening the door.

The blind man came in freely, he was at home everywhere.

"Have you been to church, Kolcho ? "

"Yes."

"Did you see Ognianoff there ? " asked the doctor impatiently.

"Well, my spectacles haven't come from America yet, so I couldn't see him. But I know he's in there, near the altar, by Frangoff."

The doctor spoke to him seriously :

"Kolcho—listen to me. This is no time for jesting. The police are after Ognianoff, and the zaptiés are watching for him at the doors. He doesn't know anything about it. He's lost if some one doesn't warn him."

"I'll go ! "

"Do, Kolcho, dear, I entreat you," said Rada, whose hopes revived.

"I'd go myself, but the police are after me too. But they'll let you in—go, will you ? " said the doctor.

"Will I ? Why, I'd give my miserable life for Ognianoff, if necessary. What am I to tell him ? " asked the blind man eagerly.

"Tell him only this : Everything is discovered ; the church doors are guarded by zaptiés ; save yourself as best you can."

He added, gloomily : "If they haven't indeed already sent some one in to get him out by a trick."

Kolcho understood the importance of every moment, and went out hurriedly.

CHAPTER XVIII : A DIFFICULT MISSION

KOLCHO went slowly down the stairs, feeling each step with his stick. But when he reached the courtyard he went on boldly and entered the porch. There he stopped, feeling giddy, and as he searched his pockets for his handkerchief he heard Sherif Aga giving his instructions :

"Hassan Aga," he was saying in a low voice, "go and tell the others to keep their eyes open. If he resists, shoot him down at once."

"Nenko, my boy, go in and call the Count—you know, Ognianoff the teacher—tell him there's a man who wants to see him at once," said Filcho the constable to some small boy, as far as Kolcho could tell.

He began to fear lest they should be beforehand with him : he raised the heavy curtain and went in. The church was thronged with people. Hajji Atanasi was chanting the last anthem and the final benediction was at hand. The crowd was unusually thick, because there had been a great many communicants and several requiem services that day. Consequently the whole aisle was blocked with people. The blind man was as it were plunged in an impenetrable forest, as dark as night, which, indeed, was eternal with Kolcho. His instinct guided him aright ; but how was he to surmount that wall of opposing hands, breasts, shoulders, and feet ? Slender and diminutive though he was, it was out of the question to think of forcing his way to the altar by Ognianoff. It would have been a difficult task for a Goliath. He pushed on for a certain distance, but stopped, wearied out. He tried here and there, in the night, to get through, but in vain ; the wall was unyielding. Indeed, many muttered angrily to him not to push, and threatened to force him back. Iron elbows crushed his feeble sides. He was exhausted. In a few minutes would come the "Walk ye in the fear of the Lord and the faith," the stream would flow out, and Kolcho would be carried away with it. And then Ognianoff was lost.   Besides—who knows ?—perhaps at that very minute the boy had reached Ognianoff by some other door, and induced him to come out unsuspecting.   He might be passing by Kolcho, pushing against him with his elbow, and Kolcho knowing nothing. He stretched out his hand instinctively to feel if there was a boy there.   As luck would have it his hand encountered a body which seemed to him that of a boy': his terrified mind at once jumped to the conclusion that it was the ill-omened messenger on his way to call Ognianoff.   In his excitement he pushed him back with all his might, saying hurriedly and almost unconsciously : " Is that you, boy ? what's your name, boy ? stand back, boy ! "   Just then the swaying of the crowd separated them.   Kolcho was in despair.   The poor, honest lad was suffering agonies.   He felt with terror that Ognianoff's life depended on a single hair, and that he, Kolcho, weak, powerless, lost, almost invisible in that sea of human beings, was that hair.   And the anthem was almost over.   Hajji Atanasi, usually so slow and tedious, was going through his chant at lightning speed. What was to be done ?   Critical moments suggest rapid decisions.   Kolcho exclaimed despairingly :

" Make way, good people—I'm dying—I'm fainting," and he pushed forward with all his might.   At this appeal every one made an effort to allow the sufferer to pass : no one wanted to crush him to death.   By this stratagem Kolcho squeezed past them and reached the altar more dead than alive.   He found Ognianoff without asking anybody—such is the marvellous instinct of the sightless.   He grasped an arm quite confidently and asked in a whisper :

" Is that you, Master Boïcho ? "

" Yes, what is it ? " answered Ognianoff.

" Bend down."

Ognianoff stooped with his ear to the blind man's lips.

When he rose again he was livid.

For a moment he was plunged in thought.   The veins of his forehead swelled out and showed the terrible mental struggle going on within.

He bent down again and whispered something to Kolcho.

Then he left the altar, moved forward, and was lost in the crowd of communicants standing there.

At that very moment the sanctuary doors were thrown open, and Pope Nikodim, with the Eucharist in his hands, began : " Walk ye in the fear of God," and the service was over.

The congregation poured out from the doors like a torrent which has just been loosed. In half an hour the last old woman among the communicants had left the church.

The only person left was the officiating priest, who was taking off his vestments.

Then the zaptiés and constables came in. The on-bashi was enraged at the non-appearance of Ognianoff. He must be hidden in the church. The doors were locked and the search began. Some climbed over the trellis partitions of the women's places ; others hunted under the altar and in the corners ; others, again, searched the sanctuary. Everything was turned inside out, every corner which could possibly serve as a hiding-place was overhauled ; the zaptiés searched behind the lecterns, in the cupboards where the vestments were kept, in the chest of eikons, in the embrasures of the windows—but no one was to be seen. Ognianoff seemed to have sunk into the ground. The sexton himself showed all the likely places, being convinced that Ognianoff was not hidden there. After a while Pope Nikodim began to join in the search, fumbling everywhere, with bewilderment depicted on his countenance. He began to look even among the books and vestments. The on-bashi himself began to be astonished at such zeal. The constable Mikhail pointed out to him that not even a chicken, much less a man, could be concealed there.

" I'm looking for something else altogether," grumbled the Pope.

" What ? "

" Why, my fur cloak has disappeared, and my hat, and my blue spectacles in it."

The poor Pope was already shivering with cold.

" Ah, I see it all, Sherif Aga," cried Mikhail.

Sherif Aga came up hot and panting.

" A thief's always a thief," added the constable with secret satisfaction : " he's stolen the old Pope's clothes."

Sherif Aga remained speechless ; when he recovered :

" Is that so, Pope ? "

" My cloak's gone, and my hat and my spectacles—they've all vanished," said the Pope, tearfully.

"He must have stolen them," said Sherif Aga, with the air of a man who has just made a great discovery.

"Of course, the Count must have put on the robe and the hat, and gone out quietly without our recognising him," said the constable.

"That's it," said the Pope. "He must have taken them while I was administering the sacrament."

"Well, I did see a Pope at the door with blue spectacles on," said one of the zaptiés.

"And why didn't you stop him, you fool?" cried his superior.

"Why should I stop him? We weren't told to look for a Pope, but an ordinary man," said the zaptié in self-justification.

"That was him, I'll be bound," cried Mikhail; "that was why he was so closely wrapped up—one could only see his spectacles. His own mother wouldn't have known him."

A loud knocking was heard at the door. Sherif Aga ordered it to be opened.

The constable Filcho and the churchwarden came in.

"Sherif Aga, the Count's in the trap," cried Filcho.

"Yes, he's hidden himself in the nuns' convent; he was seen going in," added the churchwarden.

"To the convent—at once!"

And they all hurried out.

CHAPTER XIX: A DISAGREEABLE VISIT

In a few moments the police had reached the convent gates. Sherif Aga left two sentinels there with drawn swords and revolvers cocked.

"You're to allow no one either to come in or go out," he ordered, and then hastened into the courtyard with the rest of his men.

Their entry caused a great commotion in the convent, and spread confusion and terror in all the cells. The nuns ran up and down stairs, scampered through the corridors and verandahs, with their visitors behind them, and the noise and clamour was indescribable. The on-bashi made fruitless efforts to reassure them—he called out to them in Turkish, but they could scarcely hear and still less understand what he said. Meanwhile, the zaptiés seized every

Pope they could find, as well as everybody who wore spectacles, blue or otherwise, and even two people called Bocho—all these they locked up in a small room. Amongst them were Kandoff and Brzobegounek. The latter, however, was at once released, with humble apologies, by the on-bashi as being no raya, but a subject of the Emperor of Austria. Kandoff protested from the windows against this unwarranted restraint of his personal liberty, and was in a towering passion : his companions however remained quiet, as they knew too well the customs of the Turkish police.

" Why, one would think you'd never seen a Turk before, Kandoff," said a Pope.

" Yes, but this is illegal, it's oppression, it's tyranny, it's an infraction of the most sacred of human rights."

" That sort of tyranny and oppression can't be put an end to by complaints—this is the thing for it," said Bocho the butcher, showing his knife.

In his haste Sherif Aga had not thought of inquiring who it was that had seen Ognianoff go into the convent, nor what clothes he was wearing : he had at once hurriedly begun to search the gallery where the fugitive was reported to have hidden himself. Hajji Rovoama's cell was on this gallery. The nuns were recovering from their first fright and were loud in their protestations ; they complained bitterly that they should be suspected of harbouring criminals. Hajji Rovoama was the most vociferous in her indignation ; she knew Turkish and was able to pour such a flood of abuse at the on-bashi as soon turned him to flight ignominiously. But the search went on feverishly in the other cells. Ognianoff was being hunted for so carefully that sooner or later he was bound to be discovered. Sherif Aga's reputation was at stake ; he was determined to find the culprit ; not a single cupboard or chest was left unsearched, cellars and dark corners were ransacked. All expected, in terror, every moment to hear that the unhappy " Count " had been caught in some cell.

Indeed, at one moment there were cries of " They've got him " ; but it turned out that it was Fratio, who had been found hidden under Sister Nimfidora's divan—he was at once released.

Rada, supporting herself by the beams of the gallery, was watching the search with terrible anxiety. She was in a state of frantic terror : her cheeks were wet with tears.

She took no pains to conceal her emotion—indeed, it would have been useless ; her grief convinced every one that she was in love with Ognianoff : many cast hostile glances at her, but she cared little for the opinion of these women, so cold and merciless before the misfortunes which threatened her lover. She allowed her tears to flow unrestrained.

On one side two nuns were eagerly whispering together and pointing mysteriously to Hajji Daria's cell. Hajji Daria was Sokoloff's aunt and Boïcho's chief partisan. Boïcho was doubtless in there now, and the search came every moment nearer and nearer to Hajji Daria's cell. Rada's heart almost stopped beating. She was petrified with anxiety. Oh ! God, what was to be done ?

Kolcho silently approached her—he knew her by her sobs and whispered :

" Rada, are you alone ? "

" Yes, Kolcho, quite alone," she answered tearfully.

" Don't be uneasy, Rada," he whispered.

" What do you mean, Kolcho ? And if they find him ? He's in there. You know you said yourself some one saw him go in."

" I don't think he's there, Rada."

" But everybody else thinks he is."

" Sh ! I spread the rumour myself. Boïcho told me to, in church. Let the police waste their time here. Ognianoff's at this moment as free as a wolf on the mountain."

The poor girl could scarcely restrain herself from embracing the blind man. Her face lighted up with a bright and sudden joy, like the sky after a storm.

She went quietly and joyfully into sister Hajji Rovoama's cell ; the sister at once noticed her changed demeanour, and frowned with vexation.

" I wonder if the slut knows he's not in the convent," she thought bitterly.

Then, with a look of interrogation, she said :

" Why, Rada, you've been crying ! Crying for a brigand and murderer ! Go on ; that's right, make yourself a laughing-stock before the whole world."

Rada's heart was swelling with happiness.

" Why shouldn't I cry ? " she answered boldly. " Some one may well cry for him when every one else is gloating over his fall."

This daring reply seemed to the nun inconceivably

improper. She was not used to being answered. She clenched her teeth with rage.

" Be quiet, you shameless hussy."

" I'm not a shameless hussy."

" You're a shameless hussy and a stupid idiot ; and your bloodthirsty murderer of a lover will be on his way to the gallows before the day's over."

" Perhaps ; if they catch him," answered Rada, sharply.

Hajji Rovoama started forward, mad with rage :

" Get out, you imp of Satan ; never darken my threshold again," she cried, spurning Rada from the door.

Rada went back to the gallery as if nothing had happened. What did she care for Hajji Rovoama's scorn, or for the insulting manner in which she had been turned out ? She was quite happy, her heart was at peace : indeed, she was glad at having broken off all relations with her unkind protectress. Soon, perhaps that very day, they might dismiss her from the school, and she would find herself homeless and penniless.

But what did all that matter ? She knew that Boïcho was safe, safe as a wolf on the mountain, as Kolcho said. God ! how good Kolcho was ! What a kindly and sympathetic soul, compassionate for the misfortunes of others, and forgetful of his own, poor fellow. And how many others would have remained blind and heedless before other people's sufferings. That Stefchoff for instance—the savage, who was now impatiently awaiting Boïcho's destruction ! But Boïcho was far away from his enemies now. They would have no cause to triumph ; but how happy good people would be at his escape. No, there was no one, no one in the whole world as happy as she was. While she was taken up by these bright and innocent thoughts, she suddenly saw Kolcho quietly feeling his way downstairs.

" Kolcho ! " she cried, without knowing what for.

" Rada, is that you calling ? " and Kolcho turned back.

" My God ! what did I want to call back the poor boy for, uselessly," she thought to herself with shame ; she ran towards him, stopped him, and said, " Kolcho, dear, it's nothing—I only wanted to shake hands," and she pressed his hand with warm gratitude.

The search went on. Sherif Aga, wearied out, left it to his men and proceeded to examine the wearers of Popes' hats and blue spectacles, whom he had forgotten.

R

Kandoff was still protesting against the violence done to his person in defiance of all justice.

The on-bashi, astounded, asked one of them to translate into Turkish the words of the enraged Chelebi.

" Say it again, Kandoff, and I'll turn it into Turkish," said Bencho Dermanoff, who was the best Turkish scholar present.

"Tell him, will you," added Kandoff, "that the inviolability of my person, which is the most precious of human prerogatives, in defiance of all legality and every principle of justice ——"

Bencho stopped him with a despairing wave of the hand.

"Why, the very words don't exist in Turkish. You'd better leave it alone, Kandoff."

At last the convent was freed of its unwelcome guests, who went on to search the garden and the neighbouring houses.

CHAPTER XX : THE FUGITIVE

ONCE more Ognianoff owed his life to his presence of mind.

No sooner was he out of the town than his first care was to hide his Pope's hat and fur cloak behind a bush.

The snowstorm which had fortunately come on had enabled him to pass unseen through the deserted streets : outside the town it was still fiercer. The mountain blasts whistled shrill, the ridge of the Stara Planina was as if powdered over with salt. The fields, deserted and lifeless, assumed an unspeakably dreary aspect under their icy shroud. Luckily the sun soon after penetrated the clouds and shed its invigorating warmth on the frozen landscape.

Ognianoff fled to the westward across the trackless fields and through vineyards seamed with ravines and dry watercourses. He was much perturbed. Some fatality seemed to have allied itself with Stefchoff and to be pressing relentlessly after him. In one moment he saw the whole edifice, built up so sedulously and with such tender care, crumbling in ruin before him. He saw the deacon, the doctor, old Stoyan, and perhaps other firm and devoted friends, flung into prison, Rada overwhelmed with grief, his enemies everywhere triumphant. He could not divine the circumstances which had brought about this discovery. All his worst forebodings passed before his eyes. But was the game irretrievably lost ? Would this discovery lead to fresh revelations ? His flight now seemed to him to be an act of base cowardice. He was desirous of returning, so as to assure himself of the extent of the evil : he was no longer thinking of himself : his fearlessness was quite sufficient for such an undertaking. But reflection showed that he must, at least, disguise himself first so as to be unrecognisable. So he pushed on. He determined to make for Ovcheri, a village where he numbered his most faithful adherents, and to which he most frequently repaired in his periodical journeys. At uncle Delko's he would be able to think things over quietly. But the path to Ovcheri, which was hidden away in a valley amid the solitary outskirts of the Sredna Gora, was full of dangers for Ognianoff, for it passed through the numerous Turkish villages which abounded in those parts. The news of the discovery of the bodies of the two bullies would be sure to reach those semi-brigand haunts that very day. Even if they did not seize him on suspicion they were quite likely to cut him down as a ghiaour : not a day passed without some such occurrence in the neighbourhood ; and his town clothing made such an eventuality still more probable. It was folly to be over-confident ; it would be going to certain destruction. He determined to wait for nightfall, and with this view he retreated towards the spurs of the Stara Planina, where he would be sheltered by the clustering thickets of dwarf oak.

After two hours' arduous climbing over precipices and through wild mountain passes, he reached the nearest thickets. There he found a hiding-place among the dry bushes, and stretched himself out at full length to repose, or rather to think over his position. The sky had quite cleared up. The autumn sun shone bright and warm, and the melting hoar-frost and snow glistened on the grass and the boughs. Here and there sparrows fluttered silently overhead, alighting every now and then to find some food on the ground. An eagle of the Balkans floated high above Ognianoff's head : it had scented a carcase close by, or else took Ognianoff to be such. This thought made the fugitive still more gloomy. The eagle seemed to him to be a portent of evil. He took it to be a living emblem of his unenviable fate : the bird of prey seemed awaiting its feast of blood, for which it had left its eyrie on high. For everything was possible. That wild spot was far from being safe ; it was frequently resorted to by Turkish sportsmen, little better than brigands. Ognianoff waited with impatience for sunset, and several times changed his place for a more secret refuge. The day seemed inconceivably long ; the sun still shone unwearied. And the eagle still floated overhead. Twice or three times it flapped its wings, and then stretched them out black and motionless in mid-air. Ognianoff's eyes seemed fascinated by the bird, but his thoughts were far away. Before his troubled mind passed one after another visions of the past—days of youth, days of struggles, of suffering, and of faith in a lofty ideal. And Bulgaria, which had inspired all these—Bulgaria was so fair, so bright, so worthy of all sacrifices ! She was a goddess that lived on the blood of her worshippers. Her bloody aureole bore on it a scroll of glorious names ; and Ognianoff sought for his own name among them, and fancied he saw it there. How proud he was—how ready to die—nay, to fight for her ! Death was an exalted sacrifice, but the struggle was a great mystery.

Suddenly a gunshot was heard. Ognianoff started. The Balkan echoes reverberated the sound till it died away.

" Probably some one out after game," he said to himself.

Ognianoff's relief was but short-lived. A quarter of an hour later he heard the bark of a dog at no great distance. The bark was immediately followed by a human voice. Ognianoff was involuntarily reminded of the greyhound of Yemeksiz, who had belonged to the neighbouring village. The bark seemed to him to be familiar. It was repeated, this time nearer ; the thickets rustled as if with the wind, and two greyhounds rushed towards him with their muzzles to the ground.

Ognianoff sighed with relief.

Yemeksiz Pehlivan's dog was not there : the animal had been trained to pursue human beings as well as game. That accursed creature, contrary to the ordinary nature of greyhounds, which are generally dull and gentle beasts enough, was very vindictive, as was seen at the monastery. It had appeared as Stefchoff's ally and had prepared Ognianoff's destruction. When the dogs saw him retreating into the thicket they approached him, sniffed, and passed on. Suddenly Ognianoff heard men's footsteps approaching. He fled through the bushes without looking behind him. Three shots were fired, he felt a sharp sting in the heel and trebled the speed of his flight. Whether they were pursuing him, or what was going on behind, he knew not. The valley of a stream appeared before him. He plunged into the low bushes on the bank and lay hidden there. Probably the hunters had lost him. Ognianoff lay listening for a long time, but not a sound was to be heard. Then he felt something hot and moist on his foot. " I'm wounded," he thought with terror, seeing his boot drenched with blood. He took off his left boot and saw that blood was gushing from two places, the bullet had passed right through his heel. He tore off a piece of his shirt and staunched the blood. The pain grew more intense, and a long and difficult path still lay before him. The loss of blood had greatly weakened him, and he had moreover eaten nothing that day. Soon it became quite dark, and he left his hiding-place, which was sure to be ransacked the next day by a band of Turks. With nightfall the cold became more piercing. The first Turkish village he came to was quite dark. Turkish villages become silent and deserted as graveyards as soon as night approaches. The only light to be seen was in a grocer's window. But Ognianoff did not dare to go in, though he was half starved. He pushed on for two hours more, passed through the other villages, and at length saw something white and glittering before him. It was the stream. He waded across with some difficulty and sat down on the opposite bank, because the water had chilled his wound and the pain was very great. He saw that his heel was swollen, and began to be afraid lest inflammation should set in and impede his further progress. He rose, pulled up one of the reeds growing on the bank, and proceeded to wash the wound in the manner he had learnt when he was a member of Hajji Dimitr's band. He filled his mouth with water which he blew through the reed into the wound. Having repeated this several times, he bound the place up tightly, and pushed towards the Sredna Gora, on the spurs of which he was already. The darkness increased every minute. Ognianoff was making for Ovcheri, but seemed to be getting no nearer. At last he saw he must have missed the path : he found himself in a labyrinth of bushes. He stopped in despair and listened. He was now high up in the Sredna Gora. A dull murmur of human voices reached his ears. As he conjectured, there could be no one there at that hour but charcoal-burners; indeed, he could distinguish a slight red flame. But were they Bulgarians or Turks ? He was half stunned, frozen, and exhausted ; if they were Christians there was some hope of assistance from them. He mounted a little higher and then saw clearly their fire close by : he made his way towards it. Through the bushes he could now distinguish human forms by the fire, and his ear caught a few Bulgarian words. How should he disclose himself ? He was covered with blood. His appearance might scare these Bulgarians into flight, or have even worse consequences for him. There were three of them—one was lying covered over, the other two were talking by the fire. On one side a pack-horse, half-laden, was grazing. Ognianoff strained his ears to listen to the conversation.

" Put on some more wood, there's no time for talking. I'll get out a little hay for the mare," said the elder of the two, rising.

" Why, I know that voice, that's Nencho, the son of old Ivan, of Verigovo," said Ognianoff to himself, joyfully.

Verigovo was a village on the other side of the Sredna Gora, which Ognianoff also knew.

Nencho approached the mare and stooped down to take some hay from a goatskin bag. Ognianoff moved towards him through the bushes, and said to him :

" Good evening, Nencho." Nencho started to his feet.

" Who's there ? "

" Don't you know me, Nencho ? "

The dim glare of the fire lighted up Ognianoff's face.

" What, is that you, teacher ? Come along, these are all our people ; this is our Tsvetian and that's Doïchin. Why, you're frozen to death—you've lost your way," said the peasant, leading Ognianoff to the fire.

" Tsvetian, put on some more wood. Let's have a good fire. Here's a Christian perished with cold : we must warm him up. Don't you recognise him ? "

" What, the teacher ! " cried the boy, gladly. " Wherever are you from ? " he asked, putting down some dry branches for Ognianoff to sit on.

" God bless you, Tsvetian. Glad to see you."

" The devils have wounded him ; but it's not serious, thank God," cried Nencho, angrily.

" Bah ! it's nothing."

" Father Doïchin, get up, here's a friend ! " cried Nencho, waking up the sleeper.

Soon there was a big fire blazing before them. The charcoal-burners looked pityingly and sympathetically at Ognianoff's pale face, as he briefly recounted his adventures. He soon felt the beneficent effect of the fire. His frozen limbs began to thaw and the pain from his wound decreased. Father Doïchin drew from his ragged bag a hunch of bread and an onion, and gave them to Boïcho.

" That's all I can give you, it's the only food we've got. But as for warmth, thank God, we're better off than the Sultan. Fall to, teacher."

Ognianoff felt better every moment. His being was filled with a new and inexpressible comfort. That bright golden fire cheered him up, the hospitable wood round him, the rough but kindly faces that looked so friendly, the hard, toil-stained hands stretched out to him in true Bulgarian hospitality, however humble—all this awoke a strong emotion within him. But for his wound Ognianoff would have sung aloud for joy.

At dawn Nencho, leading the horse, on which rode Ognianoff, was already knocking at a door at Verigovo. The dogs barked and Father Marin at once appeared. The unusually early hour told him some visitor out of the common had arrived.

After a word of greeting, Nencho gave the necessary explanations.

" May God cut off the heathens, root and branch ; may dogs devour them ; may the devil take their souls," cried Father Marin, as he gently helped down Ognianoff, who had suffered much from the jolting.

They took him into a remote room in the house, where Ognianoff had once before spent the night. Old Marin looked carefully at the wound and bound it up.

" I'll cure you as I would a sick dog," said he.

Soon the patient fell into a sound slumber.

CHAPTER XXI: AT VERIGOVO

OGNIANOFF'S convalescence went on satisfactorily, though not quite so fast as Father Marin had promised. The hospitable family was quite devoted to the sufferer, to alleviate whose pain everything was done. His only doctor was Father Marin, who knew something about surgery, while Marin's old wife surpassed herself daily by some new triumph of the culinary art. Casks of the white wine of the Sredna Gora seemed always forthcoming : every morning a chicken hopped headless about the courtyard, and eventually appeared at Ognianoff's table, he alone being able to enjoy this good cheer, as the Advent fasts were now being observed with the strictness usual among members of the Orthodox Greek Church.

Three weeks passed by during which Ognianoff improved daily, thanks to the unflagging attention and care bestowed upon him by the Bulgarian household. But he was tortured by an impatient desire to know what had happened at Bela Cherkva—how Rada was, what his friends were doing, and how the cause he had worked for so arduously was progressing. He entreated old Marin to send some one to make inquiries, but the old man would not hear of it.

" No, I'll send no one ; I'm going myself next week to buy one or two things against the feast. You must wait till then, my son. You keep quiet and you'll be well all the sooner. God's merciful."

" But I'll be able to go myself next week."

" Do you think I'll let you ? That's my business ; I'm your doctor, and you've got to ask my leave," replied the old man with paternal severity.

" But let them send word to Rada that I am safe."

" She knows you're safe, since the Turks haven't got you."

And Ognianoff had to content himself with this.

A few faithful villagers were allowed to come and see him : they had obtained the old man's leave after many prayers. Their simple souls thirsted for the " teacher's " inflammatory speeches ; whenever they left him their faces were flushed and their eyes bright. Ognianoff's most frequent visitor was Pope Yosif, the President of the local Revolutionary Committee. He had already been elected voïvode leader) of the future insurrection, and kept his wand of office concealed among the church vestments. Another was Father Mina, the old schoolmaster. Ognianoff was convinced that, except these few and old Marin's family, no one else in the whole village knew his secret. Meanwhile he noticed with surprise that his table was more bountifully provided every day : fried chickens, eggs cooked in butter, rice with milk, pastry, even wild duck and hares were supplied him ; wines of different kinds appeared daily. This lavishness annoyed him ; he began to be ashamed of the expense he was causing. One day in the courtyard he observed that the fowl-house was empty. He said to Father Marin :

"Father Marin, you're ruining yourself. Unless you come to your senses I shall refuse all your dainties and send to the grocer's for bread and cheese—that's quite enough for me."

"Don't you bother whether I'm ruining myself or not. I'm your doctor and know how you're to be treated, so does my wife. Don't you interfere."

And Ognianoff, much moved, said no more.

He did not know that the whole village was contributing to feast their beloved "Daskal." * The secret was kept in common, yet treachery was out of the question, so great was his popularity now. The report that he had accounted for two bullies had raised him high in favour even with the most indifferent. Heroism is of all virtues the one that strikes the public fancy the most.

However Ognianoff's wound healed but slowly, and his hot and impetuous nature was perforce condemned to inactivity : he was tortured by anxiety. Of all his visitors he found most relief in his conversations with good old Mina : the two were together daily for some hours, and Boïcho could not do without him. Father Mina was a relic of the past, the last survivor probably of that extinct race of teachers whose only books were their memory and the psalter, and who had opened the famous cellar-schools of Bulgaria. He had now completed his seventieth year, and was a grey-headed, broad, burly peasant dressed in the old-fashioned wide knickerbockers. After a long and active life he had found a haven of rest in that quiet village where he was finishing his days. He had outlived his generation, his old-world learning was of no use at the present day, his only occupation was to sing, without remuneration, in the

* "Teacher," a corruption of the Greek διδάσκαλος.

church choir : there, at least, modern education had not penetrated. On holidays the villagers gathered round him and listened with attention to his ever-attractive stories, which were, like prophecies, intermingled with scraps of Scripture. Ognianoff was delighted with the reminiscences of this aged worker, the living relic of a past epoch. When a man is in affliction, be it moral or physical, his soul turns to religion ; he finds at once a consolation in the words of the great book. It assuages his pain like a magic balsam. Ognianoff was now for the first time experiencing the soothing effects of the Scriptural language which the old man mingled with his own. When he was first brought to the sick-bed, old Mina said sorrowfully :

"Yet another Christian victim—more innocent blood shed ! How long, O Lord, shall the adversary reproach ? . . . Why withdrawest Thou Thy right hand ? Arise, Lord, judge ! Lift up Thy hands against the haughty at last."

And he greeted him and inquired into his case with warm interest. But when Ognianoff in turning round groaned from the sharp pain caused by the movement, he said pityingly :

"Keep still, my son : Blessed are they that mourn, for they shall be comforted."

"Ah ! Father Mina, we are fated to suffer ; it's not for nothing they call us apostles," said Ognianoff with a smile.

"Yours is a hard lot in this world, teacher—a hard lot ; but it's glorious and praiseworthy, for God Himself has chosen you to serve the nation. Ye are the light of the world : a city that is set upon a hill cannot be hidden. Did not Christ say to the holy apostles : The harvest truly is great, but the workers are few. Go your ways : I send you as lambs among the wolves."

These simple words imparted a sweet comfort and joy into Ognianoff's soul. He begged the old man to give him a few sacred books to read : Mina brought him the Psalms. Ognianoff began with ardour to read those inspired compositions, which are the source of such lofty poesy. These songs of battle, of despairing lamentation, and impassioned prayer awoke a response in him. The Psalms of David never left him.

At last, in process of time, Father Marin went to Bela Cherkva. Ognianoff awaited his return with feverish excitement. He was filled with forebodings of the gloomiest description. It was now more than a month since he had any news of those who were dearest to him. What had become of Rada ? After his flight to what sufferings, to what persecutions had she not been exposed on his account ? She was left alone to face the contumely of society, perhaps even the vengeance of the authorities. Poor girl, she was not fated to be happy with him. The poor child was left exposed once more to the attacks of fate, foiled in her most cherished wishes, and perhaps overwhelmed by the contempt of public opinion. Men's cruelty would impute her devotion to him as a crime, and make her atone by many a bitter pang for the short-lived joys her love for him had given her. And he was not there to console her, to defend the poor weak child.

Plunged in these dark thoughts he hailed old Mina's appearance with joy. At least there was some one to open out his soul to. Old Mina listened to him with sympathy.

"Hope—hope in God, teacher," said he. "Do not despair : the All-seeing will not desert the suffering who trust in His mercy. They who put their trust in the Lord shall see Zion. The Lord will in no wise desert the sinner who repenteth. They that sow in tears shall reap in joy."

As though in fulfilment of these words of comfort, the door opened and old Marin entered.

Ognianoff, trembling with excitement, tried to read his news in his face.

"Good evening—wait a bit, teacher—I'll tell you all about it. You're not too tired, are you ? " said he, taking off his heavy cloak.

"Those city people of yours are a funny lot," added Marin ; "they're like shadows—there's no getting hold of them."

"Didn't you go straight to the doctor ? "

"He's arrested."

"Well, the deacon at the monastery ? "

"The deacon's in hiding."

"Did you find old Stoyan ? "

"God have mercy upon him ! Poor fellow, he died the night they arrested him, from the beating he got. They say he told them the whole story, under torture." .

"Oh ! poor Father Stoyan ! But Rada, Rada ? "

"I wasn't able to see her."

" Why ?—what's become of her ? " He grew pale.

" She's there all right—don't you fret yourself ; but they've turned her out of the school."

" What ! Is she living with the nuns under the thumb of Sister Hajji Rovoama ? " cried Ognianoff, uneasily.

" No, the nun turned her out, too, without mercy."

" My God—she must be starving in the streets ! "

" No—Chorbaji Marko has put her to live with a relation of his, but I couldn't find the house, and my mates were in a hurry. But I heard she was all right."

" Ah ! that Marko's a good soul—there's no repaying what he's done for me. But what do they say about me ? "

" About you ? Why they've all got some other name for you. I couldn't make out what they were at."

" What ? the Count."

" That's it—the Count. They all say the Count was shot in the Ahievo thicket by sportsmen."

" Well, that's true enough."

" Not quite, though, because here you are alive, while they all think you're dead, and so much the better, say I."

Ognianoff started as if a serpent had stung him.

" What ? and does she think-me dead, too ? Is the poor girl to have that sorrow as well ? "

He leapt across the room as though to start off at once.

" Sit still, will you—you'll only open your wound again."

" I can walk quite well now," said Ognianoff with a determined air.

" And where are you going to walk to, pray ? " asked old Marin astounded.

" Why, to Bela Cherkva."

" Are you mad ? "

" Not yet ; but I shall be if I stop here another day. Get me out my clothes. Perhaps you'll lend me your horse ? "

Old Marin knew Ognianoff's obstinacy : he did not even attempt to restrain him.

" You can take the clothes and the horse too. Only I'm sorry for the sake of your youth," he said earnestly. " Every road's patrolled half a dozen times a day ; there's no end to their raids and researches ; do have some regard for yourself."

" Don't you trouble about me. I'll come back to you

safe and sound as a hawk—provided you'll take me in again," said Ognianoff, half in jest.

The old man cast a dark look at him.

"No ; I won't let you go," he cried, "not if I rouse the whole village, and keep you back by force. We want you here—you're like the Holy Communion to us—and you want to go, for them to kill you. Do you suppose I'm going to have it said afterwards, 'Old Marin let Daskal Boïcho, our apostle, go to his death ' ? "

"Not so loud, Father Marin—they'll hear you outside," observed Ognianoff.

Old Mina smiled under his moustache.

And Marin's face became suddenly hilarious.

Ognianoff looked at them with surprise. His last words really seemed to have amused them.

"What are you laughing at ? " he asked.

"Why, God bless you, teacher, what are you afraid of ? The whole village, down to the very children, know you're here. We've all been taking our share of your keep. We're simple folk, but we won't betray a Christian. And as for you—why, we'd sell our lives for you ! "

This time it was Ognianoff's turn to laugh when he learnt that the whole village was in the secret.

After much debate, Ognianoff overcame the scruples of his host, and his departure was decided on.

CHAPTER XXII : AN AWKWARD PREDICAMENT

An hour later a Turk—or, to be more accurate, a Turkish priest—rode out of the village of Verigovo.

A faded green turban, in rags, covered his forehead almost to the eyes ; the nape of his neck was carefully shaved ; his waistcoat of printed calico, open at the throat, had lost nearly all its buttons ; a tattered jacket with hanging sleeves was thrown over his shoulders ; the greasy leather belt round his waist contained a flintlock pistol, a short ramrod, a Sopot yataghan, and a chibouk ; on his feet he wore a pair of slippers, frayed and torn, over which were strapped Seïmen sandals, and his costume was completed by a worn-out cloak of the native shayak, reaching to his feet.

Ognianoff was thus quite unrecognisable.

Winter had now thoroughly set in : the ground was '

covered with a deep sheet of snow, from under which the rocky peaks of the Stara Planina rose black and jagged. All nature was silent and mournful : nothing living could be seen save the huge flocks of crows that flew croaking through the drowsy air.

The straight path to Bela Cherkva was towards the north-east : however, Ognianoff avoided it, for it led through Yemeksiz Pehlivan's village, which inspired him with involuntary terror. His mind dwelt on the dead man's grey-hound, into which the malignant hostility of the Turk seemed to have passed, so as to pursue and terrify Ognianoff even from the grave. Hence he determined to strike to the north, and make for the inn at Karnara, from whence he would cross the spurs of the Stara Planina eastwards, and thus reach Bela Cherkva. This would considerably lengthen his journey, but the danger would be less, though he would still have to pass through Turkish villages. When Ognianoff reached the first village the snow was falling in thick flakes, and entirely blocking the traveller's view. The intense cold had quite numbed his limbs—he could scarcely hold his horse's reins ; indeed, the animal had been guided to the village more by instinct than anything else, for no trace of the path was to be seen under the snow. He entered the deserted streets of the village unnoticed—not a soul was visible anywhere—and made his way to the only inn of the place, opposite the mosque. He was anxious to rest his horse, which was much exhausted by the journey, and also to warm himself a little. A boy came out and took charge of his horse : meanwhile, he made for the door of the inn, which seemed to be quite empty, as not a sound was to be heard. But no sooner had he entered than he saw with surprise that the room was full of Turks. To retreat was clearly out of the question. He decided to sit down, and greeted the whole company : his salute was courteously returned. He had lived long among Turks and was thoroughly conversant with their language and customs. The guests were all reclining on the matting on the floor, with their slippers off and their pipes in their hands. The room was dense with tobacco-smoke.

" A cup of coffee," he said sternly to the caféji.

He proceeded to roll a cigarette, bending over it as he did so, so as to conceal his features as much as possible. While he sipped his coffee he listened attentively to the

conversation going on in a low tone round him. For a time
there was nothing to interest him : suddenly he pricked up
his ears, the death of the two bullies had come under discussion. Such an event had never been heard of before in
the neighbourhood, and the Turks were infuriated by it. A
sudden excitement took possession of the company in the
café, which had till then been so quiet and phlegmatic.
Angry abuse and bloody threats were uttered against the
Bulgarians. Ognianoff continued to sip his coffee with a
fierce frown as a sign that he shared the general dissatisfaction. Suddenly the conversation turned on the slayer of
the two Turks, and he saw to his surprise how well-known
his own name and person were : there were already legends
current about him.

"This ghiaour of a Consul is not to be found or recognised anywhere," said one of those present.

"He's got a devil who helps him : one minute he appears
as a teacher, the next as a priest ; to-day he's a peasant,
the next day a Turk—he changes his appearance in a
moment. From an old man he becomes a boy—one day
he's short and dark—next day he's as tall as a lamp-post,
and has red hair. He's not to be caught. Ahmed Aga
was telling me they once got on his track and sent a
patrol after him into the thicket by the monastery ; he
was dressed in peasant's clothes. Well, suddenly they saw
a crow before them, nothing else, no peasant or any
one. Everybody fired, but the bird flew quietly off
with a loud croak."

"That's nonsense," said several.

"The ghiaour must be caught—only we've got to find
his nest first," said another.

"I tell you the cuckold can't be found," added the first
speaker. "I don't believe he's in hiding at all—only find
him if you can. Why, he might be here now in this very
café, and we none the wiser."

At these words, every one mechanically raised his eyes
and looked round him. Some inquisitive glances were
directed at Ognianoff.

The latter was now furiously sipping his third cup of
coffee, and emitting every now and then a thick cloud of
smoke which half concealed him from view. But he felt
the searching looks that were fixed on him and drops of
perspiration rose behind his turban. He could no longer

endure the tension of such a situation, and was eager to leave the café and breathe the fresh air outside.

" Where are you bound for, if fate wills it ? " some one asked him.

" For Klissoura, inshallah," answered Ognianoff, quietly, unrolling a long twisted purse to pay his score.

" What, in this snow and storm ? You'd better stop here, you'll get there to-morrow."

" To the traveller the road—to the frog the marsh," answered Ognianoff with a smile.

" These stories of yours are old women's tales, Rahman Aga—your ghiaour's no devil or crow, but a ' Komita ' like every other ' Komita.' "

" Well, you catch him then."

" So we will—we've scented his nest."

" If we could only get hold of him," cried several with looks of bloodthirsty ferocity.

" I'll stake my head on it that either to-day or to-morrow the Komita Boïcho will be in the trap."

" Where are they looking for the dog ? "

" He's hidden in some ghiaour village of the Sredna Gora where he's found a warm nest. Yesterday some zaptiés started for Bania and others for the Abrashlar fields—we'll get him."

" Are you after him too ? "

" Yes. We're to meet at Verigovo and begin the search there."

It was then only that Ognianoff noticed that the speaker was a zaptié—he had not observed him in the corner. The discovery of his narrow escape from Verigovo increased his dismay. Their suspicious glances fell, but the café was unendurable. He saluted the guests and went out.

When he was once more outside in the fresh air, at liberty under the snowy sky, he took a deep breath of relief, and leaped on his horse.

CHAPTER XXIII : THE SEWING-PARTY AT ALTINOVO

INSTEAD of making for Bela Cherkva, Ognianoff now turned back towards Altinovo, a village which lay in the western corner of the valley. It was a two hours' journey, but his horse was exhausted and the road was bad, so that he only just reached the village before dark, pursued right up to the outskirts by the famished howls of the wolves. • • .

He entered by the Bulgarian quarter (the village was a mixed one, containing both Turks and Bulgarians) and soon stopped before old Tsanko's door.

Tsanko was by birth a native of Klissoura, but had long ago taken up his abode in the village. He was a simple, kindly peasant and a warm patriot. The apostles often slept at his house. He received Ognianoff with open arms.

"It is a piece of luck your coming to me. We've got a sewing-party on to-night—you can have a good look at our girls. You won't find the time heavy on your hands, I'll be bound," said Tsanko with a smile, as he showed the way in.

Ognianoff hastened to tell him that he was being pursued, and for what reason.

"Yes, yes, I know all about it," said Tsanko, " you don't suppose just because our village is a bit out of the way that we know nothing of what goes on outside ? "

"But sha'n't I be putting you out ? "

"Don't you mind, I tell you. You must look out among the girls to-night for one to carry the flag," laughed Tsanko, " there—you can see them all from this window, like a king."

Ognianoff was in a small, dark closet, the window of which, covered with wooden trellis-work, looked on to the large common room ; here the sewing-party was already assembling. It was a meeting of the principal girls of the village, the object being to assist in making the trousseau for Tsanko's daughter Donka. The fire burned brightly and lighted up the walls, which boasted no ornament save a print of St. Ivan of Rilo and the bright, glazed dishes on the shelves. The furniture—as in most well-to-do villagers' houses—consisted of a water-butt, a wardrobe, a shelf, and the great cupboard which contained all Tsanko's household goods. All the guests, both male and female, were seated on the floor, which was covered with skins and carpets. Besides the light of the fire there were also two petroleum lamps burning—a special luxury in honour of the occasion.

It was long since Ognanioff had been present at a gathering of this kind—a curious custom sanctioned by antiquity. From his dark recess he watched with interest the simple scenes of the still primitive village life. The door opened, and Tsanko's wife came to him—she was a buxom and talkative dame, also from Klissoura. She sat down by Ognianoff's side and began to point out to him the most remarkable girls present, with the necessary details.

" Do you see that fat, rosy-cheeked girl there ? That's Staïka Chonina. See what a sad, sad look Ivan Kill-the-Bear gives her now and again. He barks for her like a sheep-dog when he wants to make her laugh. She's very industrious, quick-witted, and cleanly. Only she ought to marry at once, poor girl—she's getting so fat ; she'll be thinner after marriage. It's just the opposite of your town-girls. The girl to the left of her is Tsvéta Prodanova : she is in love with the lad over there, with his moustache sticking out like a skewer. She's a lively one for you—see her eyes in every corner of the room at once ; but she's a good girl. That's Draganoff's Tsvéta by her side ; and next to her Raïka, the Pope's daughter. I'd rather have those two than twenty of your fine ladies from Philippopolis. Do you see their white throats, just like ducks ? Why, I once caught my Tsanko saying he'd give his vineyard at Mal Tepe, just to be allowed to kiss one of them on the chin ! Didn't I just box his ears for him, the vagabond ! Do you see that girl to the right of fat Staïka ? That's Kara Velio's daughter : she's a great swell ; five young fellows have already been after her, but her father wouldn't have anything to say to them. He's keeping her for somebody, the old weasel—you know he looks just like a weasel. Ivan Nedelioff 'll have her, or I'll bite my tongue out. There's Rada Milkina : she sings like the nightingale on our plum-tree—but she's a lazybones, between ourselves. I'd rather have Dimka Todorova, standing over there by the shelf : there's a blooming rose for you ! If I was a bachelor I'd propose to her at once. Why don't you take her yourself ? That's the Péëff's girl standing by our Donka. She's a pretty girl, and industrious into the bargain—so they say she's as good as our Donka. She's got a sweet voice, like Rada Milkina, and laughs like a swallow twittering : you listen to her."

As she stood there by Boïcho in the dark, she reminded him of the scene in the " Divina Commedia," where Beatrice, at the gate of hell, points out to Dante one by one the condemned, and tells him their history.

Ognianoff listened more or less attentively : he was

entirely absorbed by the picture, and cared little for the explanations. The bolder among the girls jested with the lads, flirted with them archly, and laughed merrily the while. They were answered by the deep guffaws of the youths, who looked shyly across at the weaker sex. Jests, taunts, and chaff followed in one continual flow : loud laughter was called forth by jokes with a double meaning, which sometimes brought the hot blush to the girls' cheeks. Tsanko alone took part in the merry-making. His wife was busy with the stew-pan, where the supper was preparing. As for Donka, she couldn't stay still for a moment.

" Come, you've chaffed each other enough now ; suppose you give us a song," cried the housewife, as she left Boïcho and returned to her saucepans on the fire. " Now, then, Rada, Stanka, sing something and put the young men to shame. Young men are not worth a brass button nowadays : they can't sing."

Rada and Stanka did not wait to be asked twice. They at once began a song which was taken up by all those girls who could sing ; these at once formed into two choruses : the first sang one verse, and then waited while the second repeated it. The better singers were in the first choir, which consisted of alto voices, the others repeating the verse in a lower key.

The following are the words of the song they sang :

" *Well-a-day* ! *the youthful couple ; well-a-day* ! *they fell in love ;*
  Well-a-day ! *in love they'd fallen ; well-a-day* ! *from earliest youth.*
  Well-a-day ! *they met each other ; well-a-day* ! *last night they met.*
  Well-a-day ! *all in the darkness ; well-a-day* ! *just down the street.*
  Well-a-day ! *the silver moonlight ; well-a-day* ! *shone down on them.*
  Well-a-day ! *the stars were twinkling ; well-a-day* ! *within the sky.*
  Yet, well-a-day ! *the youthful couple ; well-a-day* ! *they're sitting still.*
  Well-a-day ! *yes, still they're sitting ; well-a-day* ! *in loving talk.*
  Well-a-day ! *her jug of water ; well-a-day* ! *it's frozen hard.*

Well-a-day ! his oaken cudgel ; well-a-day ! how long it's grown.
But, well-a-day ! the youthful couple ; well-a-day ! they're sitting yet !"

When the song came to an end the youths were loud in applause : it appealed to every one of them ; its pleasing refrain brought up memories of past experience. As for Ivan Kill-the-Bear, he was devouring Staïka Chonina with his eyes ; he was deeply in love with her.

"That's the kind of song to sing over again—ay, and to act all day long," he cried, in his deep bass voice.

All the girls laughed, and many an arch look was cast at Kill-the-Bear.

He was a perfect mountain of a man, of gigantic stature and herculean strength, with a big, bony face, but not over bright. However, he was great at singing—that is to say, his voice corresponded with his size. He now became cross, and withdrew silently behind the girls, where he suddenly barked like an old sheep-dog. The girls started in terror at first, and then laughed at him, and the bolder ones among them began to tease him : one of them sang, mockingly :

> "*Ivan, you bright-hued turtle-dove,*
> *Ivan, you slender poplar.*"

Another added :

> "*Ivan, you shaggy, old she-bear,*
> *Ivan, you lanky clothes-prop !*"

More giggling and laughter followed. Ivan became furious. He stared in dumb bewilderment at the rosy-cheeked Staïka Chonina, who mocked so unkindly her fervent adorer ; he opened a mouth like a boa-constrictor's, and roared out :

> "*Said Peika's aunt one day to her*
> '*Why, Peika girl ; why, Peika girl,*
> *The people freely talk of you,*
> *The people, all the neighbours say,*
> *That you've become so fat and full,*
> *That you're so plump and fleshy now,*
> *All through your uncle's shepherd lad.*'
> '*Oh Aunty dear, oh darling aunt.*

Let people freely talk of me,
Let people, all the neighbours say,
That if I'm fat and fleshy now,
If I've become so plump and full,
It's from my father's wheaten bread,
My father's white and wheaten bread ;
For while I kneed it in the trough,
A basket-full of grapes I pluck,
And drink a jar of red, red wine.' "

Staïka blushed at this bitter inuendo ; her red cheeks became as fiery as if she had dyed them in cochineal. The spiteful giggles of the other girls pierced her to the heart. Some, with assumed simplicity, asked :

" Why, however can one pick grapes and drink wine at the same time ? The song must be all wrong."

" Why, of course, either the song's wrong or else the girl's wrong," answered another.

This cutting criticism still further enraged Staïka. She threw a crushing look at the triumphant Ivan, and sang in a voice that quivered with rage :

" ' *Oh Peika, brighter than the poppy*
Is all your needlework so fine
And all my many many visits
Are all of these to be in vain ?
Come, Peika, won't you have me, dear ? '
' *Why, Yonko, why, you filthy drudge,*
Could Peika ever fall in love
With such a swine-herd as yourself ;
A swine-herd, and a cattle drover—
Some wealthy farmer's filthy drudge ;
She'd put you down before the door,
The little door behind the house ;
That, when she passes in and out,
To fetch the calves and heifers in,
If she should chance to soil her shoes,
She'd wipe them clean upon your back."

It was a crushing repartee to a savage attack.

Staïka now looked proudly round her. Her shaft had struck home. Ivan Kill-the-Bear stood motionless, as if transfixed, with staring eyes. A loud peal of laughter greeted his discomfiture. The whole party was gazing curiously at him. Tears started to his eyes from very shame and wounded vanity. The spectators laughed still louder. The mistress of the house became angry.

"What's the meaning of all this, girls ? Is this the way to behave with the lads, instead of being kind and pleasant to one another, as you ought to ? Staïka—Ivan—you ought to be cooing together like a pair of turtle-doves."

"It's only lovers who quarrel," said Tsanko in a conciliatory tone.

Ivan Kill-the-Bear rose and went out angrily, as if to protest against these words.

"Like loves like," averred Neda Liagovitcha.

"Well, Neda, God loves a good laugher," said Kono Goran, Kill-the Bear's cousin.

"Now, boys, sing us some old haïdoud song, to put a little life into us," said Tsanko. The lads sang in chorus :

> " *Alas for poor Stoyan, alas !*
> *Two ambushes they laid for him,*
> *But in the third they captured him.*
> *The cruel ropes they've fastened round him—*
> *They've bound his strong and manly arms.*
> *Alas ! they've carried poor Stoyan*
> *To Erin's house, the village Pope.*
> *Two buxom daughters had the Pope,*
> *And Rouja, a step-daughter, too :*
> *But Rouja sat and milked the cow*
> *Beside the little garden gate,*
> *While they were sweeping in the yard,*
> *And gaily cried the sisters twain :*
> *' Ha ! ha ! Stoyan,' they cried to him :*
> *' To-morrow morn they'll hang you up,*
> *Before the palace of the king—*
> *You'll dangle for the queen to see,*
> *And all the princes and princesses.'*
> *But Stoyan softly said to Rouja,*
> *' Dear Rouja, you the Pope's step-daughter,*
> *It's not my life I care about,*
> *It's not for the bright world I mourn—*
> *A brave man never weeps or mourns ;*
> *But yet, I beg you, Rouja dear,*
> *Oh ! let them put a clean shirt on me,*
> *And let them brush and deck my hair—*

That's all I ask for, Rouja dear.
For when a man's led out to die,
His shirt should spotless be, and white,
His hair should be arrayed and trim.' "

Ognianoff listened with secret excitement to the close of
the song.

"This Stoyan," he thought, "is the very type of the
legendary Bulgarian haïdoud, with his calm courage in
facing death. Not a word of sorrow, of despair, or even of
hope. He only wants to die looking his best. Ah ! if this
heroical fatalism has only passed into the Bulgarian of
to-day, I shall be quite easy in mind as to the end of our
struggle. That's the struggle I seek for—that's the strength
I want—to know how to die, that's half the battle."

Just then the kavala, or shepherd's reed-pipes struck up.
Their sound, at first low and melancholy, swelled gradually
and rose higher and higher : the eyes of the pipers flashed,
their faces flushed with excitement, the clear notes rang out
and filled the night with their weird mountain melody.
They summoned up the spirit of the Balkan peaks and
gorges, they recalled the darkness of the mountain glades,
the rustling of the leaves at noon while the sheep are resting,
the scent of the corn-flower, the echoes of the rocks, and the
cool, sweet air of the valleys. The reed-pipe is the harp
of the Bulgarian mountains and plains.

All were now listening enchanted as they drank in the
familiar and friendly sounds of the poetic music. Tsanko
and his wife, standing with clasped hands by the fire,
listened as if entranced. But the most affected of all was
Ognianoff, who could scarcely keep from applauding.

The brisk conversation and merry laughter soon broke
out again. But Ognianoff began to listen to what was being
said, for he heard his name mentioned. Petr Ovcharoff,
Raïchin, Spirdonoff, Ivan Ostenoff, and a few others were
talking of the coming insurrection.

"I'm ready for the fun now, I'm only waiting for my
revolver from Philippopolis. I've sent the money, 170
piastres. That's the price of three rams," said Petr
Ovcharoff, the president of the local committee.

"Yes, but we don't know when the flag's to be raised.
Some say we shall blood our knives at the Annunciation,
other's at St. Gregory's Day, and Uncle Bojil says not till

the end of May," said Spirdonoff, a handsome, well-built lad.

"It'll be somewhere about the coming of the cuckoo, when the woods are getting green ; but I'm ready now, they've only to give the word."

"Well, well ; our Stara Planina has sheltered many a brave fellow before now, it'll shelter us too," said Ivan Ostenoff.

"Petr—didn't you say the teacher had killed two of them ? There's a plucky one for you."

"When's he going to pay us a visit ? I want to kiss the hand that polished them off," asked Raïchin.

"He's got a start of us, has the teacher, but we must try and catch him up. I know something of the game myself," answered Ivan Ostenoff.

Ivan Ostenoff was a bold youth and a good shot as well. Popular rumour ascribed the death of Deli Ahmed last year 'to him, and the Turks had long tried to get hold of him, but so far ineffectually.

At supper Ognianoff's health was drank.

"God grant that we may soon see him here safe and sound. Take an example from him, boys," said Tsanko, as he swallowed his wine.

"I'll bet any one whatever he likes," said Tsanko's wife impatiently, "that teacher'll be here the first thing to-morrow, like a hawk."

"What are you talking of, Boulka * Tsankovitsa—why, I'm off to K—— to-morrow," said Raïchin, regretfully. "If he comes you must keep him for Christmas, and we'll enjoy ourselves together."

"What's all that noise outside ? " cried Tsanko leaving his wine and getting up.

In truth, men's and women's voices were heard making an uproar outside. Tsanko and his wife ran out. The guests rose to follow. Just then the mistress of the house rushed in, in great excitement, and cried :

"Well, that business is finished. God prosper it."

"What ? What ? "

"Kill-the-Bear's carried off Staïka ! "

* " Boulka " is the title given to a young or middle-aged wife, who on growing old exchanges it for " Baba," grandmother. Both names are followed by the feminine derivative from the husband's name, thus Tsanko, Tsankovitsa ; Avram, Avramitsa,

Every one started with surprise at the news.

" Carried her off, he has, the lad, on his shoulder, as you would a lamb on St. Gregory's Day ; now, they're at his house."

Her hearers began to laugh.

" Well, what of it ?   That's why he went away so early with his Cousin Goran."

" He laid in wait for her by the door," continued Boulka Tsankovitsa, " and carried her off.   I'm sorry for them both.   Who'd have thought it of Kill-the-Bear ? "

" Well, well, they're a pretty pair," said some one.

" She's just like a fat little Servian pig, and he's a Hungarian bull," laughed another.

" God bless 'em both ; we'll drink cherry brandy with them to-morrow," said Tsanko.

" Yes, and I shall claim my perquisite," said his wife. " I must have my embroidered sleeves, because the match was arranged at my house."

Soon after all the guests left in high glee.

CHAPTER XXIV : GOD IS TOO HIGH AND THE TSAR TOO FAR

TSANKO hastened to Ognianoff in the dark closet.

" Well, Boïcho, how did you like our party ? "

" Oh, it was wonderful, delightful, Tsanko."

" Did you take down the words of the songs ? "

" How could I ?   There's no light to write by."

In came Tsanko's wife with a candle in her hand.

" There's some one knocking at the door," said she.

" That'll be some one from Staïka, most likely.   Perhaps she wants our Donka to go to her, you must send her."

But Donka came in and said that there were two zaptiés outside, brought by old Deïko, the village mayor.

" The devil take them, zaptiés, old Deiko, and all ! Where am I to put the swine ?   They're not come after you," he said to Ognianoff, reassuringly, " but you'd better hide.   Wife, just show the teacher where to go."

And Tsanko went out.   Soon he brought in the two zaptiés, muffled up in their cloaks, and drenched with snow. They were furious.

" What do you mean by keeping us an hour at the door,

you cuckold ? " cried the first, a one-eyed zaptié, as he shook the snow from his cloak.

" You left us freezing outside while you were making up your mind to open," grumbled the other, a short, stout man.

Tsanko muttered some excuse.

" What are you muttering about ?   Go and kill a chicken for us, and get some eggs fried in butter at once ! "

Tsanko tried to say something. The one-eyed zaptié burst out :

" None of your talk, ghiaour ; go and tell your wife to get supper ready at once.   Do you suppose we're going to finish up your d——d jam tart crumbs and nutshells for you ? " he said, with a contemptuous look at the remains of the little feast, not yet cleared up.

Tsanko moved helplessly towards the door to carry out his orders.   The short one called after him :

" Stop a minute, what have you done with the girls ? "

" They went home long ago ; it's late," answered Tsanko, trembling all over.

" Just you go and fetch them back to have supper with us and pour out our raki.   What do you mean by sending them home ? "

Tsanko gazed at him in terror.

" Where's your daughter ? "

" She's gone to bed, Aga."

" Make her get up to wait on us," said the one-eyed zaptié, taking off his boots to dry them at the fire, while the water dripped from them and a cloud of steam rose.

The mayor just then came in and stood humbly by the door.

" You infernal pig ! you've led us round twenty houses, knocking at door after door, like beggars—where have you hidden your——"

And he called the girls by a foul epithet.

The Bulgarians remained silent.   They were used to this. Centuries of slavery had taught them the proverb, so degrading for humanity : " The sword does not strike the bowed head."   Tsanko only prayed Heaven that they might not molest his daughter.

" Look here," asked the one-eyed zaptié, " are you preparing for a rebellion ? "

Tsanko boldly denied the charge.

" Well, what's this doing here, then ? " asked the short

one, taking up Petr Ovcharoff's long knife, which had been forgotten on the floor.

"Oh ! you're not preparing for a rebellion, aren't you ? " asked the first, with a diabolical smile.

"No, Aga, we're peaceful subjects of his Majesty," answered Tsanko, trying to keep calm ; " the knife must have been left behind by one of the guests."

" Whose is it ? "

" I don't know."

The zaptiés began examining the blade, which was engraved with letters inlaid with gold, surrounded by a fancy pattern.

" What do these letters mean ? " they asked Tsanko.

He looked at the knife : on one side there was a wreath of flowers engraved, towards the blunt edge, containing the words " Liberty or Death " ; the other side bore the owner's name.

" It's only an ornament," said Tsanko.

The one-eyed zaptié struck him in the face with his muddy boot.

" Ghiaour !   Do you suppose I'm blind because I've got only one eye ? "

Tsanko's reply had aroused their suspicions.

" Mayor, just come here."

The mayor came in with a cake of bread on a brass platter, which he was bringing to be baked in Tsanko's oven.   He trembled when he saw the naked dagger in the zaptié's hand.

" Read this ! "

The mayor looked at it, and drew himself up in dismay.

" I can't make it out properly, Aga ! "

The short one took his Circassian whip.   The lash hissed in the air and curled twice round the mayor's neck.   A stream of blood flowed from his cheek.

" You're all a set of traitors."

The mayor wiped away the blood silently.

" Read it out, or I'll stick the knife into your throat ! " cried the zaptié.   The bewildered mayor saw there was no help for it—he must bow before them.

" Petr Ovcharoff," he read with assumed hesitation.

" Do you know him ? "

" He belongs to our village."

" Is that the fellow they call Petr the shepherd ? "

asked the one-eyed one, who evidently knew a little Bulgarian.

"Yes, Aga," said the mayor, handing him the knife, with a silent prayer of thanksgiving to the Holy Trinity that the terrible words on the other side had been passed over. But he went too fast.

"Now see what it says on the other side," said the zaptié.

The mayor bent in abject terror over the other side. He hesitated for some time. But when he saw that the short zaptié was getting his whip ready again, he cried :

"It says, ' Liberty or Death,' Aga."

The one-eyed zaptié started. "What, liberty, eh ? " he said, smiling ominously. "Who is it who makes these knives ? Where's Petr the shepherd ? "

"Whére should he be, Aga ? At home, of course."

"Go and fetch him."

The mayor moved off.

"Wait ; I'll come with you, you fool ! '

And the short zaptié took up his cloak and went out with him.

"That's right. Youssouf Aga ; this shepherd seems a thorough brigand," said the other.

Meanwhile, Tsanko passed into the kitchen, where his wife was preparing the supper, cursing the Turks as she did so : "May God destroy them—may He cut them off root and branch—may the pestilence fall on them and rot their bones—may they die of poison ! To think that I should be cooking meat and butter for them just before Christmas ! What brought the accursed heathen here, to terrify and destroy us ? "

"Donka, dear," said Tsanko to his daughter, who stood, pale and terrified, at the door, "you'd better slip out by the back way, and go and sleep at your uncle's."

"And what does Deïko mean by bringing them here again ? It was only last week he brought us two," murmured his wife.

"What's he to do, poor fellow ? " said Tsanko. "He took them everywhere. They wanted to come here—they'd heard the songs. As it is he's had five or six cuts of the whip."

Tsanko went back to the one-eyed zaptié.

"Chorbaji, where have you been to ? Just bring a little salad and some raki,"

" The shepherd's not there," cried the short zaptié at that moment, as he returned with the mayor.

" Well, we must find the rascally ' Komita,' if we have to turn the whole village upside down," said the one-eyed man, drinking.

" What do you say to giving the old boy another taste of the stick ? " asked the short one, in a low voice, adding something in a whisper.   His comrade winked with his only eye, in assent.

" Mayor, go and fetch the father here ; we want to ask him something—and fill this at the same time," said Youssouf Aga, handing him the empty raki bottle.

" It's too late for that, Aga—the shop's shut."

The only reply was a blow in the face from the one-eyed zaptié.   He was naturally a little more humane than the other, but drink, or the desire for it, maddened him in a moment.

A quarter of an hour afterwards old Stoïko appeared. He was about fifty years of age, with a sharp and intelligent countenance, expressive of determination and obstinacy.

" Stoïko, tell me where your son is—you know where you've hidden him—or it will be the worse for you."

As the one-eyed zaptié said this, he poured out and gulped down a glass of raki.   His eye flashed as he did so. Then he handed the glass to his comrade.

" I don't know where he is, Aga," replied the old man.

" You do, ghiaour ; you know quite well," cried the zaptié, enraged.

The old man again repeated his denial.

" You know, and you'll tell us, or we'll pull out your eye-teeth for you ; and if you won't say then, I'll tie you behind my horse, and you'll come with us to-morrow," roared the infuriated zaptié.

" You can do what you like to me, I've only got one life," answered the old man firmly.

" Go over there and think it over a little, then we'll talk to you again," the one-eyed zaptié said with pretended gentleness.   Their object was to extract a bribe from old Stoïko, to be suggested to him by the mayor.   It was brigandage of the worst description, but they wished to give it the appearance of a voluntary gift ; it was the system usually followed in such cases.

But old Stoïko did not move.

They looked at each other astonished at his firmness, and cast ferocious glances at the old man.

"Did you hear what I said, you old fool ? " cried the one-eyed zaptié.

"I've nothing to think about—let me go home," he answered, hoarsely.

The zaptiés could not contain themselves.

"Mayor, throw the old fool down," cried the one-eyed ruffian, seizing his kourbash.*

The mayor and Tsanko begged for mercy for the old man.

The only reply was a kick which felled Stoïko to the ground.

Then blows followed fast on his body. Old Stoïko groaned heavily for some time, then became silent : he had fainted ; his forehead was drenched with a cold sweat, he was worn out by his day's work.

They undressed him to bring him to his senses.

"When he comes to himself, let me know—I'll make him speak."

"For God's sake, Hajji Aga, I entreat you, have pity on the poor old man, he can't stand any more pain, he'll die," said Tsanko, entreatingly.

"Long live the Sultan, you rebel ! " cried the short zaptié in a passion. "You deserve to be hanged yourself for harbouring rebels in your house ; you're very likely hiding the shepherd here somewhere. Let's search the house ! "

Tsanko's face fell involuntarily. Although frenzied with drink, the zaptiés saw his confusion. He turned at once to the short one :

"Youssouf Aga, there's something wrong here—let's search the ghiaour's house." And he rose.

"At your service," said Tsanko, hoarsely, showing the way with a lantern.

He led them all over the house, leaving the closet to the last. Finally, he lighted them there too. In the blackened ceiling there was a trap-door which led to the rafters and so outside on to the roof. When it was closed it could not be noticed. Tsanko knew that Ognianoff had climbed up through it to the rafters and replaced the cover. So he led the Turks in with the utmost confidence. His first glance was towards the ceiling.

* Circassian whip.

What was his surprise to find the trap-door open !

Tsanko remained petrified where he stood. The Turks searched the closet.

" Where does that opening lead to ? "

" To the rafters," muttered Tsanko. His legs trembled under him and he had to cling to the wall for support.

The short zaptié noticed his terror.

" Just give a light here while I get up, will you ? " he said ; but a sudden thought crossed his mind, and he called to his comrade :

" Hassan Aga, you're taller than I am, get on the mayor's back."

Hassan Aga knew no fear when he had got his skinful ; drink made a hero of him. He at once climbed up over the mayor's shoulders.

" Now then, bring the light, confound you ! "

Tsanko, white as a sheet, handed him the light mechanically.

The zaptié first held the lantern in front of him, then put his head within the opening. From the motion of his body one could see he was searching with the light on every side.

At last he reappeared, jumped down, and said :

" Who is it you've been hiding there ? "

Tsanko looked blankly at him. He did not know what answer to give. He had suffered so much that evening that he had almost lost his senses. His thoughts became confused ; the question was repeated, he stammered out some meaningless reply.

" The rebel will give a proper answer at Klissoúra. There's a better prison there : he can stop here for the night."

And the zaptiés locked him up in the dark and chilly closet.

Tsanko was so overwhelmed with terror and confusion that it was some minutes before he could collect his thoughts. He clasped his head with both hands, as if to retain his presence of mind. He was lacking in determination, and suffering had at once crushed him. He sobbed and groaned in despair.

There was a knock at the door, and Deïko's voice was heard :

" What are you going to do now, Tsanko ? "

" I don't know, Deïko. Tell me what's best."

" Come, you know the Turks' weakness. You must give them something ; it's the only way to get out of it ; else they'll drag you from one court-house to another till you're utterly ruined. Poor old Stoïko could have spared himself this with a trifle. Give, Tsanko ! give 'em your white silver to get off black sorrow."

His wife came, too, weeping bitterly :

" Let's give them what we can ! Never mind, Tsanko ; it's the only way to get out of the murderers' hands. They've killed poor old Stoïko. Dear, dear ! to think I should live to see it."

" But what are we to give, wife ? You know we haven't any money."

" Let's give the necklace ! "

" What ? Donka's necklace, with the coins ? "

" Yes, yes ; it's all we have ; it's the only way to get rid of them. Why, they're asking for Donka now, the cursed brutes."

" Do what God thinks best, wife. I'm all of a muddle," muttered Tsanko from his prison.

His wife and Deïko went away.

Soon after a light shone through the chinks in the boards of the closet, and the door was unlocked.

" Come out, Tsanko, you're free," said Deïko. " The Agas were good fellows after all. They've given you back the knife as well, so there's no cause for fear. You've got off cheap."

And, bending to his ear, he whispered low :

" It can't last much longer ; either they'll finish us off, or we must them. This life can't go on like this."

CHAPTER XXV : RETRIBUTION

AT that very moment Ognianoff was knocking at Petr Ovcharoff's door. He had been unable to endure the terrible mental torture caused by the sight of the zapties' savage brutality, which he had witnessed through a crack in the ceiling : he had scarcely been able to hold back his hand from taking a bloody vengeance on the two ruffians—which would, however, have been an act of folly that might have had the most serious consequences. Half out of his senses, he had climbed his way into the street, and ran straight to Old Stoïko's house.

" Where's Petr ? " he asked, the moment the door was
opened forgetting that he was in hiding.

" Why, is that you, teacher ? " asked the poor old mother,
in tears.

" Where's your Petr, Mother Stoïkovitsa ? "

" Take care, my son, or they'll overhear you. Petr's at
Kill-the-Bear's house."

" And where's that, mother ? "

" Next door to the Pope's house—by the new door, if
you know where that is ; but mind they don't hear, my
son."

The poor woman little knew that her husband was at
that moment breathing his last. Ognianoff flew off without
a minute's delay. As he approached the Pope's door, a
noisy throng emerged from within. Ognianoff recognised
Petr's voice. He stopped them.

" What, the teacher ! " They all recognised him.

" Yes, it's me, boys—where are you going ? "

" We've been looking Ivan up," answered Petr ; " he
carried off his girl to-night, and we've been drinking their
health. You should see them together ; one would think
they'd been married for years. And when did you turn
up ? "

" Petr, I've got something to say to you."

And he took the other aside.

" Well, good-night, you fellows," said Petr, following
Ognianoff. They went straight to Stoïko's house.

" Has father come home yet ? " asked Petr.

" Not yet, my boy."

Ognianoff took him into the cellar.

" Listen to me, Petr. The zaptiés have beaten your
father cruelly on your account. They may ill-treat Tsanko
and his family still more savagely. We can't restrain the
violence of these brutes, except by force of arms. I might
have smashed their heads in just now, only I was afraid of
the consequences. We can't go to Tsanko's house."

" I must have vengeance—vengeance," cried Petr
wildly.

" Yes, and I must have vengeance, and a terrible vengeance, Petr, but it must be without danger for ourselves."

" How's it to be done ? " asked Petr, taking his gun
down from the wall.

" Patience, while I think it over."

K

" I can't stop to think ; I must go and see what they're doing to my father."

Ognianoff, himself much excited, had now to strive to restrain a man still more excited than himself from taking a natural but fatal step. If Petr went to Tsanko's house blood would flow. Ognianoff was of opinion that the hour for the decisive struggle had not yet come. It seemed to him a pity that so bold and resolute a warrior should fall prematurely and uselessly.

But his efforts were in vain. Petr roared like a tiger :

" I must avenge my father, if the whole world goes to rack and ruin."

He struggled fiercely with Ognianoff, broke from him, and rushed to the door.

Ognianoff tore his hair in despair. He was powerless to resist the other's violent impulse.

But before Petr could get to the door a knock came from outside. He put down his gun to open. Three Bulgarians, Tsanko's neighbours, were carrying in on a rug old Stoïko, or rather his body.

" Petr, my poor boy, God keep you from harm," * said one of the peasants.

The courtyard was filled with the weeping and lamentation of the women. The poor old mother was tearing her clothes and flinging herself on her husband's cold corpse. Ognianoff seized Petr, who was quite overwhelmed by this misfortune, and forced him into the cellar again ; with tears in his eyes he strove to keep him back, for after the momentary shock caused by the sight of his father, Petr was now clamouring more frantically than ever for vengeance.

" We must avenge him, brother—we must avenge him," cried Ognianoff, clasping him with both arms. " You and I have now no more sacred duty than to avenge him."

" Blood, blood ! " raved Petr, frenzied with rage. " Oh, father, father ! they've broken your poor old bones, the villains ! What will my poor mother do now ? "

" Stop, my poor fellow ; try and restrain yourself ; be calm. We'll take a terrible vengeance on the murderers ! "

Half an hour afterwards the violence of the crisis calmed down, for even the fiercest moral sufferings decrease in

* The usual Oriental form of condolence when some fatal mishap has befallen a member of the family.

time. Petr consented to remain at home, after making Ognianoff, Ostenoff, and Spirdonoff swear before the eikon that they would not leave the zaptiés alive.

"To think that Kill-the-Bear must go and choose to-night to get married," grumbled Ostenoff. "We might have done some good if we'd had him with us. Just our luck."

The plan of attack was the following :—They would lie in wait on the road that led westward to the pass of Leskovits by the road to Klissoura. They chose for their ambush the thickly wooded valley through which the river Beleshtitsa flows just before it joins the Strema. They would wait for the Turks there and attack them with their knives, after which they would strip them and hide the bodies in the thicket. But so as to prevent all possibility of their victims' escape, they would take their guns with them ; these, however, they would use only in the last extremity, on account of the danger of attracting attention by the noise. The plan was based on information obtained as to the departure of the zaptiés. They had given orders to be woke up before dawn, as at the second cock-crow they were to leave for Klissoura.

At the first cock-crow the little band started from the silent village and made for the fields. Snow was falling heavily. The whole path was covered with a white shroud. This enabled them to see their way in the dark. The adventurous party, with their guns concealed beneath their cloaks, tramped silently over the deep snow which threw its pall over everything. Not the slightest sound was heard ; one would have taken them for the nightly ghosts and vampires supposed by popular superstition to abound about Christmas time. The snow fell continuously, and deep drifts formed in the ditches, seriously delaying the march of the travellers, who, however, did not even notice them. They were absorbed by one thought—vengeance. The cries of Petr, their valiant comrade, and the lamentations of his mother and the neighbours still rang in their ears. They had only one fear : lest the zaptiés should escape them—all other emotions were put aside. For a long time they went on without a word being uttered. Suddenly they heard behind them a loud barking which broke the silence of the night. They turned round in surprise.

"Where can there be dogs this weather ? " asked Boïcho.

" It's very strange," said Spirdonoff, uneasily.

The barking was repeated still louder, and soon they saw, under the trees, a great black figure leaping and bounding towards them. The figure was not in the least like a dog : it resembled rather some monster, some gigantic bear erect on its hind legs.

Boïcho and Spirdonoff instinctively stopped at the foot of an oak tree and prepared to defend themselves against this unknown assailant. At that moment it leaped towards them.

" Ivan Kill-the-Bear ! " they all cried, simultaneously.

" Yes, it's me, you've forgotten me, God bless my soul."

It really was Kill-the-Bear in his cloak. The moment he had heard the uproar in the street he had gone to Petr and learnt the whole business from him. Without a minute's delay he had returned to his house, sent his bride home to her mother, stuck his axe in his belt, seized his gun, and hurried off to join the band and take part in the vengeance.

This powerful addition to their band gave them fresh courage. " Let's move on now," said Ostenoff.

" Forward," added Ognianoff.

" Stop a bit, wait for the other one," added Kill-the-Bear.

" What other one ? who else is there ? " they asked with surprise.

" Why, Petr's young brother Daniel, he's come with me."

" What did you bring him for ? "

" Oh ! Petr sent him, so that his brother might see what happened with his own eyes."

" What ! didn't he trust us ? we'd taken the oath ! "

" A hundred oaths go to the piastre. I don't trust you myself."

" What do you mean ? "

" Why, you went off without Kill-the-Bear, God bless his soul."

The last was an ejaculation Kill-the-Bear used at nearly every word. It expressed his thoughts and feelings much more accurately than any other words he could have thought of.

" Don't be angry, Ivan," said Ostenoff ; " we thought of you too, but you've just been married."

" Ah ! here's Daniel ! "

A youth came up panting : he was armed only with a long knife thrust into his belt.

The band had increased its numbers from three to five.

The journey was resumed as silently as before. They were going along the skirts of the Sredna Gora, just by where the peak of the Bogdan (down which flows the Beleshtitsa) rises. At last they came to the stream. It was indeed a favourable point of attack. On the right-hand side was the Strema, which the Turks had to cross : on the left was a deep gorge, thickly wooded with shrubs and under-growth, and behind it rose the mountain. The band halted here. They were about an hour's march from Altinovo, so that if it were necessary to fire, the reports would not be heard. As they took up their position in the thicket, the dawn began to appear. The snow was falling thicker than ever. The five comrades, reclining on the snow, waited patiently with their eyes fixed towards the east, from whence the zaptiés were to come. But the first sound they heard was the howling of wolves. It came from behind their heads and approached nearer and nearer. Probably the animals were making for the plains to seek their breakfast before dawn.

" They're coming towards us," said Ivan Ostenoff.

" We're not to fire on any account."

" The work must be done with our knives and the butt-ends of our guns ; do you hear ? " said Ognianoff.

His comrades listened anxiously. The continued rustling in the thicket above them showed that the enemy was approaching silently and in a body. There was a fresh howl. One could now see the black mass advancing.

" Curse the wolves ! they may ruin our whole plan," said Ognianoff.

At the same moment some wolves leaped on the open ground just behind them, and stopped. They raised their sharp muzzles, and sniffed ominously. The rest of the band appeared.

" There's eight of them," whispered Kill-the-Bear ; " you divide four among you—I'll take the rest ! "

As soon as they saw their promised prey, the famished beasts rushed into the thicket, which now became as it were a fortress, of which the assailants were wolves, and the garrison men. Knives and daggers flashed hither and thither : guns rose and fell ; the howling ceased : only teeth and claws were at work now. On one side the combatants were hungry for food—on the other side for vengeance. Some of the animals soon rolled fatally wounded in the thicket : the rest fell upon their fallen companions, whom they devoured ravenously while still living ; soon all were driven from the thicket by the frequent sallies of Ivan Kill-the-Bear, who rushed out barking like a sheep-dog and brandishing his axe which dealt many a deep wound. He reminded one of Samson when he routed the Philistine army with the jawbone of an ass.

Such of the wolves as survived were driven across to the other side of the stream, where they stopped to lick their wounds.

Fortunately no one passed while the struggle was going on.

" The wolves won't leave this spot," said Ognianoff.

" Let them stop, then, and we'll prepare a banquet for them that will make them remember Kill-the-Bear's wedding," said Spirdonoff.

" God bless his soul ! " murmured Kill-the-Bear, much gratified.

They waited for some time in silence.

The Turks did not appear, though it was past the second cock-crow. The little band had heard long before the distant sounds wafted through the stillness of the night from the neighbouring villages. It became lighter every moment ; the trees in the plain were growing more distinct. The young men began to feel anxious ; they were numbed with cold, and it seemed as though the zaptiés were not coming. They might have postponed their journey on account of the heavy snowfall during the night, or else perhaps as a precaution against an unexpected attack. It would soon be broad daylight ; the road would begin to be frequented, and then nothing could be done. These thoughts formed in the mind of each of them : a terrible impatience seized them : the situation became unendurable, a perfect torture. Ostenoff groaned in despair.

" We must wait here till they pass, whenever that may be ; we mustn't move from here," said Ognianoff, hoarsely.

" But if other people pass by ? "

" Let them—we only want two."

" But we shall have to fall upon them openly then ? "

" If we can't do it secretly we must do it openly."

" We can fire at them from here, and then be off to the

mountain. Nobody'll see us through the wood," said Ostenoff.

"That's all right. But suppose they've got company with them, other Turks ? "

"Then we shall have a real battle : we're armed, and we've got a good position," said Ognianoff. "Remember one thing—we've all sworn before God that we won't leave them alive."

"God bless their souls."

"There's only one thing I'm afraid of, boys," said Boïcho.

"What's that ? "

"They may have taken some other road."

"Make your mind easy about that," said Ostenoff. "There is no other road, unless they have gone back, which God forbid ! "

Kill-the-Bear stood up, and began to scan the horizon attentively.

"There's something coming," said he, pointing to the east.

Every one strained his eyes in that direction. Among the trees along the road could be seen two human figures on horseback.

"They're on horseback," cried Ognianoff, with annoyance.

"They can't be our two," said Spirdonoff.

"Ours are on foot," remarked Ostenoff.

"God bless their souls ! "

Ognianoff was excited and angry. He continued to look fixedly towards the advancing horsemen, who drew nearer and nearer. When they were a hundred yards off, he cried joyfully, "It's them ! I know their cloaks and their faces. The one-eyed man's on that side."

All turned, with their guns ready, towards the two zaptiés, who were quietly approaching.

"I can recognise Tsanko's horse now," said Spirdonoff.

"Yes ; and the other's mine," added Ognianoff.

"They must have taken them by force."

But Ognianoff's joy was of short duration. He saw that the Turks being mounted could now easily escape. It would be impossible to act with knives in the open, the work would have to be done from their ambush with the guns— and a gun is a treacherous weapon. Besides, it was a pity for the horses.

" Well, it can't be helped," he thought to himself.

" We must shoot them ! "

" Take care, boys, let the first aim be straight."

" When they come abreast of us we'll fire," said Ognianoff.

" I'll take the one-eyed one," said Kill-the-Bear.

" Kill-the-Bear and Spirdonoff the one-eyed man, I and the teacher the other," ordered Ostenoff. The horsemen reached the thicket.

Four muzzles were levelled and the report rang out loud and clear, awaking the echoes around. The lads gazed anxiously through the smoke. One zaptié had fallen, the other was dangling by a stirrup. The horses kicked and plunged, then stopped still.

" Teacher, which one was it who killed my father ? " asked Daniel, as he rushed the first out of the ambush.

" The one-eyed one, lying down there."

The boy flew at him, drew his knife, and commenced stabbing and hacking the ill-fated murderer of his father.

When the others came up he was still slashing at him almost unconsciously—he was like a wild beast thirsting for blood. The Turk, still living, was reduced to a shapeless and bloody heap of pulp—he had lost all semblance of human form. The blood formed in pools on the melting snow.

Ognianoff turned away in disgust from this butchery. He would have felt still more aversion had it been effected by a mere coward, but Petr's brother was brave enough : it was only a frenzied thirst for vengeance which impelled him to this act of barbarity. Ognianoff thought to himself :

" It's a savage revenge, but justifiable before God and one's own conscience. It's bloodthirstiness ; but it's a good sign. The Bulgarian's been a sheep for five centuries, it'll be well if he becomes a wild beast now. Men respect the wild goat more than the tame sheep, the dog more than the goat, the ferocious tiger more than the wolf or bear, the bird of prey more than the barn-door fowl, which supplies them with excellent food. Why ? Because they represent force, which means liberty and justice. Let philosophy flourish, human nature remains always the same. Christ has said, ' If they strike you on one cheek, turn unto them the other.' That is divine, and I bow before it. But I prefer Moses with his ' An eye for an eye and a tooth for a tooth.' That's the natural law, which I follow. It's the inexorable, sacred principle, on which must be based our struggle against the tyrants. To show mercy to the merciless is as base as to expect it from them."

Plunged in these absorbing thoughts, fierce and terrible as the hour, and completely at variance with his nature, Ognianoff remained behind his comrades, watching the pools of blood that formed in the snow by the Turk's mangled remains.

Suddenly on the ghastly mass of quivering flesh he saw a string of gold coins. He pointed them out to Spirdonoff.

" Take them for some poor man to buy his Christmas dinner with." Spirdonoff lifted up the necklace with his dagger.

" The ruffians ! what Bulgarian have they plundered, I wonder ? Why : its Donka's necklace and no other," cried Spirdonoff, in surprise and terror. He was betrothed to her.

" They must have given it as a bribe to get her father off," said Ognianoff.

" But there's only half the necklace here : the other half must have been cut off, and remained in this pulp ! "

And Spirdonoff began to search with his dagger, but the other half was not there. It was found in the short zaptié's pocket, with whom his comrade had shared the booty as well as the punishment.

Kill-the-Bear finished off the one-eyed zaptié with his axe.

The two Turks were quickly concealed in the thicket. Meanwhile Tsanko's horse returned quietly to the village, but the other, which had scented the wolves, crossed the Strema and fled, tail in the air, across the plain.

" An eye for an eye, a tooth for a tooth," Ognianoff muttered, mechanically.

As the avengers departed, the wolves approached. Nature and the wild beasts united to blot out all traces of the terrible deed.

The snow still continued to fall.

It was now broad daylight : but the neighbourhood was quite deserted. Nothing stirred as yet, either on the road, or in the fields, which were shrouded in white. No one was likely to be abroad at that hour and in such weather : thus the early departure of the Turks had been witnessed by no one. But the confederates did not wish to be noticed ·on returning to the village. Moreover, the road by which they had come would now no longer be deserted, as there were many mills along it. They held a council of war, and decided to climb the northern side of the Bogdan, which was thickly overgrown with brushwood, and reach the village from the other side of the mountain. The road was a hard and precipitous one, but not much frequented, and they would find shelter there. Daniel they sent back straight to the village.

CHAPTER XXVI: THE STORM

DEEP snow covered the path up the wooded mountain-side along which the party now climbed the valley of the Beleshtitsa. Kill-the-Bear, who knew the country well, led the way with his gun on his shoulder. Their progress was difficult, for there was no sign of a road. After half an hour's climbing the perspiration streamed from these hardy and weather-beaten youths as if they had been walking for hours. When they at last reached the first summit the snow had ceased, and soon after from the grey frozen sky the sun shone out and poured its vivifying rays on mountain and valley, the white surface of which became still more dazzling ; it flashed in the sunlight with a thousand quivering sparks ; it seemed to be powdered over with diamond dust, like the garment of a Bagdad sultana. Down in the valley, now awakened, rose thin streams of smoke over the villages, and peasants could be seen here and there making the first tracks in the slumbering roads and paths. The village of Altinovo was clearly discernible below the spurs of the mountain, and some movement was noticeable. The lads remarked a black mass—probably villagers—moving toward the outskirts of the village, where the cemetery was situated : they concluded that this was old Stoïko's funeral; they could even hear the dull sounds of the church sounding-board. But the mountain-side and the summits remained unapproached, save by themselves, and slept royally beneath their unsullied winding-sheet. The majestic Riba-ritsa, to the west of the valley, lifted its lofty towering summit to heaven, surrounded by a circle of lower peaks ; a veil of fleecy cloud, like smoke, hung as if suspended over it. Along the northern horizon stretched the straight line of the Stara Planina, white with snow and bathed by the golden sunlight. Its usually frowning aspect was softened down into a peaceful loveliness. Only the gaunt grey rocks, whence flow the crashing waterfalls, remained bare and gave a note of harshness to the view. The unbroken ridge stretched like a wall as far as the Ambaritsa ; there the chain of the Balkans began.

The confederates stopped from time to time to rest, involuntarily admiring the beauty of the wintry scene, but in silence. Petr's bereavement, and the vengeance which had followed it, weighed heavily on their minds. Only a few words were interchanged now and again, and then merely with reference to their road. Occasionally one of the wayfarers would slip on the steep ascent and be helped up by the others with great difficulty. It was then that Kill-the-Bear's great strength was most useful. Though they stopped frequently to rest, they were much wearied ; they were exhausted by hunger and a sharp icy wind, which lashed their faces and froze their noses, ears, and hands. Meanwhile the brushwood became thicker and more impenetrable. For some time they went on, but at last they came to a standstill. There was no longer any sign of a path. Before them stretched only the thick tangled undergrowth, cleft here and there by yawning chasms, and the wind became fiercer every minute.

They looked at each other in dismay.

" What do you say ? Shall we turn back to the valley and take the path that leads to the village ? " said Spirdonoff.

" No," declared Ostenoff ; " we must go the opposite way : no turning back." And the others agreed with him.

After a short deliberation they decided to retrace their steps a little and then to strike to the right and force their way as best they could through the thicket so as to reach the ridge which led to the summit, from whence they could get down to the valley on the other side.

" That's where Dicho's hut is," said Ostenoff ; " we can warm ourselves there and get something to eat."

" I'm of Ostenoff's opinion," said Ognianoff, turning his back to the wind ; " let's make for the hut, first to restore ourselves a little, and secondly, we may hear what's been going on at Altinovo. It won't do to go back blindly."

Ognianoff might have added a third reason : the sharp pain in his foot, which had been renewed by the hard exercise and the cold.

"That's true," assented Spirdonoff, "Tsanko's horse must have got back by this time and the whole story must be known."

"Oh! that's all right," said Ostenoff, "by this time the wolves will have cleared off even the bones of the zaptiés. If the Turks go to look for them they'll find only a few rags. The good old snow will have covered all traces of blood on the road, and I noticed there wasn't a drop on Tsanko's horse."

They now emerged on the bare hill-side, and again deliberated as to the direction to be taken.

Ivan Kill-the-Bear was attentively scanning the sky. His comrades waited for him to give his opinion.

"Come on, let's make for the hut at once, I don't like the look of the Ribaritsa, God bless its soul," he said seriously.

The band then turned to the north-east and began the ascent. The wind was blowing fiercely, raising the skirts of the wayfarer's cloaks, and penetrating under their clothes to the very skin. At every step the violence of the tempest increased. Ognianoff was gradually falling behind. He felt that his strength was deserting him : there was a buzzing in his ears, his head swam ; he was quite exhausted, but he would not call out for assistance : indeed, the wind would have prevented his voice from reaching the others. He was endowed with unusual strength of will, and to it he trusted to pull him through, even though his bodily strength should fail him. But a man, however strong he may be morally, must sooner or later give way to the laws of physics. The greatest effort of will, the most powerful strength of mind, cannot raise his powers beyond a certain limit. The mind may, indeed, stimulate the action of the body, but it cannot create a strength which does not already exist. All the mountain valleys echoed with the roaring of the wind, which was now a fierce hurricane : its icy breath numbed their limbs and froze the blood in their veins. The air seemed to encompass the wayfarers like a sea of ice : the sun's rays instead of warming them stung their flesh like thorns. Soon the storm broke right upon them, with thick blinding eddies of snow : it raised the snow in high whirling columns which seemed to reach to the skies. Sun and light disappeared : heavens and earth were blended in darkness and complete chaos followed, while the blinding snow lashed them in fury ; the hurricane whistled and roared : it seemed like the end of the world.

This lasted for two minutes. Then the Balkan storm passed to another peak and wrapped it in its thick veil. The sun again poured forth its pale rays from the colourless sky.

The little band had been protected by a high straight ledge of rock, like a wall, which sheltered them a little from the fury of the elements ; this had saved them, as if by a miracle, from being carried off by the storm-blast. One by one they rose, as if awaking from a sleep which would have ended in death. They were completely benumbed—there was no feeling in their hands or feet. They were indeed in great danger. The first to come to his senses was Ivan Kill-the-Bear—he cried :

"Get up, boys—we must climb the rock, or we're done for ! "

They made an effort, rose, took their guns under their arms, and began to move on. Suddenly Kill-the-Bear stopped.

"Why, where's the teacher ? "

They all looked round in dismay. Ognianoff was nowhere to be seen.

"The storm must have carried him off ! "

"He's buried in the snow."

All hastened to search for him. The precipice yawning under their feet filled them with terror. They hardly dared to look down.

"Here he is," cried Ostenoff.

At the very brink of the abyss, under the snow, two feet, clothed in sandals, were seen projecting. They scraped away the snow and dragged Ognianoff out. He was lifeless, his face was pale as death, his flesh benumbed.

"God bless his soul ! " ejaculated Kill-the-Bear sympathetically.

"Rub him, boys, rub him ! " cried Ostenoff, as he began himself to rub his face, hands and breast with snow. "He's still warm, we must bring him round."

Every one forgot his own sufferings in the desire to save their perishing comrade. The energetic friction soon restored Ognianoff's circulation, and warmed them as well.

"Let's make for the hut at once," cried Ostenoff. And

the three took Ognianoff by his hands and feet and carried him to the snow-covered slopes of the Bogdan. Here again Kill-the-Bear's powerful muscles were of the greatest assistance. At last, after superhuman efforts, they reached the hut.

CHAPTER XXVII : IN THE HUT

DICHO's hut stood on a level part of the plain, in a hollow, surrounded by lofty peaks which protected it from the wind. Towards the north side of the courtyard was stored the provision of hay and leaves for the sheeps' fodder during the winter months : this was covered over with a broad, low roof. From the hut—where the shepherds who tended the flocks remained during winter—smoke was rising cheerfully. A watch-dog flew at the wayfarers, but at once recognised Ivan Ostenoff, and withdrew satisfied. They carried Ognianoff into the warm hut, and continued to rub him energetically The shepherd-boy also assisted to save Ognianoff's life by taking off his sandals and rubbing his feet with snow. When Ognianoff and his comrades saw themselves rescued from the danger of being frozen to death, they crossed themselves devoutly and thanked Heaven for their escape. The shepherd lad heaped more wood on the fire. The four sat round it, but were careful not to attempt to warm their hands and feet as yet. The dog, true to his instinct, stretched himself out by the door to watch.

" Obreïko, where's your uncle Kalcho ? " asked Ostenoff.

Kalcho was Dicho's brother, and was in charge of the hut.

" He went to the village last night ; I'm expecting him back now."

" Give us what you've got in the bag, my lad, we're hungry."

The boy turned out all the provisions they had ; these consisted of a few scraps of hard rye-bread, some green pepper pods, and a little salt.

" Isn't there any raki, Obreïko ? "

" No."

" Well, we must make the best of it. But it's a pity there's no raki, the teacher ought to have some to pull him round," said Ostenoff, looking at Ognianoff who had clenched his hands and was writhing with pain.

" It's all right now, teacher, never fear.   What did you think of our Sredna Gora ? she's a beauty, isn't she ? "

" Thank God nothing happened to any of you," said Ognianoff.

" Oh ! she never hurts old friends like us."

" It's my belief," said Ostenoff, " that it was the Stara Planina that sent us the storm.   Kill-the-Bear was right."

" Kill-the-Bear knows what he's about, he doesn't eat chaff," roared Ivan himself in his deep tones ; the dog barked furiously, the noise having startled him.

Ognianoff looked with curiosity at Ivan.   He could not help thinking that the nickname suited him admirably.   No more appropriate designation could have been found for this big-headed, coarse, half-savage giant, who looked as if he had been suckled by a bear rather than a woman.   He gazed at his lofty figure, thin and bony, but powerful : his long, angular, shaggy head, with its narrow forehead, small grey eyes, and immense nose, very wide at the nostrils, like a beast's : his huge mouth, capacious enough to swallow a hare whole (Ivan was said to eat raw meat) ; and those long hairy, muscular arms, which were fit to wrestle with a lion. He seemed to have been intended by Nature to fight with savage animals—to which he seemed so closely akin—rather than for the idyllic calling of a goatherd.   In contrast to all this, his face bore an expression of good tempered and sheepish simplicity which made him ridiculous.   No one would have supposed that this coarse, rough, apparently undeveloped nature could know feelings of devotion, or the most humane and tender of emotions.   Yet it was so.   His very appearance that morning to join the avengers, almost comic though it was, bore witness to his kindly and valiant disposition.   He was ready to sacrifice himself.   Under the influence of these thoughts it seemed to Ognianoff that his face became more sympathetic, and even intelligent.

" I say, Ivan, how did you get that awful nickname ? "

" What, teacher ! Don't you know ? " replied Ostenoff. " He fought with a bear."

" Really ? "

" Rather—he's a wonderful hunter—and killed it, too."

" Kill-the-Bear, tell us how you and the bear rolled down the cliff together."   ·

" Do you mean to say you wrestled with it ? " asked Boïcho, astounded.

Instead of answering, Kill-the-Bear raised his hand to his neck. Ognianoff then noticed for the first time a deep scar there, newly healed ; he then bared his arm to the elbow, and showed another fearful wound, which seemed to have been caused by an iron hook. Ognianoff shuddered as he saw them.

" Ivan, tell us how you came upon the bear. You're a wonderful hunter," he said.

Ivan looked round triumphantly, his dull countenance lighted up with the proud recollection. He began his story.

" God bless his soul ! " he commenced, with his favourite expression. But the dog barked suddenly, and rushed out of the hut.

" What's Mourjo barking for ? Ivan's only just begun," said Ostenoff, in jest.

" It's uncle Kalcho," cried the shepherd-lad.

Kalcho appeared with his staff, and a bag over his shoulder.

" What, visitors ? welcome, boys ! " he cried, hospitably, setting down his burden.

" Make room for uncle Kalcho to warm himself."

" My stars, boys, but it's cold—cold enough to freeze all the wolves ! Where did the storm catch you ? "

" Here, at the bottom of the hill," said Spirdonoff.

" But what are you out for in such weather—hunting ? You ought to know that this isn't the time of year to be out on the Balkan."

" Oh, that's all right, Kalcho—we've had good sport. You haven't got any raki, have you ? " said Ostenoff.

" Raki ? oh yes, I have ; but I've got something still better."

The little flask passed from hand to hand.

" What can there be better than raki, this weather ? "

" I've got a piece of news ! " They all listened attentively.

" The wolves ate two Klissoura zaptiés this morning."

" You don't say so ? " cried Kill-the-Bear, with assumed surprise. The dog again barked at him.

" Yes, my boy, they've not left a hair of them. A band of Turks went to look for them, but all they found was their clothes and their bones by the Sardanoff hill. Hajji Omer Aga says the zaptiés must have been attacked while they were watering their horses, and tried to fly one way while the horses bolted the other way. One horse is lost. The wolves seem to have thought the Turks' flesh sweeter than the horses', and polished them off. Here's luck, boys, and the same end to all heathens. They're a race of dogs, and may the dogs eat them all."

And Kalcho took a pull at the flask. He then noticed Ognianoff, who was unknown to him, for the first time. "And who's this new chum ? " he asked, handing him the flask.

" He's from Kara-Saréli ; we met him on the Balkan. He was out after the same game as we were," said Spirdonoff.

" He's a plucky one if you like—your health, teacher," thundered Kill-the-Bear. The dog growled angrily.

Kalcho turned to Kill-the-Bear with a smile. " Why, Bear, what have you been up to, you rogue ? "

" Nothing, Kalcho, nothing."

" Nothing ? you ought to be ashamed of yourself ; carrying off a girl and disgracing the pair of you. Well, I wish you luck. Where's the game for your wedding-feast ? "

" I left it in the valley below, uncle," roared Ivan.

This time Mourjo became seriously angry.

" Come along, Ivan, tell us how you fought the bear."

" He ? " said Kalcho, looking slyly at Kill-the-Bear, " he'd better tell us how he fought Staïka."

Loud laughter followed this sally. Ivan Ostenoff wished to assure himself that the Turks suspected nothing, and added : " So that's it, is it ? they were torn to pieces by wolves. Don't the Turks say they were killed by Bulgarians ? "

" Why, the whole village knows it. Poor old Stoïko, Lord have mercy on him ! " said Kalcho, who had misunderstood the question.

" Yes, I know all about that, but what I want to know is, have the Turks any suspicion that it was Bulgarians who killed the zaptiés ? "

Kalcho looked at him with surprise.

" Who says so ? Who ever heard of a Bulgarian from our village killing a zaptié ? I tell you the wolves polished them off, and the Turks are getting ready for a big hunt to-morrow, to drive the wolves down to the fords and shoot them there. And so much the better, say I, we haven't dared to take the sheep into the fields this winter. Here's luck, boys ; may we have a merry Christmas, and may you

L

all follow the Bear's example, but not during the fast. Have a drink, mate," and Kalcho handed the raki to Ognianoff, whose forces returned under the influence of the potent liquor. He raised the flask, and said with emotion:

" Remember Father Stoïko, boys, the victim of Turkish brutality. May God rest his soul, and give us a bold heart and a strong hand to fight against Christ's enemies and pay them back a hundredfold. God forgive old Stoïko."

" God forgive him," the comrades repeated.

" God forgive him," said Kalcho, taking off his cap. Then turning in a friendly manner towards Ognianoff, he said: " My stars, mate, but you know how to talk; God must have put the words into your mouth. Things may go on for a bit yet, but there'll be trouble one of these days. Let's make friends—what's your name? They call me Kalcho Bogdanoff the Cooper," and Kalcho handed the flask to Ognianoff.

He gave him an assumed name, and drank to their friendship.

The visitors ate but little, wishing to spare Kalcho's scanty provisions: soon after they took leave of him. He followed them to the door, and again addressed Ognianoff. " Beg pardon, mate, but I've forgotten your name—never mind; but whenever you come by here again mind you come and see me—you *can* talk, and no mistake. God bless you ! "

A few stirring words from Ognianoff had strangely moved the poor goatherd. It was not that they were altogether new to him—he had shared in the hatred of his oppressors from his earliest youth; but the " mate " had spoken a word or two of the " struggle," and these words had struck on a chord hitherto untouched, and awakened new feelings within him. We shall see later what result these words eventually produced.

The confederates were soon lost to sight: they made their way down the valley to the village, which was now quite dark.

Ognianoff decided to spend the night at Dochka's inn. But no sooner had he entered the room than fifteen armed bashi-bozouks mounted the stairs: they were led by the zaptié whom Boïcho had noticed on the previous day at the café in the Turkish village.

Alas ! there was no Kalcho to warn him this time.

PART II

CHAPTER I: TOGETHER AGAIN

RÁDA could not contain herself for joyful expectation. During the whole winter she had mourned Boïcho as dead, there seemed no doubt that, as was confidently asserted by the Turks, he had been shot in the Ahievo thicket, though the body had never been discovered, and Sister Rovoama took a malicious pleasure in dwelling upon his fate, embroidering the recital with graphic and harrowing details derived from her own imagination. The poor girl, held up to general scorn and contumely as the rebel's betrothed, had taken refuge at the cottage of a lowly relative, and scarcely ventured out of doors.

And now all this sorrow was forgotten—for had not the news reached her, through the faithful Kolcho, that Ognianoff was not dead after all, that he had appeared in a peasant's disguise at a meeting of the Revolutionary Committee, which had recently resumed its sittings, and would come to her that very evening? Small wonder, then, if she counted the very moments that were to elapse before his coming, and peered anxiously from the window every now and then to see if he were approaching, and if no suspicious-looking strangers were about.

For six months have elapsed since the vengeance taken for Father Stoïko's murder. These six months have been for Bela Cherkva a troubled period; the discovery of the bodies of the two Turks at the mill had led to many arrests, and had redoubled the fury of the ruling race against the insubordinate rayas. Dr. Sokoloff had been thrown into gaol on suspicion of being an accomplice in the crime, but no evidence could be produced against him, and he had moreover a powerful ally in the person of the Bey's wife—for it may now be confessed that Hajji Rovoama's statements on this head were true for once; he was therefore released on bail, our old friends Marko Ivanoff and Micho Beyzadé being his sureties. But Lalka's marriage to Stefchoff, followed a few months later by her early death, had left the doctor a disappointed man, animated only by the desire to work at the same time for his country's liberation and the destruction of his hated rival, the notorious Turkish spy. As for the revolutionary ardour displayed so openly before, it was deemed only prudent to conceal it till the storm should have blown over, and for a time the committee ceased to meet. But with the approach of spring the suspicions of the Turks died away; all over Southern Bulgaria the revolutionary effervescence broke out once more, and the committee meetings were again in full swing.

It was only the next evening, at nightfall, that Ognianoff was able to visit Rada.

Her eyes were weary with watching. Those tedious hours, full of anxious longing, emotion, and anxiety, seemed to her to be longer than centuries.

When at last she heard Ognianoff's knock at the door, she seemed to have no strength left in her, yet she flew to open it.

The lovers clasped each other fondly and their lips met in a long passionate kiss.

A whole torrent of joy was expressed in a few repeated kisses, a few broken words.

After the first agitation of their long-deferred meeting, the two happy lovers became calmer. Their joy was inexpressible. Rada was fairer than ever, with the light of love in her face. She thought Boïcho had never seemed more handsome than in his peasant's dress which set off so well the fine and expressive features of his manly face.

"And how have you been, darling?" he asked tenderly. "Poor child—you've had much to go through. I've destroyed you, I've sacrificed you, Rada. Yet you haven't a word of reproach for me—you're always the same loving little soul, the same tender little heart, born only for caresses and kindness. Forgive me, forgive me, Rada, dear!" and Ognianoff pressed her hands in his own and ost himself in the depths of her great and flashing eyes.

"Forgive you? I won't forgive you," she cried, in feigned anger. "What do you mean? Do you suppose I am not going to mourn for you when I think you dead? Not even to send me a line! Ah, Boïcho, Boïcho, don't die, for God's sake! I can't do without you. I want to be always with you—to watch over you as the apple of my eye—to love you—oh! so much—and to rejoice in you. You've suffered terribly, Boïcho, haven't you? Ah! how foolish I am! I haven't even asked you what you've been doing all these months—these terrible centuries, as they've eemed to me."

"I've wandered far and wide, Rada, and gone through much danger ; but there's a God for us, too, and so we've met once more."

"No, no—you must tell me all about it—I want to know. Such terrible stories they told about you, one more frightful than the other. My God ! how can people be so unmerciful as to invent such things ! Tell me, Boïcho. Now you're with me safe and sound I can listen boldly to everything you've gone through, however terrible it may be."

And she looked at him beseechingly, with inexpressible affection and sympathy.

Boïcho had not the heart to refuse her request. She was quite right. And besides he was only too ready to disburden his soul to some friendly hearer, some responsive heart : the memories of sufferings endured, of misfortunes gone through, possess a special charm when related in hours of happiness. Boïcho recounted in simple language his adventures since he had left Bela Cherkva. In Rada's clear childish eyes were reflected the emotions of her soul as she listened to him ; he read there now fear, now kindness and compassion, now joy and triumph : she swallowed eagerly every word, she endured and went through everything, and did not once take from him her glance which cheered and comforted him so sweetly.

"Oh ! Boïcho ! some one must have betrayed you !" she cried in dismay when he came to the story of his being attacked by Turks at the inn at Altinovo.

"I can't tell—I won't accuse a Bulgarian. Perhaps I betrayed myself in the Turkish café by some imprudent act."

"Well ? Go on !" she asked impatiently and excitedly.

"I heard from my room the steps of the Turks, and understood at once that they'd come after me. Everything grew dark before my eyes. I saw there was no hope : I was lost. I took out my revolver and stood by the door. I had six bullets—five for them and the sixth for myself."

"My God ! my God ! to think that all the while I knew nothing—perhaps I was laughing here at that every moment."

"You must have been praying for me, Rada, for God once more had mercy on me and saved me from inevitable destruction."

"Did He perform a miracle, Boïcho ? "

"Yes, a miracle, if you like. He blinded the Turks.

Instead of coming into my room, they entered the first room by the courtyard. I found out afterwards that immediately after me some cashier had arrived from Philippopolis, a Greek, and they had given him the next room to mine. He seems to have been very much like me in appearance, and this confused the zaptié, who had seen me the day before."

Rada sighed with relief.

" I heard them talking loudly, and understood that there was some mistake and that they'd be upon me in another minute. Only a minute divided me from them, from death. I don't remember now how I pulled the window open and flung myself into the road below—not the road, that is, but the river, which was frozen. The ice broke and I plunged into the cold water up to my knees. While I was struggling to reach the dry land, I heard a deafening noise—five or six guns were fired at me from the window. Then I turned to flight, a mad unreasoning flight. How long I fled in the dark—where I passed—I have no idea."

" Were they pursuing you ? "

" Yes, I heard them for some time, then all became still. I was in the depth of the forest. It was night and the wind was blowing hard. My clothes were frozen as stiff as boards. I went on for two hours to the westward, always through the thickets, and at length reached the village of Ovcheri, more dead than alive. There some kind people took me in and gave me food and shelter ; one of my toes was frostbitten, but thank God ! . . . . I stayed there for a fortnight, but I was afraid of bringing trouble on these poor people—I seem to draw misfortune on every one—and I made my way to Pirdop, where Mouratliski's brother was employed as a schoolmaster. I stayed with him for three months, during which time I was dangerously ill."

" Poor Boïcho ! You've wandered over the mountains and in the fields all the winter—you're a perfect martyr," said Rada compassionately.

" He's as true as steel, that brother of Mouratliski's—he looked after me like a mother."

" There's a noble-hearted Bulgarian ! " said Rada, gratefully.

" Yes ; and a great patriot ; he's repaid me threefold all that I'd done for his brother."

" And did no one recognise you ? Oh, Boïcho, do take care, even here ! "

Boïcho had taken off his cap, and the bandage over his eye. He went to the looking-glass, replaced them both, and then turned towards her, greatly metamorphosed.

" Do you recognise me now ? "

" I should recognise your face under a mask ! See how he's looking at me ! How funny you are, Boïcho ! " and she laughed merrily.

" You know me because you love me ; but how should strangers ever find me out ? "

" Ah, hatred has sharp eyes—take care ! "

" For that kind of acquaintance I've always got this ready," said Ognianoff, raising his cloak and showing the butt-ends of two revolvers, and the handle of his knife fixed in his belt.

" Man of blood ! The sister Hajji Rovoama was quite right ! " laughed Rada.

" If I'm a man of blood you're the opposite extreme—you're an angel ! "

" Don't make fun of a poor girl."

He sat down again.

" Well, go and tell me how you got here. And who are these Mouratliskis ? " asked Rada, who had now heard the name mentioned twice.

" Brzobegounek's brother."

" What, the Austrian here ? the photographer ? "

" Yes, Rada, it's an assumed name ; his real name is Dobri Mouratliski. He's as much an Austrian as he is a photographer. He's escaped from the revolt at Stara Zagora. I sheltered him here and concealed him under that name. He's an old and thoroughly devoted friend of mine. You can rely on him entirely in case of need."

Rada looked at him in dismay.

" Why should I rely on strangers ? There's no necessity. You know I've got my savings to live on."

" Yes ; but you needn't look on him as a stranger."

" But haven't I got you ? "

" I must be off again, Rada."

" Going ? where are you going ? Are you going to leave me again ? "

" This very night, in two hours' time," said Ognianoff, looking at his watch, and replacing it in his pocket.

Rada grew pale.

" So soon—why, I've hardly seen you ! "

"I must be at K. before dawn. I've got a mission. Besides, it's not safe for me to stay any longer at Bela Cherkva. I'm sorry I couldn't even thank Marko for all his kindness to you, and, for that matter, to me too. Ah! there's some noble hearts among us, Rada, and that makes me love Bulgaria still more. I love her so well because she produces such charming creatures as you."

"Oh, Boïcho! why are you going, darling? But no, better go, and take me with you. You must go—you've devoted yourself to Bulgaria. Take me away from this black town; put me in some village where I can see you often—or, if you like, let me do something for the nation as well. I'm a Bulgarian too, and your ideals are mine, Boïcho, and if you die for Bulgaria I'll die with you. But don't let us be separated—it's terrible to remain alone, to have a thousand terrors for you, to hear bad news of you continually! Oh, God! how good it is now we're together!" And she placed her hands on his shoulder.

"Rada, I can see for myself how sad a position you're in here," said Ognianoff, feelingly. "I can guess what you don't tell me. My enemies persecute you still, don't they, dear? There's more than one Hajji Rovoama here, I know. And you endure all silently—you suffer heroically, for my sake. Poor dear angel! The great cause which has so entirely absorbed me does not leave me a minute to take thought of your position. I'm thoroughly selfish—it's my fault. Forgive me, darling!"

"Ah! Boïcho, Boïcho, if you leave me alone again something tells me I shall lose you for ever! I shall never see you again," continued Rada, and her eyes grew moist. She added in low, beseeching tones, "Don't leave me here, Boïcho. Whether you live or die I want to be with you; I won't be in your way. I'll assist you, I'll do everything for you; only let me see you oftener."

"No, you can do nothing. The revolution demands a man's strength, bloodthirstiness, merciless ferocity, and you're a perfect angel. Besides, you've done your duty; the flag you've worked with the lion on it will inspire and encourage us. That's quite enough for a Bulgarian girl."

Then, as a thought struck him, he added:

"Listen to me, Rada, will you come to Klissoura and stay with Mouratliski's wife? I'll arrange it all. There may be danger there, too ; but at least you'll be free from the intrigues here."

" I'll go wherever you like, if I can only see you."

" I'm acting as agitator in the villages round, and I often pass through. Next time I come to Bela Cherkva it will be to raise the rebellion. We shall see one another till then, Rada ; afterwards, God knows if I shall come out of the struggle alive ; it will be a great and bloody struggle. If God only blesses our cause ; if our country—this much-enduring country of ours—only rises from the struggle bloodstained but free, I shall die happy. My only regret would be that I should be leaving you, dear. For my love for you is boundless, my whole heart is yours ; but my life belongs to Bulgaria. And I shall know that at least there's one heart in the world that will pity me and shed tears over my unknown grave."

A cloud passed over Boïcho's face.

Rada seized his hands with emotion.

" Oh, Boïcho, you mustn't die. God will preserve such heroes as you for Bulgaria, and then you'll become famous. And I—oh ! how happy I shall be then ! "

Boïcho shook his head incredulously.

" Well, darling," he said, " we're in God's hands," and taking her hands in his own he added :

" Rada, whatever happens, I want to have a clear conscience. I may perish ; indeed, I feel that I shall."

" Oh, Boïcho ! don't say that."

" Listen, Rada ! I may perish, because I'm going to face death ; but I want to have my mind at rest as regards you. You have united your fate with mine—the convict, the outcast : you've made me very happy with your love : you've sacrificed for me something dearer than your life—your good repute ; and you've been cruelly punished for it by the world ; you've forgotten all for my sake. If I die I must know that you're at least an honest woman before God and the world, if not a happy one. I want you to bear my real name, the name of Kralich. There's nothing dishonourable attached to that name, Rada. When you come to Klissoura I shall call in the Pope to give us the nuptial blessing, and I shall try to provide for your future maintenance. My father's a wealthy man ; he loves me and will carry out the last wishes of his only son. I'd have done it here, only it's not possible now. However, we can do it elsewhere. I've no ring to give you, Rada, neither of gold nor of iron—the iron I carry is for the enemy. But there's no need of that : above us is God, the great and just God of Bulgaria, the God of crushed and broken hearts, of suffering humanity, He sees and hears us."

And taking her by the hand he knelt down :

" Let us pledge ourselves before His presence, He will bless our holy union." She knelt beside him.

Their lips uttered sounds heard only by the Almighty.

*   *   *   *   *

When Ognianoff left the house the street was quite dark. In turning the corner he met and almost ran against a nun. He recognised the sister Hajji Rovoama. She was going to her brother's house. Some fatality had brought her to Rada's door just as Ognianoff went out.

Hajji Rovoama fixed her eyes on the peasant, but did not recognise him. However, she turned in to the Lilovitches' house on some pretext to try and find out who the stranger was.

The next day, Rada set out for Klissoura.

CHAPTER II : EXTREMES MEET

CHORBAJI YORDAN was growing older and weaker every day, and the death of his daughter Lalka had been a heavy blow to him. A gastric disorder, which had during many weeks confined him to his bed, had further affected his character very much, and rendered him more impatient and exacting than ever.

That morning the weather was delightful, and he had ventured out as far as a garden he had at the outskirts of the town. It was a good, broad piece of ground, surrounded by high walls, and abundantly planted with fruit-trees, flowers, and vegetables. The walk, and the fresh air and sunshine combined, invigorated the old man, who had been compelled for so long to keep to the house. His step was firmer as he walked home. But just as he reached the house of Ghenko Ghinkin, his son-in-law, he felt a sudden weakness, his legs seemed to be giving way under him. He turned in to Ghenko's house to rest.

At the door stood Ghenko Ghinkin, still shyer, more timid, and more of a nonentity than ever. He was carrying a baby a few months old in his arms, which was screaming lustily as he rocked and dandled it in approved nurse-fashion.

Yordan made for the garden seat, overhung with flowers, and seated himself heavily, as he said with a frown :

" Confound you, have you become a wet-nurse ? What's become of her ? "

By " her " Yordan meant his daughter.

Ghenko became confused—which was indeed his normal condition—and muttered incoherently :

" She's busy—she said I was to nurse Yordancho—she's got plenty to do to-day."

" She didn't tell you to wear a petticoat at the same time, did she ? " asked Yordan, contemptuously. " Ghina, get me a cup of coffee, will you ? " he cried, without looking for her.

" She's busy baking—she's busy, father—that's why I'm nursing the baby. Coffee ? I'll get you a cup of coffee in a minute. I know where she keeps the coffee, and the sugar, and all," stammered Ghenko, as he set the baby down on the old man's knees and vanished.

The child began to scream louder than ever.

Yordan became furious. He put the child in a corner of the seat, stood up, and shouted :

" What the devil do you mean ? Are you a perfect fool ? Ghina, come here directly ! "

" Why, father, good-morning ? How are you this morning ? All right ? You're quite right in going out such a fine morning," cried Ghina from the threshold, smiling cheerfully.

She had on a large blue apron, her sleeves were tucked up to her elbows, the green handkerchief on her head was pushed back, and her face was powdered over with flour. She looked very well, and reminded one of some of the types so common in paintings of the Flemish school.

" What are you doing ? What does that wet-nurse of a husband of yours mean ? Why are you as white as a miller ? Isn't there any one here to give one a cup of coffee ? " grumbled the old man in angry and authoritative tones.

" I'm very sorry, father ; the fact is I've just set to work. I'll get you a cup of coffee in a minute. Ghenko ! wherever have you got to now ? Take Yordancho and put him in his cradle this minute ; he ought to be asleep long ago."

" What are you working at ; what's this you're baking ? "

" I've got a lot to bake—every one must take their share—we're Bulgarians and patriots too, aren't we ? " said Ghina, as she laughed boisterously.

" Bulgarians ? patriots ? What in the world do you mean ?   What are you baking ? " asked her father, angrily.

" Why, biscuit, father."

" Biscuit ? "

" Yes, of course. Why not ? "

" What do you want biscuit for ? Are you going to the country ? "

Instead of answering, Ghina burst into a loud giggle.

Yordan looked at her in deep displeasure. He had never been able to endure his daughter's perpetual and meaningless laughter ; no two persons could be more thoroughly different than she, with her gay temperament, and her father, with his choleric nature.

She approached nearer, and said in a whisper :

" Who thinks of going to the country nowadays ? We're getting the biscuit ready for something quite different ; it's for the boys."

Yordan looked at her utterly bewildered.

" What boys ? "

" Why, the brave Bulgarian boys, father, when they go out on the Balkan."

" What boys are you drivelling about, woman ? " asked Yordan, more and more surprised.

Ghina came still nearer, and said :

" For the insurrection : hasn't the committee ordered it? "

And she burst out laughing again.

Yordan leaped to his feet. He could not believe his ears.

" What insurrection, woman ? what committee ? Do you mean for a revolution ? "

" Yes, a revolution ! We won't have this brute of a Sultan to reign over us any longer," said Ghina, boldly, but she started back the next moment, for her father had raised his stick to strike her.

The old man, quite pale and trembling like a leaf with rage, cried with all the force he could muster :

" What, you donkey, you empty-headed chatterbox, you're going to make a revolution ! You're tired of your distaff and your needle, and you must needs begin to bake biscuits to feed all the bandits and ragamuffins in the place. Aren't you ashamed of yourself, you lunatic ? She won't have the Sultan any longer, if you please. There's a hussy for you ! And what's the Sultan done to you, I should like to know ? Have they taken away your child ? Have you been oppressed in any way ? She's ready to let her house and child go to rack and ruin, but she must pull down the Sultan ! And what are you thinking of all the time, you miserable creature ? Are you of the same mind ? Are you going to follow the flag too ? " asked Yordan sneeringly of Ghenko, who was looking on, terrified, from the door.

Ghenko Ghenkin stammered out something, and fled back towards the house. Ghina was already taking off her apron and arranging her dress, for she saw that her father's shouts had attracted the neighbours. When she saw Ghenko she caught up a slipper and seized him by the throat.

" You good-for-nothing ! what do you mean by saying I was baking ? "

Ghenko, in the proud consciousness of his dignity as a husband, did not condescend to answer his wife, but managed to escape her grasp and ran into the room. Locking the door securely, he breathed again, now that he had placed that rampart between his back and his wife's slipper, and cried triumphantly :

" Hit me now, if you can ! I'm your husband and you're my wife. Just let me see you hit me ! "

But Ghina was not listening to him. She had gone out into the courtyard, because her father had gone away excited and angry.

When he got home he was much exhausted. He passed through the yard panting with fatigue, and sat down to rest on the bottom step of the staircase.

Chorbaji Yordan was utterly amazed by what he had heard. True, though he had long been confined to the house, yet some rumours had reached even to his ears. The secret of a forthcoming insurrection was everybody's property—even the deaf had heard of it. It was supposed to be in preparation somewhere towards Panaghiourishté, among the mountains and the woods, according to what Yordan had heard, so the flames would break out far enough away from his roof. But to-day, from what his feather-brained daughter had told him, he saw that Bela

Cherkva was also on the point of an eruption. What could the Turks be about? Were they deaf or blind, not to see how the Empire was being undermined? he thought.

On his right he heard children's voices. They came from a window, a little over his head, by which the cellar was lighted. Yordan rose and began to go upstairs. As he reached the third step he mechanically stopped and looked in at the window. There he saw his two youngest children, of whom the eldest was but thirteen years old, standing by a bright fire, and busily concocting something. So deeply were they absorbed by their task that they did not notice their father's head peering in.

One of the boys was holding an iron saucepan over the fire, and watching its contents with the greatest attention; the other boy was taking from it with a kind of shovel certain dark lumps, of which there was already a whole heap in front of them. They were busily engaged in making bullets: one of them was melting the lead in the saucepan, the other held the mould.

"You young thieves—you vagabonds!" cried Yordan, the moment he saw what his sons were about, as he turned back, shaking his stick at them.

The boys hurriedly left their laboratory, and fled like the wind out of the cellar into the street, where they disappeared.

"They've ruined me, the thieves—the murderers—curses on them; they're getting ready for the revolution too!" cried Yordan, as he hurried upstairs rapidly, for anger had galvanised his muscles.

On the verandah upstairs he met his wife in deep mourning.

"What, Dona, aren't you in it too?" he asked with a look of suspicion. "The whole family's gone mad—they'll ruin me—they'll break my heart, at my time of life, too!"

He gasped, quite exhausted.

His wife looked at him in amazement.

"Pencho, Pencho!" he cried; "what's become of him? I want to see what he's about. If the little ones are making bullets, he must be casting cannon-balls—a set of rascals!"

"He's not here," said his wife; "he's gone to K."

"What the devil is he doing there?"

"Perhaps he's gone to take the £100 to the tanner."

"What! to Tossoun Bey? He was to have gone to-morrow. What does he mean by going without asking leave first ?".

And Chorbaji Yordan went to his desk. He opened it hurriedly and began to fumble in the drawers among the books and papers. But the money-bag was not there. Instead of it he came upon a Lefaucheux revolver among the papers.

" What's this pistol doing here ? Whose is it ? Who's been meddling with my desk ? I'm looking for my money-bag and in its place I find a revolver ! "

" You know no one ever touches your desk except yourself and Pencho," observed his wife.

" There's a scoundrelly son for you—there's a vagabond ! I'll never make a man of him. He's an enemy of the State, a revolutionary, if you please. Not a doubt of it : he must have persuaded the little ones to make bullets. All of 'em at work : all busy weaving the rope for their own necks ! What's the meaning of all this infernal nonsense, eh ? Why, every one'll become a rebel, down to the very cats, if this goes on ! Where's Kiriak ? "

" He's here, making up the bundles."

Yordan went hastily towards the room where Stefchoff was.

CHAPTER III : FATHER-IN-LAW AND SON-IN-LAW

STEFCHOFF, who since his marriage had become a regular inmate of the house, was making up, with the assistance of the two workmen, the bales of home-manufactured braid ready to be sent off to the Eski Jouma, a fair on St. Gregory's day. So as to be more at his ease he had thrown off his coat and fez ; his face, though flushed with the exercise, still preserved its usual repulsive expression of harsh and unsympathetic indifference.

He let go the string with which he was fastening the bales when he saw Yordan come in, excited and trembling, with deep furrows on his brow.

" What, Kiriak, are you doing there ? " he cried as he opened the door. " It seems you and I are the only loyal subjects of the Sultan left in the house. Every one else, down to the very cats, have joined the rebels ; they're buying revolvers and making bullets. Fire and sword are being prepared while we're sitting here getting our goods ready for the fair. I've been ill all this while ; but you must have heard and seen all this, yet you go on letting me sink so much money in these goods, in such brigand times as these."

The two workmen went out quietly.

Stefchoff stared at him in amazement.

" What are you staring at, you idiot ! " cried Yordan ; " I tell you my whole family has taken up with the ' Komita,' the family of Chorbaji Yordan, the Sultan's most faithful subject, the friend of Kaïmmakams and Pashas. What do you suppose common people are about, if my relations have become insurgents ? A set of ruffians are busy forming committees under our very noses, and we stand looking about us like a parcel of fools ! "

And Chorbaji Yordan, with his anger increasing every moment, began to recount the discoveries he had made that day.

" You must have known this kind of thing was going on ; what do you mean by not mentioning a word of it to me all this time ? "

" I didn't want to trouble you while you were ill."

" Have you spoken to the Bey about it ? "

It should be noticed that although the secret was common property, Stefchoff was the very man who knew least about it, partly because everybody avoided mentioning the insurrection before him, and partly because he himself despised the whole business, and did not seek to conceal his contempt for the patriots and their proceedings.

Stefchoff's face flamed with sudden anger.

" I'll tell the Bey all about the scoundrels this very day ! " he cried, enraged.

" You ought to have done so long ago ! "

" They meet in Beyzadé's garden. Let the police seize them there and examine them. After a couple of hundred blows from the stick they'll confess their mother's milk. You're right, I ought to have stopped these rascally plots against the State long ago, and I would have done so, but for all the trouble we've had. If anybody isn't satisfied with the government here, let him go off to Russia with the teacher Klimet; don't let them try and burn our houses down."

Stefchoff opened the door and whispered for a moment to some one outside.

" Do you know who the fools are ? "

" Sokoloff's the leader of them," said Stefchoff, his face flushed with malice.   In his hatred against the doctor was mingled a burning, fiery jealousy ; it was the only way in which that stony heart could be affected by love for the departed.

" What ? is that scoundrel still at it ? "

Stefchoff went to his coat and took something from the pocket.

Yordan watched him attentively.

" Here's a letter I found in the street yesterday, just by your house."

" What letter is it ? "

" It's signed by Sokoloff, and addressed to some vagabond of the same kind at Panaghiourishté."

" What's it all about ?   Fire and sword and all that sort of thing ? "

" Not at all, it's quite innocent in appearance, but I'll take my oath it's all got some hidden meaning," said Stefchoff, putting the letter away carefully.   " However, Samanoff will tell us what it all means, he's such a sleuth-hound, he'd scent out a rebel a thousand yards off."

Downstairs Yordan's wife was superintending the preparations for dinner.

At that moment Ghina came in.   Her mother at once proceeded to vent her rage upon her for having so angered her father.

" What are you angry about, mother ?   You ought to be pleased.   The Chorbajis ought to be the first to give the example."

" Silence, Ghina ! " screamed her mother.   " You're mad !   I won't listen to you ! "

" I'm not mad, but I'm a Bulgarian and a patriot ! " retorted Ghina, boldly.

" Bulgarian and patriot ?   Is that why you beat your husband every day of your life ? "

" I beat him because he's my master.   That's another matter altogether ; that's a matter of internal policy."

" You fool !   Do you want to be more Bulgarian than your father ?   If he was to find out that you get newspapers from Sokoloff to read, he'd beat you to a jelly, for all that you're forty years old."

M

" Mother, it's not true !   I was thirty-five last Christmas. I ought to know how old I am."

But this dialogue was interrupted by the servant-girl.

" Mrs. Dona, will you come upstairs ?   Father Yordan is worse," she said anxiously.

" There you are—I told you so.   My God ! " cried his wife, as she hurried to her husband, leaving her saucepan on the fire.

As she ran upstairs she heard Yordan's cries of pain.   He had suddenly been taken with colic in the room upstairs, and was writhing and tossing with anguish on the floor. His face was distorted and convulsed : loud and despairing groans issued from between the old man's clenched teeth, without, however, assuaging his sufferings : they filled the people of the house with dismay, and could be heard in the street.

One of the workmen was immediately sent for Dr. Yaneli, but he had gone to K., and would not be back till evening. They then had recourse to domestic remedies.   But neither compresses, nor friction, nor poultices were of any avail. The sufferer continued to writhe and groan with pain.

Yordanitsa did not know what to do.

" Shall we send for Dr. Sokoloff ? " she asked, turning inquiringly towards the sufferer.

Stefchoff muttered something with an air of disapproval.

" I sent for him last year myself, and he did me good," she retorted.   Then turning again to her husband, " Yordan, let me send for the doctor."

Yordan made a sign of dissent with his hand, and went on groaning.

" Do you hear ?   I'm going to send for Dr. Sokoloff," repeated Yordanitsa, persuasively.

" I won't have him," faltered out the old man.

" You won't have him, but I won't listen to you ! " said Yordanitsa, resolutely.   And, turning to one of the workmen, she said :

" Chono, go and fetch Dr. Sokoloff at once ! "

Chono rose and went to the door, but just as he reached the threshold a piercing cry from Yordan stopped him.

" I won't have him !—do you hear ?   I won't have the rascally brigand in my house ! "

Yordanitsa looked at him in despair.

" Do you want to die, then ? " she cried.

" Yes, I do !   Get out of my sight, d——n you ! " roared the old man.

Two hours later the crisis passed slowly away.   When he saw the old man was better, Stefchoff dressed himself and left hurriedly for the Konak.

CHAPTER IV : A SPY IN 1876

WHEN Stefchoff went into the room he found the Bey was not alone : Samanoff was with him, and the two were playing at backgammon.

Samanoff was the accredited spy of the Turkish Government, and drew his pay regularly at the Konak at Philippopolis.   He was a man of about forty-five years of age, but looked older.   He had a huge, prematurely wrinkled face, dark and thin, lighted up by a pair of black eyes, which, though rather dim, were always on the move ; his expression was savage and repulsive.   His moustaches were cropped short, and his hair fell in a dark and greasy mass from beneath his tall fez, which concealed his increasing baldness.   He was dressed in a dark brown suit of the native tweed, very shabby, the black-cloth collar of which was shiny with grease.   He was tall and powerfully built, but stooped considerably, as though under the weight of public execration.   The whole appearance of the man was suggestive of poverty and cynicism.   He usually lived at Philippopolis, but made frequent tours in the neighbourhood.   He was a native of Bela Cherkva, and knew everybody.   He, too, was known and dreaded by all who had any grounds for fearing detection.   His arrival always struck dismay and aversion in those who met him, yet, though he knew this, it did not seem to affect him.   He faced the most contemptuous glances boldly and fearlessly, as much as to say, " What then ?   One trade is as good as another.   I must live too." He had already met some of the principal residents and extorted money from them on pretence of a loan.   Naturally no one ventured to refuse a request from so honourable a borrower and so amiable an acquaintance.   He evidently knew that something was going on at Bela Cherkva, for he asked of every youth he met, with a diabolical smile, " How are you getting on with your preparations ? " and in order to increase still more the confusion of his victim, he would add, "It'll all end in failure" : on which he would leave him in terror. With this ill-omened and malignant outspokenness he drove every one from the streets as he passed by.

Stefchoff's face beamed with satisfaction when he found his powerful ally seated with the Bey. He greeted them with a gratified and familiar salutation, and drew up a chair to watch the game, shaking hands with Samanoff as he did so.

The old Bey, dressed in a short cloth coat lined with fur, continued to devote the utmost attention to his game, silently saluting Stefchoff as he came in. When the game was over, Stefchoff at once proceeded to business. He told the Bey in detail all that he had heard of the revolutionary effervescence which had again broken out at Bela Cherkva.

The Bey had also heard something of some such movement on the part of the rayas, but he had considered it a childish affair, unworthy of attention, and had allowed it to go on unchecked, as was the cue of the Turkish authorities just then.

Now, however, that Stefchoff took the mask from his eyes he was surprised by the widespread nature of the evil. He turned sternly and inquiringly to Samanoff.

"Petraki Effendi, what does this mean? Everything's ablaze round us and we're playing at backgammon all the while!"

"I've only been here a few days myself, but I know all that Kiriak's just told you, and more besides."

"You know it, and you don't inform me of it! Upon my word, you're a valuable servant of the State," cried the Bey, much dissatisfied. "This gentleman has shown himself to be a far more loyal subject of the Crown."

"I've only done my duty, Bey Effendim."

Samanoff's brow grew clammy. He said with much vexation :

"Whatever there may be going on here, it's not a patch on what they're doing elsewhere. If there's a straw smouldering here, there's a haystack blazing towards Panaghiourishté. But the Imperial Government isn't deaf or blind—it knows what's going on—it's biding its time—it's got its reasons for it. It would be a great mistake for us to start the whole thing and compromise ourselves on the strength of a mere trifle. What we see at Bela Cherkva is only the shadow of the smoke that's rising in clouds else-where. My opinion is that we should watch them carefully and do nothing rash."

These words pleased the Bey, because they corresponded with his inclination for inactivity and his hatred of all responsibility.

Stefchoff noticed this to his annoyance. He saw that Samanoff sought by means of this cunning explanation to conceal his own negligence and want of zeal for the interests of the State.

"Petraki Effendi talks at his ease," he said spitefully, "he has neither family nor interests here—he doesn't own a ragged carpet in the town. If there's an outbreak to-morrow, he's nothing to lose."

"It's false, I protest," cried Samanoff, angrily.

"You're right, Kiriak. I must have the cuckolds arrested at once," cried the Bey.

Stefchoff's face was triumphant.

"Well, on thinking it over, I'm of the same opinion. Let the donkeys be caught," said Samanoff with a sudden change of manner.

"Then we're agreed," said the Bey, with a sigh of satisfaction.

"Yes, let's have at them this very night," said Samanoff.

"Where do they meet ?" asked the Bey.

"At Micho Beyzadé's."

"At Beyzadé's ? I see it all now. A man who's more Russian than the Russians must be a traitor. Is he their leader ?"

"No, Doctor Sokoloff," answered Stefchoff.

"What, Sokoloff again ? He's succeeded the Consul then ?"

"The Consul's affair was mere child's play compared with this new business of Sokoloff's, Bey Effendim."

"And who are the others ?"

"Two or three dismissed schoolmasters and a few other vagabonds."

"I know their names," said Samanoff, "and where their weapons are stored, and their agents at Panaghiourishté. They've got their own post. More than that, they've established a kind of government, which issues decrees, judges, and condemns to death. I've thought it over ; perhaps it will be best that we should show some activity and give an example to the other authorities, only we must go about it manfully. I'll search their pockets and put them through their first examination to-night myself. After that you may do what you like."

Samanoff's face assumed a still more ill-omened expression. His words greatly surprised the Bey, who at once changed his opinion of Samanoff; he saw in him a zealous and trusty servant of the State.

" I'll see that you're properly rewarded for this, Petraki Effendi," said the Bey in a protecting tone.

Even Stefchoff was struck by the spy's knowledge of the organisation of the committee. He saw clearly that Samanoff was now burning with impatience to prove his zeal and earn his reward, and had for this reason offered to take a prominent part in this dangerous business. This suited Stefchoff admirably, for he was still desirous to remain in the background so as not to be exposed to the vengeance of the revolutionists.

The Bey looked at his watch.

" Are they there now ? " he asked.

" Yes, in the cellar. They meet in the garden when it's fine, and drink their raki while they talk treason."

" Well, what do you think ? "

" They always leave Micho's house at nightfall. Let the zapties wait outside and arrest them as they come out, and then bring them here in a body."

" That won't do," said Samanoff; " you'll only arrest them without any proofs, and they can deny everything. No, they must be caught in the room at Micho's while they're sitting there, at the very scene of the crime, so to speak. Let's take them with all their papers, protocols, and other documents. Then, it'll be all as clear as day, black on white; there'll be no denying it."

This advice pleased the Bey. Even Stefchoff was delighted with the idea. The spy was a most able man, and his zeal was no less conspicuous than his ability.

" Only we must wait till nightfall," added Samanoff; " these raids can only be carried out in the dark."

" That's settled," said the Bey triumphantly, as he clapped his hands.

A zaptié appeared.

" Is the on-bashi here ? "

" Sherif Aga will be here directly, sir."

" Send him to me as soon as he comes in," said the Bey.

The zaptié saluted and went out again.

" Dear me, I was forgetting," said Stefchoff, as he turned to Samanoff ; the spy was plunged in thought, and the deep wrinkles in his brow seemed to bear witness to the dark designs which he was revolving in his inmost mind.

Stefchoff drew a letter from his pocket, and unfolded it.

" What's that ? " said Samanoff, suddenly awaking from his reverie.

" A letter from Sokoloff to Panaghiourishté."

" You don't say so ! "

" It must have been dropped by some one. I found it in the street just by our house."

" What does it say ? " asked Samanoff, bending over the letter.

" It seems to be written in a secret code ; it's addressed to a certain Lonka Neïchoff. He's quite a common peasant, a cobbler at Panaghiourishté, who passes through here every week on his way to the market at K. But I'm certain it's meant for some one else—most likely the committee at Panaghiourishté."

" What's the paper you've got ? " asked the Bey inquisitively, for they had been talking Bulgarian.

Stefchoff explained.

" Read it, read it, and we'll see," said the Bey, preparing to listen attentively.

Stefchoff read out the following lines :

" DEAR LONKA,—I hope you're all quite well again now, and that your wife's got over her illness. You must keep on giving her the pills you have from me. How's business with you ? It's more than a fortnight since I saw you, which I suppose is on account of your health. When you come back, buy me 10 piastres' worth of belladonna at Yanaki's pharmacy, as mine is run out.

" Give my love to all your people.

" (Signed)   SOKOLOFF."

" No doubt the letter's in code language," said Samanoff.

" Now translate it into Turkish," said the Bey.

" To tell you the truth, it means a great deal or nothing at all, according to how you understand it," said Stefchoff to the Bey, and proceeded to translate it.

" Stop a minute," said the Bey at the very beginning, " by pills he must mean bullets."

" Maybe it's bullets," acquiesced Samanoff.

The Bey puffed vigorously at his cigarette with a proud and self-satisfied air and resumed his expectant attitude.

Stefchoff continued.

" Hold hard," once more interrupted the Bey, " he asks how business is. I see it all—he means ' how are your preparations going on ? ' We're not such fools as he takes us to be." And the Bey winked significantly at Samanoff, as much as to say, " Don't you make any mistake—Husni Bey's an old fox, and you must get up very early in the morning to take him in."

Stefchoff went on once more. When he came to the words " I suppose it's on account of your health," the Bey again stopped him and turned inquiringly to Samanoff.

" Petraki Effendi, all this about illness and health seems a trifle obscure. What do you make of it ? "

" I think that for ' illness ' we must read ' health ' and *vice versa*," said the spy with an air of importance

The Bey became pensive. He assumed the air of a man who has fully understood the deep significance of this dark saying.

" I think we've got 'em now," he said triumphantly.

When Kiriak resumed his translation and reached the word " belladonna," the Bey started up with excitement.

" Oh ! this time there's no doubt—it's quite clear—old Debela Bona's in it. Ah ! every time I see the old she-buffalo go past something tells me she's plotting against the State."

The Bey was referring to a poor old woman, sixty-five years of age, known as Debela (Fat) Bona who passed by the Konak morning and evening, with unfailing regularity, on her way to church.

Stefchoff and Samanoff smiled. They explained to the Bey that what was meant was a drug used in medicine.

" Go on, go on," said the Bey, somewhat crestfallen.

Stefchoff continued :

" My love to all your people—Sokoloff. That's all, sir."

The Bey cried :

" My love to all your people. That's quite clear. In a word the letter smells of treason from beginning to end."

" Yes, but there's nothing to be made of it," said Stefchoff dissatisfied.

" It is a trifle obscure," said Samanoff.

" Obscure ! of course it's obscure," said the Bey ; " but we'll make the doctor himself explain what we can't understand."

" Yes, but it would be interesting to find out what it all means beforehand," said Samanoff, gazing fixedly at the letter. " Give it to me—I'll decipher it. I've got a key at home for all revolutionary letters." And he put the letter away in his waistband.

" That's right, Petraki Effendi."

Stefchoff rose and bowed before taking his leave.

" Then it's all settled ? " he asked.

" Quite settled—for this evening," said the Bey ; " you can go to bed quietly—my kind regard to Chorbaji Yordan."

Stefchoff left the Bey with a countenance beaming with satisfaction. As he got to the door of the Konak Samanoff caught him up.

" You won't make any mistake this evening ? You'll superintend the raid on these gentlemen," said Stefchoff.

" That's all right—don't you fret yourself," said the spy ; adding rapidly, " Kiriak, lend me a lira till to-morrow ; I'm a little short."

Stefchoff frowned, and felt in his waistcoat pocket.

" Here's a couple of roubles for you—that's all I have."

Samanoff took the money, but added in a whisper :

" Come, come, I must have more than this. If I was to whisper a word to Stranjoff of what you've been doing to-day, you'd find yourself in a pretty mess." And he smiled ominously.

Stefchoff looked at him uneasily.

" Samanoff," he said, " if I hear to-morrow that Sokoloff and his associates are under lock and key, you shall have ten liras from me, I give you my word."

" Right you are. Now just give me three or four piastres small change to pay for my dinner ; I don't want to change the roubles this evening. Thanks. Good-bye." And Petraki turned down a side street to go to the inn where he was staying. Just by Hajji Tsachoff's house he met Pope Stavoi, and stopped him.

" Your blessing, Father ! " And he kissed his hand.

" How are you ? How are things going with you ? Is the

money coming in ? Which are you having most of just now—births or deaths ? "

" Well, marriages, I think," answered the pope with a forced smile, trying to pass on, for the spy's piercing look terrified him. Samanoff grasped him by the hand, and gazed at him fixedly.

" Nice time for marriages, this, when to-morrow or next day we may have another row." And he winked significantly at the pope. Then, suddenly changing the conversation : " Father, can you lend me fifty piastres till to-morrow morning ? I'm rather hard up just now."

The pope's face contracted. " A pope has no money. I'll give you as many blessings as you like," he said, trying to get off with this jesting rejoinder.

Samanoff looked at him sternly, and said in a low tone :

" Hand over the fifty piastres. Your son Gancho's secretary to the committee. I've only to say one word, and you're all done for."

The pope grew deadly pale. He took out a coin, and left it in the other's hands, pretending to shake hands with him.

" Good-bye, Father. Don't forget me in your prayers."

" Anathema," muttered the pope as he moved away.

The rain was still falling.

" My boy, bring me a little live charcoal in a chafing-dish (mangal), will you ? " said Samanoff to the waiter who followed him into his bedroom.

The waiter stared at him with surprise, as much as to say : " What can you want to warm yourself for this weather ?"

" Now then, hurry up with that charcoal ! " repeated the spy, taking off his coat, which was drenched.

The waiter brought some charcoal on a shovel, and placed it in a pan which he drew from under the bed.

" That's right. You may go now ! " And he locked the door after the boy.

He then took the letter from his waistband, unfolded it, turned the back of it—on which nothing was written—towards the fire, and waited patiently. When the paper was thoroughly heated he withdrew it, and examined it carefully : his face was expressive of lively curiosity mingled with satisfaction. The paper, which was quite white and clear a moment before, was now covered with thick yellow characters. As is well known, the letters sent by the various committees were written in sympathetic ink, and the letters were visible only when the paper was warmed. On the other side they usually wrote a series of innocent and meaningless sentences, so as to throw the authorities off the scent in case the letter should fall into strange hands. But, as usual, a secret which is known to more than two persons is no longer a secret, and the vigilant Samanoff had long since found it out.

The letter was signed by the vice-president, Sokoloff, and contained an account of the decisions and plans of the Bela Cherkva Committee.

After he had attentively perused the fatal letter, an indefinable smile appeared on Samanoff's repulsive countenance. He took out his pencil and wrote something on the blank space under the vice-president's signature.

And he went out hurriedly towards the Konak.

CHAPTER V : THE CHERRY-TREE

NEXT morning the sun again shone forth brightly in the deep blue sky.

The gardens were odorous with perfume, and the rosebuds were beginning to shed their fragrance around : the forest trees gaily crowned with white gave a festal appearance to every courtyard in Bela Cherkva ; the nightingale's note was everywhere audible, the swallows flashed through the air, rejoicing in the sun's rays. All nature was full of life and youth. Heaven and earth united to form a soul-rejoicing picture of vernal bloom and loveliness.

At that moment Marko Ivanoff stopped at the bottom of a dark and quiet street at the outskirts of the town, and knocked at a door.

It was at once opened by a strapping youth in peasant dress.

" Is it here they've brought the trunk ? " asked Marko in a low voice.

" Yes, yes, master ; come in," and the lad stepped back and pointed to a door. " There they are, walk in."

Just then the door opened, and the first thing that Marko saw in the room was a trunk—the trunk of a cherry-tree.

Kalcho, the goatherd (an old acquaintance of the reader's), mounted on a pile of wood, was busily engaged in hollowing out one end of the cherry-tree, which was firmly fixed below. His perspiring face showed that the task was no easy one.

" Well done, Kalcho, my man ! " said Marko, watching the process with interest ; " you're getting on, I see."

" Bless you, everything's easy when you know how to do it," said a voice.

Marko turned to the left, and saw Micho Beyzadé leaning against the wall.

Chorbaji Micho Beyzadé was a short dark man, dressed in loose Turkish knickerbockers and a woollen jacket. Like his contemporaries, he had had little or no education, but an active and eventful life had made him a man of wisdom and experience. His dark, twinkling eyes gave an intelligent look to his face, which was shrivelled up and seamed with many wrinkles. His peculiarity, which had become a by-word among his friends, was his unbounded partiality for politics, and his unshakable conviction that the fall of Turkey was at hand. Naturally, he was a Russophile, but to a fanatical, ridiculous degree. Every one remembered how one day at a school examination he had flown into a violent passion because a pupil had said that the Russians had been defeated at Sebastopol. " You're mistaken there, my lad," said Chorbaji Micho, angrily ; " Russia can't be defeated, you know ; you'd better ask the master who taught you to give you back the money you've paid him." But the teacher happened to be there, and proved, book in hand, that the Russians were defeated in the Crimean War. Micho cried out that his history was incorrect, and, as he was on the school-committee, he took care that the teacher was never engaged again.

He was naturally of a nervous and excitable disposition, and lost his temper the moment anybody ventured to oppose his confirmed convictions. He would then flame with passion, and use the most uncomplimentary language to his opponents. To-day, however, he was cheerful enough.

" Hallo ! Micho, how are you ? " said Marko courteously, holding out his hand to the president of the committee.

" We've got a meeting on to-day, and I thought I'd come round on my way and see how Kalcho's getting on."

" Where's your meeting to be, in the fields ? " asked Marko, sitting down with his eyes still fixed on the trunk.

" It's to be at the Green Dell."

The Green Dell was the name given to a valley on the bare hill to the north of the town, which was the first spur

of the Stara Planina. The committee changed its place
of meeting every time. That day the Green Dell had been
fixed upon.

Kalcho, heated and perspiring, continued to bore away
at the tree with a gigantic gimlet. He frequently withdrew
the tool to clear away the shavings, looked down the hole,
and went on again. The hole now reached to about the
requisite point—that is to say, a foot from the thick end of
the trunk, where the touch-hole was to be. Kalcho cleared
the shavings out carefully, peeped down with one eye, blew
through it, and looked at his visitors with an air of satisfaction. They also rose and looked down the cavity.

" Why, it's big enough to take a ten-pound weight," said
Micho, " but we'll fill it with shrapnel, it'll polish off all
the more heathens. Your cherry-tree will do marvels."

For the committee had decided that, in the absence of
proper cannon, which it was found impossible to obtain, an
attempt should be made to construct field-pieces out of the
hollowed stems of cherry-trees, bound round with iron
hoops, such as were said to have been used in the Polish
and Carlist insurrections.

Marko's face beamed with triumph. For, to tell the
truth, the cherry-tree was from his garden. During the last
few weeks, a complete change had taken place in Marko's
ideas. The revolutionary effervescence which had broken
out in Bela Cherkva had at length extended to him also.
He began by taking an interest, next he was surprised, last
of all his warmest sympathies were enlisted. If this kind of
thing was going on everywhere, as they said, perhaps, after
all, the whole of Turkey might catch fire, he thought. Was
it not possible that the knell of the Empire had sounded,
when even the very children thought only of arming themselves ? Who knows—who knows ? This thought calmed
his apprehensions and increased his confidence in the
future. Resolute and sensible as he was, without the
slightest imagination, at last he was overcome by the
general excitement, and began to believe. The epidemic
had extended even to that sober but honest Bulgarian
soul.

But this mental process was not accomplished in a
moment. Firm convictions are obtained only through the
influence of a whole series of facts and impressions. At first,
the autumn before when he had seen the growing savagery

and atrocities of the Turkish population, he had thought to himself, "This life isn't worth living, it can't go on like this."

It was the first step.

Later on, that spring, after Kableshkoff's appearance, when he saw the excitement that reigned among the youths, who were so resolutely preparing for a hopeless but noble attempt, he said one day to his wife :

"After all, who knows ? They may be mad, but the mad succeed sometimes."

Finally at Easter, when they were talking at the café of the terrible difficulties in the way of such an attempt, and the awful consequences it might lead to, Marko said crossly to Alafranga :

"Mikhalaki, a man who counts up the cost of the pipers and drummers never gets married at all."

It should, however, be noted that Marko was in reality in favour of the preparation, but not of the revolt. He was not enthusiastic to the last degree, like Micho, nor had he such a blind and unshakable faith in the result of the struggle as to risk everything upon it, like Ognianoff. Bela Cherkva ought to be prepared, so as to repel the bashi-bozouks when they should attack it with the inhabitants of the numerous Turkish villages in the valley of the Strema. It was quite surrounded by them and they already eyed it askance. If the revolt broke out all over Bulgaria, that would be a different matter. But who could affirm that that would be so ? In any case, Bela Cherkva ought to be prepared.

So he insisted on the armaments. Afterwards, time would show, he said. Three days before Nikolai Netkovitch had come to him and related his unsuccessful attempts to obtain the trunks of a few cherry-trees.

"You can cut down my cherry-tree," he said. But whether through human egoism or through parental solicitude, not unnatural indeed under the circumstances, he refused to allow his sons to have a hand in the matter. He wished them to be preserved from the torrent which he had been powerless to resist for himself. He wanted to do what was impossible. "One in the family is enough," he thought. The revulsion in his feelings had not become complete as yet, hence these hesitations and inconsistencies. In a word, Marko represented the moderate element in the national party, an element worthy of respect everywhere save in revolutions, which seek to attain their ideal by violence and extremes. Sometimes it may act as a brake on the wheel, but too often its effect is unfelt.

Kalcho was busily engaged in smoothing the inner surface of the cherry-tree, so as to make a real cannon of it. He completed the touch-hole, and blew through it while a stream of dust and shavings emerged from the mouth.

" Well, that's what you may call finished ! and a good account it'll give of the Turks, I'll be bound," said Kalcho, triumphantly.

" Well done, Kalcho, you'll be at the head of our artillery. Now all we want is Father Lilo, the smith, to put the iron hoops and caps on it, and then, there you are," said Micho.

" My stars, what a noise it'll make," said Marko.

" We'll put it on the hill above the Green Dell ; we can command the whole valley from there. Wherever they show themselves, we'll mow them down without mercy, it's a wonderful position."

A sound of steps was heard outside.

" It's one of us," said Micho, who had given the lad outside orders to admit no one who was not in the secret.

Popoff, the secretary of the committee, appeared. He saluted Micho and Marko.

" What is it, Gancho ? " asked the president.

" I thought I'd look in on my way to the Green Dell to see how the artillery was getting on."

" All right ! We must all be at the meeting to-day, to decide whom we're to send to Panaghiourishté. They want us to send a representative. I'm for Sokoloff."

" What do they want a representative for ? " said Marko.

" For the general assembly there."

" General assembly ? What do you mean ? "

" Why the assembly, man, that's going to decide when the revolt's to break out."

" They'll probably fix upon the first of May," said Gancho. Marko started.

" Oh, that's too soon. Better wait till the roses have been got in," remarked Micho.

" What, are we going to rise then, too ? "

" It'll break out everywhere on the same day."

" Don't let's have any folly."

" Folly or no folly, it's got to be," said Micho shortly.

" You don't suppose we've been preparing all this time for nothing, do you ? " added Gancho.

" I've always understood that we were arming only to defend ourselves against the bashi-bozouks, and to see what happens elsewhere. I'm very much afraid that we shall be left to pay the piper alone," said Marko.

" It would be a shame and a disgrace for Bela Cherkva to delay for a moment—the whole nation will rise on one day—and Turkey will be done for ! " cried Micho excitedly.

" Do you know positively that that's so ? " he asked.

" Know ? Of course I do ; I'm not a child. That's why I've pressed you to join the committee—to read the letters with your own eyes, and to listen to what Kableshkoff says. Why, the very spies are with us. Look at this letter we got last night from Samanoff, written on the back of one of our own, which came into his hands, Lord knows how : it's a miracle, I tell you."

The letter was the one we have already seen Samanoff explaining to the Bey, and afterwards deciphering by himself. He had sent it back to the committee, to their dismay and subsequent relief, with the following lines on the back :

" MR. VICE-PRESIDENT,—If I were you I would not leave my letters lying about in the street, where Stefchoff may find them. To-day I received this letter from him before the Bey, to whom we translated into Turkish the other side about the belladonna : this side I deciphered myself, alone, before the fire, so you need not be alarmed. Another storm was hanging over your heads for this evening, but it's passed over. You may thank me for that ; only you'd better meet somewhere else, and more secretly, in future. Good luck to you !

" The Bulgarian traitor and spy,

" PETRAKI SAMANOFF."

It should be added that the unfortunate Samanoff had never as a matter of fact been guilty of political treachery so far, all rumours to the contrary notwithstanding ; he had undertaken the spy's calling with the sole aim of getting money from the Turks as well as the Bulgarians. In order to levy blackmail upon the latter he had used countless threats, but he never went further than that. Self-respect he had none, but conscience was still alive within him.

Clearly he had not been intended by nature for a spy, but circumstances had remorselessly driven him into that tortuous path. Before returning the letter to the committee he had skilfully persuaded the Bey to postpone the police raid.

He eventually died in prison in Asia, just as the San Stefano amnesty was signed.

Marko shook his head distrustfully.

" It's one thing to know something's going to happen, and quite another for people to tell you so. Think well over it before doing anything rash. Don't let us have a second Stara Zagora."

Micho lost his temper.

" This is a different thing altogether, Marko. Don't be a child. I tell you the whole country'll be ablaze. Everything's arranged and organised—they've only to tell us the day."

" Well, if the whole country's ablaze, I'll take my gun too. But suppose we're the only ones ? That's what I want to get at."

" We shan't be the only ones—the whole country'll rise ! "

" Who knows ? "

" I tell you it will, Marko. Do you want me to take my oath to it ? "

" No."

" You're a regular unbelieving Thomas."

" I want to feel it with my finger, like he did. We're staking our heads, man ! "

" Make up your mind to it—we're bound to conquer ! "

" Why ? "

" Because Turkey must fall—the time's come."

" Why must it fall ? "

" Because it's written that Turkey must fall ! "

Marko thought that Micho was as usual alluding to the prophecies of Martin Zadek, a Russian " Old Moore " who was perpetually preaching the downfall of the Ottoman Empire.

" I don't believe in these new prophecies. The almanack prophesies rain and storm, and the weather's perfect—it's all bosh."

" No, no, Marko, Zadek's a different thing altogether—even the learned believe in him," said Micho earnestly.

N

" Oh bother ! it's always Zadek—can't you leave Zadek alone ? "

Micho flared up.

" If you won't have Zadek, I'll show you another prophecy still deeper and clearer than even Zadek's ! "

" Whose is it ? "

" It's from the Divine Providence. Only the Holy Ghost can have inspired it. No human mind can have found it out."

And Micho began to fumble in his coat-pocket.

Marko watched him with surprise.

" Dear, dear—I've left my pocket-book at home," said Micho, much vexed—" but never mind, I think I can remember it. If this won't convince you that Turkey's doomed, I shall wash my hands of you. A deaf man can't hear the sound of the big drum."

And Micho took out his writing-case, dipped his pen in the ink, and again began to search his pockets.

" Have you got a bit of blank paper about you ? "

" No," said Marko, after searching in his own pocket.

" Never mind, I can write here."

And Micho bent over the cannon and began to write on the smooth planed surface at the butt end.

Marko watched him with curiosity.

Soon certain signs appeared—they consisted of Church-Slav characters with their equivalents in arabic numerals * in regular alternation—in the following order :

$$\text{T.} (=300)\ \text{У} (=400)\ \text{Р} (=100)\ \text{Ц} (=900)\ \text{I} (=10)\ \text{A} (=1)$$
$$\text{К} (=20)\ \text{Е} (=5)$$
$$\text{П} (=80)\ \text{A} (=1)\ \text{Д} (=4)\ \text{Н} (=50)\ \text{Е} (=5)$$

These letters, read in words, formed the following sentence : Турцїа ке падне—Turkey will fall : the figures added up denoted the fateful year 1876 !

Who was it who first discovered this marvellous combination ? Who first rescued from oblivion this ray of light, this inexplicable freak of chance ? No one ever knew. The younger people laughed at it as a mere capricious coincidence—the older spoke of it as a revelation. Thus prejudice or superstition explains what reason is unable to understand.

* In the Slavonic alphabet, as instituted by SS. Kiril and Metod, each letter has a numerical equivalent, as in the Greek and other alphabets.

Micho Beyzadé supplied the key to the double sense of the enigma—Marko's waverings were at an end.

He was speechless with surprise.

Micho's triumph was complete. A proud self-satisfaction beamed from his black eyes, and the faint sarcastic smile with which he gloated over Marko's amazement seemed to express pity for his unbelief—and triumph—and joy—and enthusiasm all at once. He seemed to say to Marko, "Now, then, let's hear what you've got to say! Martin Zadek's no good—but how about this, eh? What do you think of Beyzadé now?"

While the two notables were discussing the point, several of the members of the committee had come in unobserved. They had also looked in on their way, to superintend the completion of the Bela Cherkva Krupp. The others soon followed in the same casual manner, so that all the members of the committee were there, except Dimo Bezporteff.

"I can't find Bezporteff anywhere to-day," said Ilia Stranjoff; "he must have fallen asleep in some dram shop."

"Ah! it's a bad thing to get drunk aimlessly like that," remarked Pope Dimcho, as he took a pull at his pocket flask of raki.

The members could not sufficiently admire or praise the new gun. It lay before them like some great monster without head or feet, with one eye in its back and a frightful gaping mouth, ready to vomit forth fire and lead. On its bright new surface could be read the cabalistic words written by Micho—the "mene, tekel, upharsin" of the Ottoman Empire :

"Turkey will fall—1876."

"Boys," said the president, "didn't we agree to meet at the Green Dell to-day?"

"Yes, yes; let's be off!"

"But here we are all together? Why not hold the meeting here? If you ask me, I prefer this, especially with that before us," pointing to the gun.

The president's proposal met with universal approval.

"Well, then, let's begin."

"But where are you going to sit?"

"Here's my armchair," said Micho, mounting on the gun.

And the sitting commenced.

CHAPTER VI : MARKO'S PRAYER

MARKO left Kalcho's workshop deep in thought : what he had seen and heard there had made a great impression on him.

"Who knows ? who knows ? " he thought, as he passed through the market-gardens which abounded at that side of the town.

He went along by the river, to the east of Bela Cherkva, where it pours down, with many a foaming cascade, from the Balkan. There he cast a glance at his own kitchen garden and the hole, not yet filled up, where the cherry-tree had stood ; he smiled grimly at the sight. From there he turned back through the gardens towards the principal street in the town, which joined the road to K. As he passed by the cabins of the carpet-weavers, in the dusty plain at the outskirts of the town, he saw a great Khoro* in full swing. There was evidently a wedding in the neighbourhood, and all the poor and hard-working population seemed to have joined in the festivities, for the Khoro was unusually long.

"That's the way of the world ! " he thought to himself ; " over there they're getting cannon ready, and here they're marrying without a thought of the morrow."

But he at once observed that the revolutionary element was not unrepresented even here : the dance was being conducted by Bezporteff, an ardent patriot, though too fond of the bottle, who, although slightly lame, was a renowned dancer. He was waving a white handkerchief as he danced —in a somewhat wild and eccentric fashion, it must be confessed—and imparted to the endless human chain, which followed him, the strangest figures and windings—at one moment the Khoro formed an irreproachably regular semicircle, at another it wound round him like a sleeping serpent, and again it untwisted and extended in a straight line or took some other fantastic shape. The broad soles of his shoes came down with a vigorous stamp at every new figure.

Marko slowly approached the Khoro, which was at its height, and then observed that Bezporteff was very drunk and was tugging the whole column after him with such ardour that one would have thought he was leading the assault on some fortress. His enthusiasm had spread to

* Khoro, the national dance of Bulgaria.

the farthest extremity of the column, where the five-year-old children were. At his bidding the musicians had ceased playing, and the dancers themselves sang as they danced, keeping time with the song. Marko heard the following verse of the song :

> *Kalina, can you tell me, dear,*
> *Will brother Kolio come to-day ?*
> *Will brother Kolio come to-day*
> *And bring a birthday-gift for you ?*
> *A necklace for your neck so white,*
> *A waistband for your waist so slim,*
> *A kerchief for your hair so bright,*
> *And slippers for your tiny feet.*

And the dance went on with fresh vigour.

Marko stopped beneath the eaves of the smithy to rest a little and enjoy the gay sight.

Suddenly Bezporteff noticed him. He at once left the Khoro and hastened towards him, still waving his handkerchief and keeping time to the music. On his pale, elongated and bony face, with its red moustache and twinkling grey eyes, was depicted a certain wild glee and excitement produced by intoxication.

"Hurrah ! Marko ! Hurrah for you and for Bulgaria ! and all her brave sons ! Stand us a glass of wine, Marko. Thanks ! Hurrah ! Beg pardon, Marko, I'm as drunk as I can be—that's so—but I know what I'm about. Yes, I'm a true Bulgarian. I see the sufferings of the nation—that's why I say, ' We've had enough slavery and drunkenness : we'd better die than go on like this.' They may say : ' You're as drunk as a Russian sapojnik ' (cobbler). Whoever says that is a traitor. My heart's sore for Bulgaria, that poor slave of the Turks. All we want is our rights—the rights of humanity. ' We seek not fame nor riches, we seek not land nor wives.'* But you may say people do get married, how about that ? Well, I answer, that's the way of the world. If the word's given to-morrow : Forward, march, set fire to your houses, and off we go to the Balkan ! A man who's afraid of the birds doesn't sow millet—you know what I mean ! Long live all patriots like you—I'd kiss their hands and their feet. But as for Yordan Chorbaji

---

* These are the first two lines of a patriotic song by M. Stamboloff, the famous Prime Minister of Bulgaria.

—I'd like to give him a good hiding with my belt. And Stefchoff ? the devil take the fellow ! . . . But a dog may sleep under a rock—sooner or later. Why, I'm as drunk as a—as a . . . It's love for my country that makes me drunk. The hour's nigh. I'm alive to-day—but to-morrow I may be dust—ashes—nothing. It's a fool of a world, and that's the truth. And whoever dies for the nation will live for ever and ever. Hooray ! long live Bulgaria ! And what am I ? an ass who's afraid of cold water."

Bezporteff stopped suddenly, for he saw that a Turk was riding by on horseback, an unusual sight of late. Pointing to the Turk, he began to sing :

On to the struggle : the enemy draws near ;
Beats every heart, but it beats not from fear !
Courage, the brave band grows stronger and stronger,
We'll be submissive rayas no longer !

"Forward, forward ! " cried Bezporteff, as though he was urging on some invisible band, and rushed at the Turk.

The Turk, seeing Bezporteff making for him, stopped.

Bezporteff reached him, seized his arm, and cried :

"Turk, where are you going ? How dare you pollute this sacred soil ? This soil is Bulgarian—your country is not here, but in the wilds of Asia. Be off there at once ! Down, you brute, and kiss this soil. If you don't, the devil take your Sultan, and his pages, and his paramours ! "

The Turk did not understand what Bezporteff said, but he saw that he was very drunk : he became alarmed and spurred his horse, but Bezporteff caught at the bridle.

"What do you want, Chorbaji ? " asked the Turk, in dismay.

"Get down or I'll drink your blood," shouted Bezporteff fiercely, as he drew his glittering knife.

The Turk had some weapon or other in his belt, but he forgot it, and got down trembling and submissive.

"What do you want, Chorbaji ? " he repeated, terrified by the vindictive look of his assailant.

"Where are you going, Turk ? "

"To K."

"And when are you going to Mecca ? "

The Turk lost his presence of mind entirely—his voice seemed to stick in his throat—he could scarcely falter out :

" Chorbaji, leave me alone."

" Come along and we'll go to Mecca together," raved Bezporteff ; " wait till I get on your back—you've ridden on the Bulgarians for a thousand years." And Bezporteff nimbly leaped on his back and clasped him tightly round the neck—" now then, step out, for Mecca ! " he cried.

And before the whole crowd, amid shouts and laughter, the Turk set out, spurred on by Bezporteff.

The horse followed its master sadly.

" Who knows ? who knows ? " thought Marko to himself on his way home—he had not yet recovered from the shock of surprise caused by the events he had just witnessed. He had lived for fifty years, and could remember the time when Bulgarians were forbidden to wear green, and were obliged to dismount if they met a Turk : he had himself seen, undergone, endured so many degradations as a raya that now he could not believe his eyes. He saw that before the whole crowd, in sight of a thousand spectators, a Turk had dismounted from his horse at the bidding of a lame, drunken Bulgarian ; that this Turk had forgotten his weapons and his nationality and had submitted to be ridden by Bezporteff like a beast of burden through the town. And all this so simply, so suddenly—so terribly suddenly ! And yet it was not altogether by chance, or a mere drunken frolic—it would have been impossible a day before—to-day it was possible, and every one applauded as if it were the most natural thing in the world. What did all this mean ? Why was the raya so bold, and the ruling race so submissive to-day ? Had the death knell of the Empire really rung, and were Beyzadé and the youngsters right after all ?

" Who knows—who knows ? "

In his reverie he stopped to look at the children just released from school. They were Merdivenjïeff's pupils, and were formed in a long column two abreast. They kept step as they marched, like soldiers, under the command of officers who marched at the side : the general was at the head. Marko's Asen held a stick with a red handkerchief tied to it—this was their flag.

Marko stood amazed.

" They've all gone mad, from the old greybeards to the very school-children ! " he thought, " all gone mad ! "

He took Asen by the ear, and asked him with a smile :

" And what's that you're carrying, you young monkey ? "

This reminded him that, at any rate, his elder children had remained unscathed, that he had not noticed the same fermentation of spirit among them as had spread to every one else, himself included.

" Thank goodness, they're out of it at least. God bless 'em ! I'm in for it, that's quite enough ! "

But a bitter thought occurred to him ; he added sadly :

" What, haven't the rascals got blood in their veins ? Have I brought them up to be traders ? But no—no—let 'em keep aloof, one in a house is enough."

The sun was just approaching the meridian.

Marko reached his home uneasy and annoyed, went into his room, and examined his pistols which were hanging on the wall. Next he opened a large closet concealed behind the door, with the intention of putting new flints to two old pistols which had come down from his grandfather, and long ago had been thrown aside as useless. The closet was quite dark ; he tried to feel for what he wanted, but it was impossible ; he had to light a candle to see—when he brought the light, what was his surprise ! Instead of the two old pistols, he found an array of guns, pistols, and revolvers, a complete arsenal ; at the same time it seemed to be a kind of military store—in a corner hung heavy cartridge-cases, sandals, boots, uniforms of European cut trimmed and braided, and other strange and suspicious-looking articles.

He called grandmother Ivanitsa, who at once appeared.

" Why, mother, who's been opening the closet ? Who's been up to all these games, I should like to know ? "

The grandmother looked at him with surprise.

" Who's been opening it ? Do you think I have ? Why, all of them, Vasil, Dimitr, Kiro, they're all in and out the whole day up to something. Who knows what they're doing in there in the dark ? "

Marko became confused.

" The devil take the young brigands," he cried, scratching his head.

He examined carefully, with the light, the contents of the closet, and muttered, with an indescribable expression on his face :

" Mad—mad ! God bless 'em ! "

And he closed the door again.

He went straight to the eikonostasis, and knelt humbly before the image of the Saviour. He was uttering some prayer not to be found in his missal. He was praying for Bulgaria !

For the first time in his life he was praying for Bulgaria !

CHAPTER VII : A NATION INTOXICATED

IN truth, as spring went on, the revolutionary movement made giant strides. The whole of Western Thrace, where the excitement was most general, resembled a huge volcano, the dull rumbling of which announced the coming eruption. A stream of apostles and agitators traversed mountain and plain and organised the contest. Everywhere they met with the same welcome—everywhere arms were opened to receive them, hearts to absorb their words—the whole nation thirsted after the stirring language of freedom, and was impatient to bear its cross to the new Golgotha. A long list of workers had already prepared the soil, and had even sown there the seeds of a love for freedom. These workers, beginning from Païssi, a monk, and ending with Levski, a deacon—both saints—had sown and watered the field ; the former had shed upon it his blessing from Mount Athos, the latter from the gallows. Twenty years before, Rakoffski had ventured in a village to advocate the revolt—he had to fly for his life, disguised in woman's dress, from the fury of the villagers. Now, when villagers heard that an apostle was coming, they sent out deputations to welcome him and herald his approach. They listened, they swallowed thirstily every word of that life-inspiring speech, even as the parched throat does the refreshing draught. In response to the appeal, " Be ready, we must die ! " the church gave its pope, the school its teacher, the field its ploughman, the mother her son. The idea struck its roots everywhere with invincible force—it spread over all alike—over Balkan and valley, over the hut of the poor shepherd and the cell of the monk. Even the Chorbajis, who formed a close caste opposed to all national development, even these fell under the sway of the idea with which every brain was on fire. True, they took a comparatively small part in the patriotic movement, but they did not hinder it, for they did not betray it. Treachery and baseness were rife enough later, but after the catastrophe, as always happens in such cases.

In vain would certain writers, blinded by party spirit, seek to claim a monopoly of patriotic ardour only for the sheep-skin clad and shod peasant, in defiance of historical truth. No, the revolutionary spirit, like a flaming seraph, spread its wings over peasant and university student—kalpak and fez, priest's cap and tall hat alike.   As in all the progressive struggles of Bulgaria, science and the cross were in the front rank.   The martyrology of modern Bulgarian history proclaims this truth.   True, the principal contingent, as at all times, was furnished by the mass of the people.   But it gave what it could—that is, numbers.   Thought and soul could only be supplied by the intelligence.   So the effervescence increased daily and spread over everything.   Every day it assumed greater dimensions and acquired fresh strength. The preparations went on with unremitting ardour ; young and old displayed equal zeal.   The peasants left their fields untilled to cast bullets, the citizens neglected their business. Secret posts went day and night between the different committees and the central committee at Panaghiourishté ; young lads spent the day in drilling with their guns, under the command of centurions and decurions ; the women knitted stockings, made cartridges, and baked biscuit ; the bootmakers worked only at knapsacks, cartridge cases, military boots and such revolutionary gear ; even the village mayors, vekils, and other local functionaries eagerly took part in the preparations.   In every village the depot of arms, bullets and gunpowder grew larger daily—the gunpowder was supplied by the Turks themselves—cherry-trees, hollowed out, planed, and fitted with iron hoops, formed the artillery.   The silken standard embroidered with lions, fancifully braided uniforms, bright ecclesiastical vestments, and crosses were the adornments of the impending contest. The influence of this general infatuation was felt even in the children's games : tops, hoops, kites were left for the more thrilling joys of playing at soldiers with wooden swords and guns.   The old people, amazed, said it was a visitation of God.   In truth, it was the only divine manifestation by which people were persuaded to join in the movement, if we except the miraculous logogram, " Turkey will fall—1876," which spread rapidly abroad and convinced the most sceptical.   That year, spring was extraordinarily early ; the whole of Thrace resembled the Garden of Paradise.   The rose-gardens were one mass of scented bloom, more luxuriant than ever before or since. Field and vineyard alike promised miraculous harvests, destined, alas ! to rot unreaped.

As for the inaction of the Turkish Government, in face of such open and unconcealed agitation, such boisterous preparations for the revolt, it is to be explained only by their blindness and utter contempt of the despised raya. " They're merely hares at play," said the complacent Effendis. " They're only the Hurrahers . . . ," * said the haughty rulers, smiling grimly and contemptuously. There are words which mark an epoch. The " Hurrahers " were the expression of the awakening of the nation when it emerged victorious from the thirty years' struggle for its ecclesiastical autonomy. But the hurrahers who saluted with their cheers the establishment of the Bulgarian Exarchate in 1870 had in 1876 become revolutionaries, and prepared bullets and cannons to welcome Bulgarian liberty.

The Turks, however, could not discern the change : they were unable to march with the times or to see the progress in the ideas of the people. Indeed, if they had understood, it was now too late—their dungeons were not vast enough, their fetters too short, to curb the gigantic idea, the invisible " King Marko " † lurking in the mountains.

Posterity will be astonished—nay, the very contemporaries of the age, with a whole series of historical examples before them, stand aghast before this moral intoxication, this sublime infatuation of a people preparing to contend with a mighty empire still great in its military resources— preparing with the hope, too, of victory, and with such means, ineffectual even to a point of ridicule, ready to take the field in the very " jaws of hell," as Marko Ivanoff had said not long before, without seeking for any ally save its own enthusiasm—a will-o'-the-wisp, which flames and dies out, a phantom, an illusion. History has but rarely furnished an example of such self-confidence—verging on madness. The Bulgarian national spirit has never risen to such heights, and may never again reach them.

Especial attention has been devoted to this prelude of the struggle, for it alone is striking, and may be taken as the

* An allusion to the boisterous crowds whose loud acclamations heralded the establishment of the Exarchate and the liberation of the Bulgarian Church from Greek domination in 1870. The Turkish expression is " Dajiveījilerdendir " from " Dajivéï," the Bulgarian " Hurrah ! "

† A Bulgarian legendary " King Arthur."

example of a great idea fostered in a fertile and favourable soil. The struggle itself by which it was followed was unworthy of the very name.

Nor will it be described in these pages. The story is naturally taken up with a single episode of the contest, which follows later, and which gives a glimpse of the revolution, that utter downfall of the brightest hopes.

CHAPTER VIII : TROUBLE UPON TROUBLE

RADA's departure for Klissoura had been quite sudden and unexpected. The day after her meeting with Boïcho, she had found a peasant from Klissoura waiting for her : he was returning in his cart from K. and had been requested by Boïcho, whom he had met on the road, to drive Rada to Klissoura : so she set out with him in haste. It was not altogether a sorrow for her to leave Bela Cherkva, for she had of late been pursued by the attentions of the Russian student, Kandoff, who had also joined the revolutionary committee. All her attempts to escape from his persistence had been unavailing. While she still mourned for Boïcho's loss she could not listen to Kandoff, and now that her lover was restored to her these attentions were doubly distasteful. Moreover, the loss of her only friend, Lalka, deprived her of the only companion she had in the town, where she had suffered so much already.

She took up her abode with Gospoja Mouratliska, who had not long before settled at Klissoura. The good woman had readily granted Ognianoff's request to take in the homeless girl.

The windows of the house looked northwards upon the whole town of Klissoura, the valley, and the Stara Planina. The majestic peak of Ribaritsa (known hereabouts as Vejen), which still wore its winter coronal of snow, towered above the city nestling on its southern slopes : here and there the flocks of the nomad Wallachian shepherds grazed on the grassy hillocks, which were dotted with the roughly enclosed penfolds : to the east the town was surrounded by high jagged rocks and crumbling ravines—in part bare, in part covered with vineyards and rose-gardens. A narrow path wound its way to the summit and led to the heights beyond, known as Zli Dol, over which passed the road to the valley of the Strema. Klissoura was surrounded by hills on the other two sides also : it nestled in a deep valley, covered with verdure and fruit-trees and rose-gardens which filled the air with their perfume. In winter it was lonely and mournful, but now it was a delightful spot, shady, cool, and fragrant.

Kandoff reached Klissoúra the day after Rada, and proceeded to the house of a relative, on a visit—a specious pretence for being near Rada.

The next day he called on Rada. His visit overwhelmed her with confusion, which was heightened by rumours of the impending outbreak of the revolt at Koprivshtitsa and her ignorance of Boïcho's whereabouts. In her affliction Kandoff's coming was most ill-timed.

" Why, Gospodin Kandoff, how is it you're here ? What's the matter ? " she asked uneasily.

" They talk of rebellion," said Kandoff dryly.

" Whatever's going to happen ? My God ! and Boïcho isn't here. Nothing's been heard of him."

Kandoff looked listlessly out of the window towards the Ribaritsa.

" And what do you think, Gospodin Kandoff ? " asked Rada impatiently.

" What, I ? "

" Yes ! "

" About the rebellion ? "

" Yes, about the rebellion."

He answered carelessly, without even turning towards her:

" The rebellion, the rebellion ? Oh, they'll fight, guns will be fired, people will be killed, all for the liberation of Bulgaria."

" And how about Klissoura ? "

" I suppose there will be fighting here too ; it doesn't matter."

" What do you mean, it doesn't matter ? And you ? "

" Oh, it doesn't matter about me."

Kandoff answered with the same indifference as if he was describing the customs of the people of New Zealand. But black despair was hidden under this apparently listless manner, this cold indifference to the events which would decide the fate of Bulgaria. However, neither he nor Rada felt this.

" And what will you do when the insurrection breaks out ? " asked Rada.

" I'll do whatever is necessary."

" What do you mean ? Won't you fight ? "

" There's only one thing for me to do, Rada, and that's to die," answered Kandoff gloomily.

Just then there was a low knock at the door, repeated thrice.

" Boïcho ! " cried Rada, as she ran to open.

Ognianoff entered, disguised as a peasant, dusty and footsore. He was on his way back from Panaghiourishté. He had been present at the general meeting at Mechka, where the first of May had been decided upon for the outbreak of the revolution. He was now hurrying to Bela Cherkva to take the last measures necessary for the preparations during the few days which still remained, and to raise the standard of revolt at Bela Cherkva on the appointed day. He was passing through Klissoura to take a last farewell of Rada. But just as he reached the house at the outskirts of the town, which served as a refuge for the apostles, he found a letter from Bela Cherkva : he hurried to Rada before seeing any one else.

He stood still, and threw a cold piercing glance at Kandoff, who stood quietly at the window.

Rada murmured a few words expressive of her joy at his arrival, but when she saw Ognianoff's altered countenance, she stood as if transfixed.

" I must apologise for disturbing your conversation at this early hour," said Ognianoff, deadly pale, with a bitter smile.

He scarcely looked at Rada.

" Boïcho, what is it ? " she asked, in a quivering voice, advancing towards him.

" Come, come, miss, we've had enough of pretence : this is shameful," said Ognianoff coldly.

She rushed towards him to embrace him. He turned away.

" You must really spare me these tokens of tenderness," and turning to Kandoff, he said in tones that quivered with emotion :

" Gospodin Kandoff, I cannot find words to thank you for your courtesy in responding to an invitation to come all the way from Bela Cherkva."

His anger would not allow him to proceed.

Kandoff turned from the window.

" Invitation ?   What do you mean ? " he asked coldly.

" What do you mean, Boïcho ? " repeated Rada in amazement.   " Mr. Kandoff has come to stay with his relations.   He——"

She broke down and burst into tears.

It was the first time she had ever been obliged to tell a falsehood, unavoidably, against her will.   During their short meeting at Bela Cherkva she had not had time to tell him of Kandoff's strange attentions, which she did not venture to repel.   And now Ognianoff found him in her room, and at this early hour.   Evidently something must have reached his ears of the student's visits, and some accursed chance had contributed to fortify his doubts before she had time to dispel them.

Rada hoped that Kandoff would say something to free her from her difficulties, but he remained silent.

" Gospodin Kandoff, can't you tell me something that will amuse me ? " asked Ognianoff spitefully, with a contemptuous glance at his rival.

" I've nothing to say—I'm listening to you," answered the student coldly.

" Oh ! this is disgraceful ! " cried Ognianoff, eyeing both of them.

Kandoff grew still paler than before.   His wounded pride pierced through his gloomy apathy.

" Ognianoff ! " he cried fiercely.

" Shout a little louder—try and frighten me ! " answered Boïcho in the same tone.   He was trembling with rage.

Rada forced herself between them in terror, lest he should commit some rash act ; she knew his impetuous character.

" My God !   Boïcho, what are you about ?   Wait till I explain everything," she cried in tears.

Ognianoff cast a withering glance at her.

" It's not worth while, Rada ; don't stoop to shed tears, crocodile's tears, that you're always so ready with.   I thought, poor fool, that you were innocence itself.   I've wasted so much love on you—I've thrown my heart into the street.   What blindness ! "

" Boïcho ! " cried Rada, sobbing in despair.

" That will do—there's nothing more between us henceforth.   The mask has fallen.   What infatuation !   To think you could love a vagabond like me, with only torture and the gallows to look forward to, when there are chivalrous lovers waiting for you, with sounding phrases, deep learning, and loyal sentiments! My God! what a base world this is ! "

He turned to the door.

" Ognianoff, take back the words you've said ! " cried Kandoff, following him.

Ognianoff stopped.

" Take them back ? I repeat them—it's base and disgraceful ! It's a foul abuse of friendly confidence. Do you deny the evidence of my own eyes ? " he cried, with a glance of scorn and hatred.

" Take back your words, or death ! " roared the student, boiling over with passion.

" Death ? that can only frighten revolutionaries who wish to save Bulgaria from behind a woman's petticoats ! "

Kandoff rushed at Ognianoff and tried to strike him on the head. All his long pent-up sufferings and tortures gushed forth in a flow of rage against the man who had indirectly been the cause of them.

Ognianoff was a powerful man. He flung Kandoff back against the wall, and took two revolvers from his belt.

" I won't fight like a street-porter—take this pistol," and Ognianoff handed him the weapon.

Rada, in a frenzy of fear and despair, opened the window that looked on to the street, and screamed aloud in the hope of attracting the attention of the passers-by.

At that moment the sound of the church bells burst out, loud and ominous. Their echoing ring pierced the air. Ognianoff stood motionless, as he held the pistol towards his opponent. Heavy footsteps were heard outside, and the door was thrown open. A number of the townspeople burst into the room, armed to the teeth.

" The Revolution's begun ! Long live Bulgaria ! " they cried.

" Where are the people to meet ? " asked Ognianoff, with emotion.

" Outside the town, on the Zli Dol, near the monastery. Make haste." And the insurgents hurried out again, with a cry of " Long live Bulgaria !" and began the song " On to the struggle ! "

The bells rang out wildly.

Ognianoff turned to Kandoff.

" I'm busy just now. If I come out of this alive I'll give

you your satisfaction. For the present you can keep the young lady company to prevent her being frightened.''

He rushed out.

Rada, quite overcome by this fresh shock, fell fainting on the divan. Gospoja Mouratliksa, whom her screams had brought to the room, was busy trying to restore her to consciousness.

Kandoff listened to the bells like a man in a dream ; at last he bent his eyes to the ground, and saw a crumpled letter, which had fallen from Ognianoff's hand. He picked it up and read it. It was an anonymous letter, drawn up in venomous terms, and bidding Boïcho be on his guard against Kandoff, who had never ceased his attentions to Rada, which it hinted were favourably received, and who had now followed her at her own request to Klissoura.

Kandoff tore up the base calumny and spat upon it, after which he went out.

CHAPTER IX : THE REBELLION

It was now five days since the rebellion had broken out at Klissoura.

Every other employment had ceased ; every other interest was forgotten ; unusual excitement was depicted on every face. The whole town was in a state of frenzy and expectation, and bristled with arms ; the very air in the streets appeared oppressive. During those five days the people of Klissoura seemed to have gone through five centuries of fear, hope, ecstasy, and despair. All that they saw, and did, which before had seemed so far away in the future, now appeared as an evil dream, a gloomy fancy of some disordered mind.

On the 20th of April, the Klissoura delegate at the General Assembly at Mechka had returned from Koprivshtitsa—which had revolted on that day—embraced his family and relations, and informed them that the hour for the rebellion had struck. Soon the chief confederates assembled in the school, and after singing the song, " On to the struggle, the enemy draws near," Karajoff delivered an impassioned harangue, and Klissoura, amid shouts of enthusiasm and the ringing of the church bells, declared itself in a state of rebellion. Letters were at once sent to the committees of the other Balkan towns, enjoining them

o

to support the movement begun at Klissoura and Koprivshtitsa, by following their example : decurions and officers were appointed, weapons were hurriedly fetched from houses, the zaptiés were fired at and pursued, but without success ; they managed to reach the Balkan. All the men were summoned to the heights above the town. On each of these strategical points was placed a guard of from fifteen to twenty men to preserve the city from a surprise ; trenches were dug for their protection. Almost all the men in the town between the ages of eighteen and fifty were drafted into these garrisons. No one was now allowed to enter or leave the town ; food and other necessaries were brought to each man at his post by the remaining members of his family. The rebels were armed with such weapons as each could procure for himself.

On the next day, a solemn service was held in church at which the women and priests (for the men were at the fortifications) prayed on their knees for the deliverance of Bulgaria from bondage ; the principal townspeople, who had taken up the movement with enthusiasm, elected a council of war, as well as a commander-in-chief of the rebels. At noon the lion-embroidered standard was planted with much solemnity on the summit of Zli Dol, and a special guard appointed to defend it. The rest of the day was spent in naming the commandants of the different fortified positions, excavating a powder-store, and settling other matters important for the arming of the insurgents and the defence of the town. But the news they were able to obtain from the outer world was not reassuring : no other town had risen, except in the Sredna Gora. Night found the insurgents somewhat despondent.

On the 22nd of April, the insurgents killed two Turks— travellers. Blood had now been shed, and the die was definitely cast. But in vain did they seek to descry from the heights smoke rising from the burning Turkish villages in the valley of the Strema, which was to be the signal that Kableshkoff had induced the Bulgarian villages in that neighbourhood to rise. They began to look for some place of shelter and refuge in the mountains for their families, and sent to Koprivshtitsa for assistance.

The rebels were gradually losing courage. St. George's Day (April 23) did not inspire them with gladness, and the bells which summoned the pious to prayer sounded dull and mournful, more like a passing bell. But suddenly the chimes became louder and triumphant; faces beamed with joy; Voloff had arrived from Koprivshtitsa with reinforcements consisting of fifty men, mostly peasants from villages in the Sredna Gora. He marched straight to the church, where a "Te Deum" service was solemnly celebrated. The bells rang out still more joyously. After the service, Voloff and his little band, accompanied by the priests chanting hymns, proceeded to the heights. There several Turks and gipsies, who had been captured, were sentenced to death as spies. He executed one of them himself, with his sword; when all was over, Voloff returned alone to Koprivshtitsa. The rest of the time was taken up in completing the trenches.

On the next day, discouragement again set in. In vain the outposts strained their eyes in watching for the eagerly desired fires in the valley. Kableshkoff's expedition had returned to Koprivshtitsa unsuccessful. The few travellers who managed to reach Klissoura during the first few days of the insurrection declared that in the valley everything was peaceful, and that there was no sign whatever of an impending outbreak. Since the previous day there had been no more travellers. In place of these, groups of Turks could be observed on horseback in the distance; they fired, and again retreated. The discouragement increased. The promises of the most sanguine (whose number decreased every day), news of fictitious successes, severe reprimands, all were alike ineffectual to restore the general confidence.

This lamentable condition of the defenders of Klissoura became still further intensified on the 25th of April. They saw that they were left to themselves—that is, to unavoidable destruction. It was evident. The handful of defenders which the town could supply, at most about 250 men, was not sufficient to repel the frightful horde of bashi-bozouks who would fall upon them from east and west. How could any fresh reinforcement be hoped for from Koprivshtitsa, which was itself in need of aid? Discouragement and despair gained ground every moment. Discipline was growing weak; complaints, mumurings, regrets, the forerunners of demoralisation, replaced the enthusiasm of the first days of the revolt. The enemy had not yet been seen, but all felt that he was near, terrible, inevitable. The revolutionists now resembled an army which has been defeated without a battle, a trembling herd of deer, crouching in some corner from which there is no escape, and hearing the roar of the advancing enemy. A few preserved their presence of mind, still fewer clung bravely to the last hope of success. To their moral sufferings were added physical hardships ; icy winds blew down at night from the Balkan, and numbed the garrisons in their damp trenches, where they were obliged to spend the night without even the comfort of a fire. These poor shopkeepers and cloth-spinners, who had lived all their lives by peaceful toil, suddenly turned into rebels and bristling with arms, were really to be pitied. Confused grumblings and sighs were to be heard at night in the trenches, where everybody trembled with cold and dismay.

"God bless the kingdom, dear ! " had been the greeting of the old women to one another, when they met in the streets.

"Ah ! we're ruined, my lad ! We're done for ! " the most fervent of the confederates now groaned.

Despair increased every moment. It was clearly stamped on each haggard face. However, there was no talk of retreat or flight, but the thought of it was in every heart.

Such was the mental condition of the garrisons at each of the trenches. Such or almost such it was at Zli Dol, the principal point of the defence.

CHAPTER X : THE BATTERY OF ZLI DOL

THE peak of Zli Dol, at the north-east end of the town, was a valuable strategical position. It commanded the surrounding valleys, and was the key to the pass which led from Klissoura to the valley of the Strema. From there one saw an apparently endless series of bare undulating rocks stretching to the east, along which the outposts were stationed.

The garrison of Zli Dol was the most numerous of all. It had been reinforced by Voloff's Sredna Gora peasants—the remnants of bands which had been repulsed—and was preparing to greet with a shower of bullets the first onslaught of the enemy.

The garrison was unusually alert to-day. A certain boldness was noticeable on the faces of the men. Yet they were not turned in the direction from whence the enemy might be expected, but towards the valley in which Klissoura lay nestling. Every one was gazing expectantly along the path which led up to the ravine. An insurgent of gigantic stature was carrying a long, white, cylindrical article of some sort on his shoulder. Behind him a woman, stout and plump, in peasant dress, was toiling under the weight of a load which seemed very heavy.

It was this pair that had attracted everybody's attention, and there were some grounds for this excitement : they were carrying the artillery up to Zli Dol.

It consisted of nothing more than a cherry-tree cannon, which the giant was carrying on his shoulder.

The ammunition—consisting of scraps of iron, bullets, nails, &c.—were on the woman's back.

The eyes of the rebels flashed with satisfaction : a general enthusiasm prevailed on Zli Dol.

At last the giant reached the summit, bathed in perspiration, which streamed from his forehead and neck.

" God bless its soul ! " he exclaimed, as he set the fatal weapon on the ground.

The garrison flocked round with curiosity to examine the cannon. There were twenty more like it, destined for the other forts, but they were still in the town. This had been brought up to test its strength, its report, and the distance it would carry. It was taken up to the very summit, whence it could command the pass and the bare peaks. It was filled with powder, firmly fastened into the ground by means of stakes, and a trench was dug behind it to protect the gunners.

The insurgents burned with impatience to hear the voice of the first Bulgarian cannon. All were inspired with childish glee and unspeakable enthusiasm. Some even wept.

" Listen when the Lion of the Balkan roars, boys. His voice will shake the Sultan's throne, and proclaim to the whole world that the Stara Planina is free ! " cried the commandant of the garrison of Zli Dol.

" The sound will stir up our other brothers in the valley of the Strema—it'll remind them of their obligations—they'll rush to arms and fall upon the common enemy ! " said another.

" We command the whole valley from here ; only let the tyrants show themselves, we'll blow them to pieces."

"We won't leave one of them alive, God bless their souls !" said Ivan Kill-the-Bear, who was still fanning his heated face with his cap.

For the giant who had carried up the cannon was our old acquaintance Kill-the-Bear ; his wife had brought up the rest. They had settled at Klissoura a month before, having found work there, and had joined in the revolt.

The gunner, with his lintstock in his hand, was preparing to set to work.

"Wait a bit, Delcho, we mustn't frighten the women and children, we ought to give notice first," said Niagoul, the cloth-worker.

"Quite right," said others, "let's send some one to cry the news in the town—there may be women near their confinement."

"Why send to the town ; we should only lose time ? Better get some one to cry from here; who's got the loudest voice ?"

"Kill-the-Bear, Kill-the-Bear," cried those who knew the wonderful strength of his lungs.

Kill-the-Bear readily undertook the fresh task. He asked what he was to say, committed it carefully to memory, and went half-way down the hill to be a little nearer to the town. He drew himself up to his full height, swelled out his chest, raised his head, and cried in stentorian tones :

"Now then, you people ! Take notice that we're going to fire the Bulgarian cannon, to try it, God bless its soul ! Women and children needn't be frightened. There are no Turks yet to be seen, God bless their souls !"

He repeated this announcement several times, with a minute's pause between each. The Balkan echoes replied to his powerful voice. It penetrated to every house in the town. After this reassuring warning, they set to work. Delcho made a fire, lighted a truss of straw at it, fastened it to his long pole, and approached it to the touch-hole. The straw burned and crackled ; clouds of grey smoke rose in the air ; in their feverish expectation of the report, the insurgents drew back to some distance ; others threw themselves down in the trenches so as not to see anything ; some even stopped their ears with their fingers and waited. Several seconds passed, during which the strain on their nerves was frightful, inexpressible. The grey smoke continued to rise from the straw, which seemed powerless to ignite the gunpowder.   Hearts were beating furiously.   The torture became insupportable.   At last a white flame appeared at the touch-hole, and suddenly the cannon emitted a faint, angry, dull sound, like the crack of a board that is being split, or a sharp cough, and the whole battery was covered with a cloud of smoke.

The cannon had cracked, and the charge was carried only a few paces from the mouth.   Many of the insurgents did not even hear the report.

One of them said, in jest or in earnest, that he had taken the sound for Ivan Kill-the-Bear coughing.

This unfortunate result brought out only too clearly the shortcomings of the artillery.   They hastened to improve the other cannon, by binding them firmly round with strong iron hoops, and lining some of them inside with tin.   That day two guns were taken up to each fort ; they were loaded to the muzzle, and firmly fixed in the ground.   Every gun was destined to serve only once, and in a particular direc-tion.

It should be added that no one thought of giving notice in the town that the Bulgarian cannon had gone off.   So the poor old women waited expectantly till the evening, with cotton-wool in their ears, for the explosion which was to cleave the air and shatter all the windows in the town.

CHAPTER XI : DISCOURAGEMENT IN THE FORT

NEXT morning, as Ognianoff was anxiously scanning the horizon through his field-glass, a decurion advanced towards him.

" What is it, Marcheff ? "

" Things are as bad as bad can be," whispered the de-curion ; " demoralisation's spreading all over the fort."

Ognianoff started.

" Whoever discourages the others will be punished by death," he said fiercely.   " Whom have you noticed, Marcheff ? "

The decurion mentioned four names.

" Call them up at once ! "

The accused appeared.   They were elderly men—cloth-workers or tradespeople.

Ognianoff glanced at them sternly, and asked :

" So it's you, is it, who're discouraging the garrison ? "

"We're not discouraging anybody," answered one of them sharply.

"You know the punishment imposed for such conduct at critical moments like these ? "

They did not answer. But their silence was expressive of obstinacy rather than fear.

Ognianoff was boiling over with rage, but he made an effort to restrain himself, and said quietly :

"Go back to your posts, men. We've begun our revolution and it's too late now to cry off. We've to face the enemy here : no one has any business to look back towards Klissoura. You'll preserve your families and your houses much better by stopping here than by going back to the town. Don't place me in a difficult position, I entreat you."

The insurgents did not move.

Ognianoff looked at them with amazement. This was clearly a protest.

"Have you anything else to say ? "

The insurgents looked at one another ; at last one of them said :

"We're not meant for this kind of thing."

"I never had a gun in my hand before in my life," said another.

"No more have any of us," said the third.

"We can't shed blood."

"You're afraid, are you ? " asked Ognianoff, thinking to shame them with this question.

"Well, it's not a sin if we are."

"Yes, we are afraid," said the first, angrily.

"We've got wives and children."

"You don't suppose we've picked up our lives in the road, do you ? " said the boldest of them.

"What are your lives and your families, and your houses, compared with the liberation of Bulgaria, and especially compared with the honour of Bulgaria ? " asked Ognianoff in a voice that quivered with rage. "I ask you again : don't show yourselves to be cowards, and force me to take strong measures against you ! "

"We're not meant for guns and rebellions ! "

"Well, what do you want ? "

"We want to be set free, to go home."

" We've never fired at another man ; it's not our business."

Ognianoff saw that their obstinacy was not to be overcome by soft words.   He was bursting with rage, but managed to keep calm.   He recognised with sorrow that only deep discouragement and fear could embolden these cowards to confess aloud to their commander that they were afraid without blushing.

From this to open panic and flight there was only one step.   He resolved to be pitiless.   The infection could not be allowed to spread to the others.   Discipline before everything.

" My men, will you return to your duty or not ? " he asked resolutely.

And with a gloomy frown and a beating heart he awaited their reply.

At that moment shouts were suddenly heard behind him. He turned round and saw, in the plain below, Kill-the-Bear pursuing a gipsy.   The other insurgents crowded to the edge to watch the race, and cheered on Kill-the-Bear, who, in spite of his gigantic strides, could not succeed in reaching the bare-footed and agile gipsy.   Some raised their guns to aim at the latter, but Ognianoff ordered them to desist. Clearly the fugitive had been concealed at Klissoura till then, and was trying to escape to some Turkish village. The gipsies, who had managed to escape during the first few days, had been the first to give notice to the Turks of the revolt, and details respecting the numbers, &c., of the garrison.   By nature and interest they were faithful allies to the Turks, and such they showed themselves to be both here and elsewhere in similar circumstances   Kill-the-Bear continued to pursue the gipsy with enormous strides, but the gipsy maintained his lead, and the two were getting further and further away from the fort.   The gipsy was almost out of gunshot range.   Suddenly he stopped bewildered : before him appeared two insurgents from the outposts, and he found himself between two fires.   At that moment Kill-the-Bear reached him, made one bound at him, and the two rolled over together on the ground.   Shouts of satisfaction were heard from the fort.   Many cried :

" Bring him here—here ! "

Kill-the-Bear, enraged at his pursuit, forced the gipsy on

before him with a torrent of imprecations, which were clearly audible at the fort.

The fugitive was placed under arrest.

The insurgents crowded round him with faces that boded no good. Every one recognised the gipsy. He had twice before attempted to escape from Klissoura—the first time from the Konak with a secret message for the village of Rahmanlari, given him by a Turk kept in the town, but had been punished only by a closer confinement. Now there could be no question of pardon.

The commandant of the fort turned to the decurion, and they consulted for some time in whispers.

" Yes, yes," finally said Ognianoff. " Any mercy or indulgence would now only be injurious. The sight of death may inspire the cowardly with a little boldness. But the Council of War must pronounce its verdict. Marcheff, go at once to Zli Dol and report what has happened. My own opinion is that the penalty should be death. Go at once."

The decurion went out.

Ognianoff turned sternly to an aged insurgent :

" Father Marin, put this gipsy under arrest."

He then addressed two younger men :

" My lads, take these gentry, the cowards, to that side of the fort ; take away their guns, and keep them under arrest until further orders."

The four demoralised insurgents grew pale, but offered no opposition and proceeded quietly to the place of arrest.

CHAPTER XII : A BAPTISM

OGNIANOFF was excitedly pacing up and down the edge of the fort : his gloomy thoughts were reflected in his face.

He turned mechanically to look at a group of insurgents who were zealously digging the new trench ; after a word or two of encouragement, he mounted the rampart again, scanned the eastern horizon and, with a still darker expression of countenance, returned to his former place.

" What a nation ! what a nation ! " he muttered.

Marcheff returned.

" The sentence is—death ! " he cried, panting.

" The Council of War has decided, has it ? "

" Yes, death without delay ! " said Marcheff aloud, adding something in a whisper.

Ognianoff made an imperceptible sign of satisfaction.

The words " Death without delay " were heard all over the fort : they were repeated from mouth to mouth, and reached to the corner where the prisoners stood under arrest.

They were pale before ; now their faces became as white as a sheet.

They began to see that their fate was sealed. The Council of War appeared to them as something terrible, majestic, unavoidable—like Fate itself. God alone stood above it.

An insurgent approached Ognianoff :

" The prisoners are begging for mercy."

Ognianoff replied coldly :

" The sentence has been pronounced ; it's too late now." Then, in commanding tones, he added : " Braïkoff, take Niagoul, and Blagoï, and Iskroff, and march the four prisoners to the valley down there, to undergo their penalty. The judgment of the court-martial must be carried out to the letter."

Braïkoff, much moved, proceeded to carry out the orders of the commandant of the fort.

Not a voice was raised in defence of the condemned : no one wished to appear to share their ideas. Every one felt that his life was at the mercy of the court-martial—the only tribunal, and one from which there was no appeal.

The condemned insurgents, conducted by the four men told off for the duty, passed through the fort and down the valley.

" Take the gipsy down there as well ! " cried Ognianoff.

Then, in a whisper, he gave certain instructions to the decurion, who hastened after them.

The place selected was a moist, green meadow, through which flowed a little brook. It was surrounded by rocks. The whole garrison flocked to the heights above to witness the execution.

To the left of the brook was a withered oak : two of the insurgents conducted the gipsy to the tree, and bound him to it with his red waistband.

Fear had rendered the wretched man speechless. From his clenched lips blood was flowing.

Close by the bank stood the other four condemned men, awaiting their turn. Their features were distorted with terror.

Marcheff cried :

" Bring them here, too ! "

The victims looked at him helplessly. Three of them were unable to move : the guards were obliged to drag them to the spot.

Marcheff placed them in a row ten paces distant from the bound gipsy, evidently that they might witness the terrible spectacle which their own fate would shortly supply to their comrades flocking together on the heights above.

They were not bound ; but terror had paralysed their forces, and not one of them even thought of flight, which would, indeed, have been impossible.

A minute's dead silence followed.

" Advance ! " cried Marcheff to the six armed insurgents who had brought the prisoners.

They advanced firmly.

Marko then cried in loud and solemn tones :

" The gipsy Mehmed, of Klissoura, having been guilty of three attempts at escape from prison with the treacherous design of betraying the Bulgarian cause to the Turks, is condemned to death by the supreme tribunal as an example to all other traitors ! " Then, turning towards the other four : " Men, turn towards Mehmed ! "

They did as they were ordered, automatically.

" Give each of them a gun ! "

The insurgents, much excited, handed them their guns. The condemned men took them, their faces stupefied with terror.

" Now fire at him when I give the word three. One !— two !—three ! "

A report was heard and a cloud of smoke arose.

The gipsy was still standing upright against the tree. Not a bullet had touched him. The firing-party had evidently not aimed at him. But he was as pale as death.

" For shame, men ! Try again ! "

And he repeated the command. The guns again rang out. This time the gipsy was writhing in his death agony.

Sounds of applause were heard from above.

" That is to be your punishment, men, for this once. You've had your baptism of blood. You have to thank the indulgence of Ognianoff and the court-martial."

When the four men understood that they were saved, they first looked piteously round them like men awaking from some terrible dream. A faint smile of pleasure was only just visible on their leaden faces, still pale with terror. Fresh sounds of applause rose from the fort.

CHAPTER XIII : THE VALLEY OF THE STREMA IN FLAMES

" STRANGE—strange, it's inexplicable ! terrible ! Nothing all this time ! What can they be doing ? What's Bela Cherkva about ? They're as silent as the dead ! Silent ! Oh ! this silence is terrible. I don't dare to think about it ! Have they folded their arms and thought prudence best, after all ? Yet there's Sokoloff there, and Popoff, and Bezporteff —all my boys ! All eager and experienced lads. What can they be waiting for ? Are they waiting for me ? Yes, but if I can't come—if I'm knocked on the head—won't they do anything at all ? or are they deaf and blind ? Can't they see ? Klissoura in open revolt, Koprivshtitsa in revolt, Panaghiourishté in revolt, the whole Sredna Gora in flames ! Only the valley of the Strema still slumbering! Can anything have happened ? is there any special impediment ? But it's not possible : if Bela Cherkva can't rise itself, at least it might send us ten or a dozen bold lads to encourage the others. And yet, not a sign ; and disaffection spreading among us every day. And after such thorough preparations, too ! Can this be going on in other places also ? If so, God have mercy upon Bulgaria—only utter ruin awaits her ! "

Filled with these dark thoughts, Ognianoff, disguised as a Turk, was cautiously making his way down the Stara Réka to the valley of the Strema.

On the 20th of April, as we have already seen, he had arrived at Klissoura, on his way to Bela Cherkva, with the intention of raising the insurrection there on the day appointed for the general rising. However, matters had come to a head the very day of his arrival at Klissoura. He had been overwhelmed by the outburst of the revolt at a moment of terrible mental agitation, and had flung himself blindly into the movement, trying to forget his pangs in the excitement of the struggle, and perhaps to meet death fighting for the liberty of his country. But the enemy gave no sign of life. All communications between Klissoura and the valley were cut off. Ognianoff had during five days and nights

worked with untiring activity at the organisation of the
defences, burning with impatience to hear that Bela
Cherkva had risen.   But Bela Cherkva was quite peaceful,
like the other towns and villages in the valley.   Ognianoff,
with a bursting heart, cursed the chance which had brought
him to Klissoura.   He saw the fearful effect produced on
the insurgents by this ominous silence, which paralysed the
whole movement.   In vain he sought to encourage his
comrades with solemn asseverations that Bela Cherkva
would certainly rise, and that the other towns would
follow its example.   Finally he began to despair himself,
and to foresee with terror the collapse of Klissoura and
of the whole revolt.   He then resolved upon a bold,
almost reckless undertaking—to make his way through the
infuriated Turkish villages to Bela Cherkva and force it to
rise.

He was exposing himself to terrible peril.   But the revolt
of Bela Cherkva would supply the spark which would kindle
all the other places ready to rise along the whole length of
the Stara Planina.   The forces of the Turks would be
divided.   Klissoura would be saved—the revolt extended
far and wide—and, who knows ? the revolution triumphant !
Many great events in history have been due to trifling
circumstances.   The result was, therefore, well worth the
risk—and if any one could achieve it, Ognianoff was the
man.

It was past noon when he reached the valley, which was
now in full bloom, bathed in shade and verdure.   Clear
crystal brooks flowed down the hillsides past the branching
oaks.   The air was heavy with the perfume of the roses,
like the boudoir of some royal favourite.   The valley
beneath that azure sky and in the joyous rays of the sun
was enchantingly lovely—like an earthly paradise.   But the
wayfarer saw nothing of all this—he would have preferred
to have seen it in flames.

His path lay through the Turkish village of Rahmanlari,
the nearest to Klissoura.   He approached it fearlessly.   As
he passed through the rose-gardens at the outskirts of the
village, he was stopped by some armed Turks, who were
evidently on guard.

" Where are you from, brother ? "

" From Altinovo."

" And where are you bound for ? "

"For Ahievo ; are things quiet there ? "

Ahievo was the nearest Turkish village to Bela Cherkva.

"Yes, thank God."

Ognianoff felt a sharp pang at his heart.

"You'd better stop at the village ; we're going to attack Klissoura to-morrow."

"Thanks—we'll see.   Good-bye."

And Ognianoff entered the village.   There he found great excitement prevailing, the streets were crowded, groups of armed Turks were standing about, the cafés were thronged, the grocers' shops and the inn were full of people.   Evidently there were several hundreds of Turks there from neighbouring villages, come to take part in the attack on Klissoura. Rahmanlari was the place of meeting.   Though overwhelmed with a terrible presentiment of what was in store for Klissoura, Ognianoff was still more anxious for positive information respecting Bela Cherkva : he yet hoped that it might have risen at the eleventh hour.   He had almost made up his mind to enter the inn, which was kept by a native of Bela Cherkva.   But he was afraid of treachery and did not go in.   He went on, eyeing the various groups of Turks, undecided which he should approach.   He happened to reach the door of the mosque, into which worshippers were crowding ; he looked in and saw that it was nearly full.   Something extraordinary was evidently going on there.   Ognianoff guessed that the khoja was going to preach a sermon to excite still further the fanaticism of the already infuriated crowd.   An insurmountable curiosity impelled him to squeeze himself in among the throng of worshippers.   He was not disappointed—at that moment the preacher mounted the wooden bench which serves as the pulpit in Mussulman places of worship.   Ognianoff saw at once that it was no common village khoja, but a softa, who had probably come on purpose from K.

Amid profound silence, the softa began :

"Brethren and true believers !   There was a time in the glorious reign of our great Sultans when the whole world trembled at the name of the Osmanli.   East and West bowed down before them ; kings and queens prostrated themselves to lick the sacred dust before the throne of the Khalif.   Then Allah was great, and great was His sainted prophet Mohammed.   But it seems we have greatly sinned before God, we have given way to drunkenness and adultery, we have fraternised with the unbeliever and adopted his laws. And so God has abandoned us to be destroyed by the vanquished, to be trampled on by the downtrodden. Ay, Allah! Allah! grant us the flaming sword of the angel Azraïl that we may drench east and west with the blood of Thy foes—that we may redden the seas and glorify the heavens. This is my prayer, true believers! Whet your knives and make ready your weapons, for the hour has struck, and we shall wash away our shame with the blood of the Ghiaours, to the glory of the one and only God of Islam.''

In this spirit the orator began his impassioned harangue, which was a long one, and which his hundreds of hearers received with rapt attention and increasing enthusiasm.

'' So this is what's going on,'' thought Ognianoff, as he went out into the street. '' The croakers were right after all. While we were preaching the insurrection against the Turks, their apostles were preaching the extermination of the Bulgarian nation. The struggle will be a terrible one—it will be nation against nation. Bulgaria is not broad enough to contain the two races side by side! Well—so be it—no retreat! The die is cast! Oh! God! protect Bulgaria in her holy struggle!''

And he began again to walk up and down the market-place. The service was over and the congregation flocked out: they formed in small groups, all evidently still under the influence of the words they had been listening to. Ognianoff drew near one of these groups to catch what was being said. He soon understood the position of affairs. At first the rising at Klissoura had terrified the Turkish population of the neighbouring villages, because they were convinced that there were Russian troops at Klissoura. Under the influence of this idea, they had begun to prepare for flight with their families and such portable property as they could collect. But they soon learnt from Turks who had succeeded in escaping unharmed from Klissoura—as well as from the want of daring shown by the insurgents—that they had to do with common rayas, mostly cloth-workers, and a few schoolmasters; and this at once restored their confidence and courage. They resolved to settle accounts with the people of Klissoura without waiting for the regular troops. Ognianoff also heard that the villagers of Rahman-lari had ascertained through skilfully planned reconnaissances the disposition and approximate strength of each garrison. Tossoun Bey was expected to arrive the next morning from K. with a band of bashi-bozouks, and then they would at once attack the revolted city.

These discoveries terrified Ognianoff. He now recognised still more clearly how indispensable it was to hasten the rising in other Bulgarian towns.

Tossoun Bey must be anticipated.

He set out eastward. He passed unmolested through the Turkish village of Tekkié. It was guarded only on the western side, a sign that no danger was expected from the east. Here also great activity was noticeable ; here also Tossoun Bey's arrival was being awaited ; the villagers were to join his horde.

"There's not a minute to lose ! Bela Cherkva—Bela Cherkva. Tossoun Bey must first of all try his strength against its walls of iron. They'll rise—yes, yes—they'll rise the moment I get there. If I can only get hold of Bezporteff we two will proclaim the rebellion, and in half an hour I'll have five hundred men under the colours. Bela Cherkva must revolt, even though it means her ruin. Forward, forward ! Oh, God, give me wings ! "

And Ognianoff tore onwards to Bela Cherkva. In two or three hours he would see from afar the white chimneys of the town, and the pyramid-like frontal of the church. His heart beat with insensate joy.

Not far from the village he had just left the path lay through a thickly wooded gorge which lay in a cleft of the rocks. When he reached the valley he seemed to hear distant sounds of drums and cymbals. Probably some wedding was going on in a Turkish village, most unseasonably as it seemed. But soon all grew silent and he forgot what he had heard. As he emerged at the opposite end of the gorge the drums and cymbals echoed again, this time quite close by. He climbed the heights, astounded : from the summit he saw a spectacle which petrified him with dismay.

The whole path before him was dark with Turks, marching on to the sound of that barbaric music. Several red banners waved in the air. The horde was moving on without any order, tumultuous and noisy. In the sun guns, scythes, axes, pitchforks, gleamed on the shoulders of the bashi-bozouks. Most of them were in their waistcoats and shirt-sleeves, on account of the noonday heat. The wave

P

had emptied the Turkish villages through which it had passed. There was no semblance of discipline throughout that frenzied horde ; but a fierce, savage object united them, inspired them, drove them onward : they all sought alike blood and booty. For the first, they carried their guns and scythes ; for the second, a whole train of waggons followed behind. This rabble, drunken with fanaticism, moved on to the sound of the drums and cymbals, advancing slowly but irresistibly like a swarm of locusts.

Before them rode a tall, thin, dark man, with a white turban : he was their leader.

He beckoned to the gipsy musicians to stop.

" Come here, Mussulman ! " he cried to Ognianoff.

Ognianoff approached, bowing low.

" Where are you coming from ? "

" From Tekkié."

" What's going on there ? "

" Nothing—all's well, thank God ! "

" What do they say—are there many of them at Klissoura ? "

" A good many, they say—God save the Sultan ! "

" Who are they ? "

" Moskovs, they say."

" Silence, you pimp. They're nothing but rascally rayas."

" Beg pardon, Bey Effendi."

" Where are you going ? "

" To K."

" Turn back and come along with us."

Ognianoff involuntarily turned pale.

" Bey Effendi, won't you let me——"

" To the rear," cried Tossoun Bey, spurring his horse.

The host moved on again—the drums and cymbals struck up—Ognianoff was forced along with them.

It would have been absurd to resist or to try to pass through the mob which blocked the whole path. The wretched man, with despair in his soul, let himself go with the throng. He was utterly overcome—his last hope had vanished. He went on mechanically, as in a dream, driven forward by the noisy crowd, whose numbers and fierce merriment increased every moment. And the human wave pushed on, on, to the bare peaks behind which lay Klissoura.

CHAPTER XIV : A FRESH ATTEMPT

In the evening Tossoun Bey's horde reached Rahmanlari, still more excited and fanatical. It was met there by a fresh detachment of Turks who had flocked in from the surrounding villages. Tossoun Bey would march against Klissoura the next day with a force of about two thousand men.

The village was a mass of light. It would scarcely contain these new arrivals. As the night was a fine one, most of them lay down to sleep in the streets.

Ognianoff unwillingly followed this example.

He lay down by himself on a mound near the inn, which was kept by a man from Bela Cherkva.

Though it was late, there were still lights in the windows of the inn, which was crowded.

Ognianoff was resolved not to sleep. He determined to make an attempt to escape from that hornet's nest of Turks into which he had fallen—to-morrow this would be impossible.

Deep in thought, he fixed his eyes on the brightly illuminated windows of the inn. He was trying to contrive some means of passing through the numerous guards that protected every exit from the village.

He hoped that this would easily be accomplished owing to his costume and thorough knowledge of the Turkish language. But, alas ! what would his escape avail, even if he was successful ?

Bela Cherkva remained peaceful, and nothing could save Klissoura from destruction.

To try to make his way to Bela Cherkva that night was almost out of the question ; the guard on the east side of the village had strict orders to let no one pass, so as to keep back any casual deserters. Next day it would be still more impossible. Indeed had it been possible, he would not have gone to Bela Cherkva now. He felt he had no right to be absent from Klissoura at so terrible a moment. His absence would be considered as a cowardly desertion. No, it was not to be thought of. But how could he send word to Bela Cherkva ? Could he not make one last attempt ? And he strained every nerve to try and hit upon some plan.

At last an idea struck him. He decided to propose to the innkeeper to send one of his sons to Bela Cherkva next morning : the messenger might for safety's sake be accompanied by some travelling Turk, as to-morrow was market-day at K.

The plan seemed a feasible one, though the difficulties in the way of its realisation were very great, but its importance was·worth the effort and the risk. For the danger was undeniable : he must begin by revealing himself to the innkeeper, and place his fate in the man's hands.

Fortunately he knew him and his family, one of the sons having been his pupil : this somewhat encouraged him.

He rose from the mound, passed boldly through the gates of the courtyard, traversed the yard, and drew near to a small window in a little room at the end of the yard next to the stable : there he began to walk up and down, waiting till chance should bring out one of the family. He did not venture to knock at the window or the door, for fear of the noise being overheard by the Turks.

For a long time he paced up and down before any one came out. The innkeeper and his sons were doubtless busy in the inn, and there was no one but his wife and the younger children in the room. So at last he resolved to knock at the door.

But chance came to his aid. The door opened and a female figure appeared. Ognianoff recognised the innkeeper's wife. She was going towards the stable with a measure of barley under her arm. Either she did not see him in the dark, or more probably she took him for a Turk who had come to look after his horse.

Ognianoff went up to her, and said clearly in Bulgarian :

" Good evening, Sister Avramitsa."

She turned round in surprise, or rather in terror.

" Don't you know me ? " he added in a fawning voice, and, to quiet her fears, he hastened to disclose himself to her.

" I'm Ognianoff, your son Nanko's teacher."

" What, the Count ? " she asked, astounded, putting the measure of barley under her other arm. " What are you doing here ? "

Then, as she suddenly understood his situation :

" Come in, come in. Wait till I fill the horse's bag with barley, and we'll go in."

Half a minute later Avramitsa and Ognianoff had entered a dark little room. The innkeeper's wife struck a match and lighted a tin lamp, which at once cast a dim light over the room and her visitor.

"There's a way out into the garden by this door, and from there you can get over the fence into the street. It may be useful for you to know it," whispered Avramitsa, pointing to a trap-door so small that a man could scarcely crawl through it. "But what have you come here for?" she asked.

"I was going to Bela Cherkva from Klissoura, but Tossoun Bey met me beyond Tekkié, and turned me back."

In response to her hospitality Ognianoff felt himself obliged to be perfectly sincere with her. He could do nothing without her assistance.

Avramitsa looked compassionately at him.

- "Dear, dear! the poor people: it's terrible to think of what's in store for them. All this band's going to Klissoura."

"Klissoura must fall, Sister Avramitsa: it'll be reduced to dust and ashes. I did my utmost to save it, but it's no good. I can't get through to Bela Cherkva."

"What good would that be? What could you do there?"

"I'd have got Bela Cherkva to rise, and the villages round it as well; and Tossoun Bey would have had to come back."

"The Lord destroy the black gipsy! But what are you going to do now?" asked Avramitsa again, not knowing what Ognianoff wished her to do.

"Where's your Nanko—is he here?"

"Yes."

"And Kousman?"

"He's here too."

"Where are they?"

"In the shop helping their father—to see that these scoundrels don't steal anything."

Ognianoff thought for a moment.

"Couldn't we send one of them—either Nanko or Kousman—to Bela Cherkva to-morrow morning?"

The mother looked at him with dismay.

"He might go with some Turk from here whom he knows. It's market-day at K. to-morrow, and there must be plenty going from Rahmanlari."

"Yes, but it's terrible just now, teacher."

" It won't be terrible if he has a Turk with him. Besides, everything's quiet over there. No one'll touch him."

" And what do you want to send him there for ? "

" Just to take a letter for me to a friend of mine ; he can be back here again by noon."

Avramitsa thought of Boïcho's words a moment before, and guessed what was the message he wished to send by her son to Bela Cherkva. Her face became still gloomier.

" Well, teacher, I must ask their father's leave first."

" Sister Avramitsa, please don't say anything about it to Avram. Can't you send word quietly to Nanko to come and see me ? "

Ognianoff knew that his former pupil idolised him, and would do anything he asked him.

The woman's face grew stern.

" No, no ; I'll do nothing without Avram's leave."

" But he'll never let the boy go."

Evidently the good will she had borne him a moment before had disappeared. Before her mind appeared the thousand dangers which might befall her child if he went to Bela Cherkva. She began to tremble before this strange and terrible man. She regretted inwardly that she had not at once sent him about his business, and began to look around her uneasily. But her kind heart would not allow her to yield to the cruel thought which suggested itself to her.

Ognianoff remarked her violent agitation. He saw that it was impossible to settle so important a question with a weak, irresolute woman. Time was going by, and he must begin to think of his escape. He resolved to know the worst.

" Well, Sister Avramitsa, go and call the master ; I want to talk to him for a minute."

Avramitsa was at once relieved.

" I'll go and whisper to him. You stop here, and remember the trap-door, if you hear anything wrong."

And she went out.

CHAPTER XV : AVRAM

OGNIANOFF remained alone. He resolved to be quite open with Avram. He must have complete confidence in the man, and trust to his honour. The object he had in view was worth a hundred lives like his own, if it could only be attained. At all events, Avram was a Bulgarian ; he might refuse his request, but he would not betray him. He heard steps in the passage outside : he guessed that this must be Avram. And he waited quietly by the door.

The door opened and the innkeeper came in. His fat, ruddy countenance was smiling all over. He closed the door behind him.

" Oh ! welcome, Count, welcome ! How are you ? all right, eh ? That's a good idea of yours to come and see us, and have a talk ; well, I *am* glad. We're all glad to see you, the wife's glad too, and won't the children be glad when they know ? Why, Nanko hasn't seen you for six months : he's always saying how kind you were to him. Welcome, welcome—well, I never."

And his joy and rapture seemed boundless.

Ognianoff was overjoyed. He went boldly to work, explained in a few words his position to Avram, and repeated the proposal he had made to his wife.

Avram's face continued to beam with satisfaction.

" Of course, of course—that's all right—why not ? It's not worth talking about ? Who wouldn't do as much for the nation ? "

" Thanks, thanks, master Avram," said Ognianoff with emotion ; " at this great moment every Bulgarian is bound to make some sacrifice for the country."

" And who wouldn't help ? There isn't a single Bulgarian who wouldn't. Whoever refuses to assist in a sacred cause like that deserves God's curse. No, no, that's all right. Which boy shall we send ? "

" Better send Nanko, he's the oldest and the sharpest."

" Very well, that's all right, he's your pupil. He'd give his head for you. Won't he be glad when I tell him ? Have you written the note ? "

And Avram's voice trembled with joyful excitement.

" I'll write it in a minute." And Ognianoff fumbled in his pockets. " Haven't you got a bit of paper ? "

The innkeeper took out a piece of paper, handed it to Ognianoff, and said :

" There you are—you write the letter, while I give a look round at the shop. These fellows are regular thieves."

" Make haste back, master Avram, and bring my Nanko with you. I've already told you I must be off myself."

"I'll be back in a minute." And the innkeeper, with one last smile at his visitor, opened the door and went out.

Ognianoff scribbled off his note in a moment. It consisted of the following lines :—

"The insurrection's ablaze ! Don't delay a moment ; proclaim the revolt at once ; send a detachment to fall upon Tossoun Bey's rear, and another to raise the villages. Courage and confidence ! I will soon come to you to die for Bulgaria. Long live the revolt.—OGNIANOFF."

He congratulated himself on his success. He would never have expected to find such readiness and patriotism in Avram. He now listened impatiently for the father's and son's footsteps. The noise and bustle of the street scarcely reached that remote room. The lamp was burning down and emitted thick clouds of smoke.

Suddenly, he heard a piercing, heartrending shriek—a woman's wail—in the next room.

Ognianoff shuddered.

He recognised the voice as that of Avramitsa.

What was the meaning of this lamentation ?

He was seized with involuntary terror.

He listened intently in the semi-darkness ; he thought he heard steps retreating in the corridor outside.

He rushed to the trap-door and tried to open it. But it resisted his efforts ; it seemed to be firmly fastened. It was a terrible position ; his hair stood on end.

"They've betrayed me ! " he thought to himself.

At that moment he heard a noise at the trap-door as if the lock was being tried with a key. Suddenly it opened, and the night air blew fresh through the aperture. Ognianoff peered into the dark hole which opened on to the garden. He then distinguished a human form.

It was Avramitsa.

"Fly ! " she whispered low. In the dim lamplight Ognianoff could see that she was bathed in tears.

He crawled through and hastened across the garden.

"This way," whispered Avramitsa, pointing to a plum-tree in the hedge. And she vanished in the darkness.

Ognianoff leaped over the garden hedge and found himself in the back street, which was quite deserted.

He passed hurriedly along the street, which led him past the front door of the house.

There he ran against a throng of armed Turks. They passed through the gates and made straight for the end of the yard.

Ognianoff went rapidly on till he too was lost to sight.

CHAPTER XVI : NIGHT

IT was long after midnight when Ognianoff, after many hair-breadth escapes, returned to the fort.

The garrison was still awake ; the men lay rolled up in rugs and blankets brought from their houses. They were talking quietly as they watched the moonless, starlit sky. Ognianoff penetrated noiselessly among them and lay down exhausted, physically and mentally. He was trying to gather his wandering thoughts, or at least to get a little sleep, which he required so much, so as to be able to face the next day boldly. But his thoughts were dispersed like a swarm of startled bees, and sleep fled from his eyelids. It is not easy to sleep on the eve of a battle, or rather a disaster.

By his side a low conversation was going on among a small group of insurgents lying there : the conversation attracted his attention.

" Do what you will, we're all done for," said one.

" Ah, they've deceived us, they've deceived us," sighed another.

" What fools we were to listen to the scoundrels ! We've burnt our own houses down over our heads," declared a third.

" What did we want with a revolt, I should like to know ? "

" It's too late now to cry over that."

" Well, what then ? "

" We must find some way out of it."

" There's only one way out of it, and that's to leg it," said a voice which was familiar to Ognianoff.

" Yes, yes, Hook-it's mother doesn't weep."

" No, but Hold-hard's will," added another.

" We'd better cut it to-morrow, towards Vrlishnitsa."

" Better do it now."

" No, we can't, we'd be stopped by the patrol."

" To-morrow, to-morrow."

" To-morrow everybody'll take to their heels, they'll show us the way."

" Only take care Ognianoff doesn't see us, the dog ! "

" Oh ! he cleared out this morning."

" Did he ? "

" Yes, we're the only fools left behind."

Ognianoff leaped to his feet and cried :

" It's a lie, you wretches, here I am ! "

At that terrible voice coming from out of the darkness they all disappeared.

Ognianoff had listened to the conversation with mingled disgust and terror. There could be no doubt that it expressed the general turn of mind of the insurgents at that fort as well as the others. The voice of one of the speakers seemed to be familiar to him of old, but he could not call to mind where he had heard it.

" My God, my God ! " he thought to himself, drawing his cloak carefully round him to keep out the chill night air. " What a state of things : what disenchantment : what a disaster ! Who can care for life, or wish to live any longer, after this ? To-morrow we'll have to fight, and I can see what will be the end of that. The panic's in their hearts, the fear of death has paralysed their arms and their minds, and yet they were ready to meet death when they first came. The nation was fearless—it hoped—it believed, like a child, and now it trembles like a child. The cowardice of one has infected many. Bela Cherkva and the rest have demoralised Klissoura. It's cowardice—it's base treachery against the common cause. That intriguing city is only good for producing traitors and treachery ; it can beget a Kandoff, an Avram, a Rada ! Ah ! how that girl has poisoned the last few hours of my life—how I seek death ! how gladly I'd welcome it ! How proudly and gladly I would have died, convinced that at least one honest tear could be shed over my unknown grave ! But to die when everything in this world is dead to you, when you see your two great idols in the mire, your beloved ideals trampled on—Love and Revolution ! Ah ! how hard and hopeless it is to die now ! And yet how desirous, how indispensable it is for hapless wretches like me ! "

The mountain wind whistled shrilly down the slumbering valley. A dull and ominous rustling arose from the thickets around, which the darkness made still more weird. All the peaks, valleys, and hills around, all Nature, seemed to be sobbing in terror. The stars twinkled hastily and uneasily in the sky. But for the hooting of the owls, no sign of life was audible. From time to time the insurgents would wake up and peer into the night, only to fall asleep again, and see in dreams the ghostly phantoms of terror, while the wind imprinted its icy-cold kisses on their brows.

Only one human form seemed still awake on the trenches. This man, this insurgent, paced up and down without stopping—quietly, regularly, mechanically. He seemed completely absorbed in his thoughts, and to be moving quite unconsciously. One would have taken him for a sentinel, but the guards were in front, at some distance from the fort. Hours passed on, and the solitary walker still kept on his pace unaltered. From time to time his figure became invisible against the dark background of the opposite rocks, then it shone out again in the bright starlight. The second cockcrow sounded at Klissoura. This seemed to awake him. He started, and remained for some minutes motionless, turning towards Klissoura : then he made an almost imperceptible sign without moving from his place. Suddenly a tiny flame flashed before him and was at once extinguished : it was accompanied by a loud snap, which was not repeated. It was clearly the flash of some flintlock weapon, which had failed to ignite the charge. The man had fired at something. But at what ? The slight flash and noise attracted no attention from the sleeping insurgents, numbed with cold. Meanwhile, the ringing note of the cocks of Klissoura penetrated the night air and filled the lonely mountains with its cheerful sound, the forerunner of dawn, of the golden sun, of life, and the renewed festival of spring.

CHAPTER XVII : MORNING

IN spite of his agitation of mind, Ognianoff at length fell asleep and slept soundly for two hours. Such slumber, they say, is enjoyed by the condemned the night before their execution. At dawn he woke, and scanned the horizon carefully. Nature was awaking : the morning star still stone in the bluish-grey heavens, which were getting brighter and brighter towards the east : there a red, fiery glow rested on the summits of the mountains, like the glare of some distant fire. Dark mists still overhung the steep precipices of the Ribaritsa, but its crown of snow was growing rosy under the reflection of the eastern dawn. Only the Bogdan was still wrapped in mist and wore a cold and forbidding look. But slowly the mist dispersed, the light became brighter and more powerful, and the green hills, forests, and valleys around smiled joyously beneath the blue heaven of that spring morn. Here and there the morning nightingale's note could be heard in the glades.

Ognianoff rose, glanced at the sleeping garrison, wrapped in furs and cloaks, and proceeded in the direction of Zli Dol. He was going to confer with the Council of War.

Soon he was lost to sight in the valley through which his path lay.

It was now broad daylight, and the sun had fairly risen.

The insurgents in the fort were now all afoot and beginning to work at new trenches, under the supervision of the decurions. They seemed bolder now. Marcheff had whispered to them that Ognianoff had reconnoitred as far as Tekkié, and that he knew positively that Bela Cherkva would rise that day. This news slightly restored their courage. The lads were more at their ease now, their faces seemed even cheerful, and some went so far as to sing songs. The humour which is indigenous to the soil was not slow to appear. Jests were made at the expense of the four Klissouriots who had been sentenced to fire at the gipsy on the previous day.

"Fancy not being able to hit Mehmed at five paces! and having to fire a second time : poor fellow, his sins are upon you now. The one minute you lengthened his life by was like a hundred years of torture. All his sins are forgiven him now," said one.

"Confound you," said another, "you've made a martyr of him. Now he's in Paradise with Mohammed."

"It's not true," said a third. "Dicho and Stamen the Crow threw them in the ditch there—I saw him myself—and now he's with the frogs."

They all laughed.

"So near, and not a single bullet in him!" cried another ; "why I could have spit on him at that distance."

"I'd bet anything you never aimed at him!"

"Of course not—my grandmother could have hit him at that distance."

" We did aim at him," said one of the four.

" Well, you aimed pretty badly then."

" Just as I was firing, I winked, and——"

More laughter followed.

" What are those fellows beckoning for ? " said some one, turning to the east.

They all looked in that direction.

The outposts were giving the conventional signal that they had seen the enemy. At the same time two men hastened from thence to the Zli Dol battery, to report to the Council of War what they had seen.

Just as these reached the fort in question, two bands of mounted Turks, each about twenty strong, came in sight from the direction of Rahmanlari. One band was following the path, the other took to the thicket. The insurgents gazed anxiously to see if any fresh forces appeared behind these, but nothing could be seen.

At once two detachments of infantry more numerous than the Turks hurried down from the forts to meet the enemy. The larger detachment came from Zli Dol.

" Who's their leader ? " asked the insurgents of each other, looking curiously at the commander, who was very like a Turk.

" Why, Ognianoff, can't you see ? " said several all at once.

The Turks stopped when they saw the Bulgarians advancing, and retreated.

" They've taken to their heels," said some one joyfully.

" We'll fight 'em to-day."

" It seems to me they'll have trouble with Bela Cherkva yet," declared another.

And the fort was busy with activity and cheerful conversation.

CHAPTER XVIII : THE FIGHT

NOON came and went. The sun was now at its highest.

The men in Ognianoff's battery had finished their dinner and were hurriedly putting away in their knapsacks the scraps that remained. Anxiety was depicted on their haggard, dusty faces, unwashed for the last week, discouragement was again visible there : a slight success in the morning had given them a little confidence, but only for a moment. They knew that if the decisive struggle did not take place that day, it would inevitably be on the next. They felt that the storm was gathering over them with terrible rapidity. And from time to time they cast uneasy glances towards the east upon the bare heights, whence the distant outposts appeared.

The sun was very hot. On the right-hand side of the battery, which had been marked out and prepared on the previous night, Ognianoff was busily engaged with several insurgents who were rapidly throwing up another trench. A reinforcement of ten men had been sent to the fort on the previous day and the trenches required to be enlarged.

" Teacher," said a peasant, fifty years of age, who came up just then.

Ognianoff turned round.

" What is it, Father Marin ? "

The peasant from Verigovo gave him a paper, roughly folded in four.

" There's a letter come for you ! "

" Who brought it ? " asked Boïcho before opening it.

" Ivan Kill-the-Bear. He was looking for you here last night, but he couldn't find you, so he gave it to me to give you when you came back."

" Did he say who it was from ? "

" From the schoolmistress." ·

Ognianoff felt a pang at his heart, as if a serpent had stung him there. He crushed the letter convulsively with the intention of throwing it away ; but it occurred to him that this would be noticed, and he placed it in the pocket of his tunic. He returned to his work hurriedly and feverishly to deaden the feeling of torture which the sight of the letter had caused him.

" What does this Rada want of me, at this moment, too ? Can't I be left alone, to see the struggle, to meet death at last, so that all may be over ! "

Just then something unusual had evidently occurred. All the insurgents flocked to the edge of the fort and gazed towards the east.

Ognianoff raised his head and glanced in that direction. The outposts were making signals of distress. Several guns were fired, a sign that the enemy was advancing in force.

Soon they began to retreat rapidly from their posts, crying :

" They're coming—crowds of them ! "

The fort was thrown into a state of confusion. The garrison flocked hither and thither, panic-stricken.

" To your posts, I command you," cried Ognianoff, seizing his Martini from the heap where all the guns lay piled.

At this order the insurgents started and each returned to his place in the trenches.

At critical moments the courage and presence of mind of one man act like magic on the mass : any one who wishes may then command them.

Several men from the outposts arrived just then, wearied out by their rapid flight. Ognianoff met them.

" What did you see ? " he asked.

" Turks—a terrible horde advancing—there must be a thousand of them. The road's black with bashi-bozouks."

Ognianoff made a sign to them to be silent.

" Hold hard ! " he cried, seeing that several of the garrison had again left the trenches.

" Crowds, crowds of them ! " muttered several, as they raised their heads over the rampart.

" To your places—every one to his arm ! " commanded Boïcho authoritatively. They all returned to their posts.

" Here they come ! "

In truth far away on the main pass where it emerges on the summit of the mountain the head of a thick column could be seen : its length increased every moment—it resembled a gigantic caterpillar. This was Tossoun Bey's horde. The nearer it approached the more numerous and redoubtable it appeared. The Turks were marching four abreast : twenty small flags and three great banners, white, red, green and other colours, waved over the column. It soon filled the whole road from the Tower to Bela Voda— a distance of a mile and a half.

Confusion again prevailed in the ranks of the garrison. No one could be induced to remain at his post. All looked despairingly at the advancing enemy.

Only Ognianoff's fierce glance restrained them a little.

The black column continued its march along the road, till it reached the fountain, about gunshot distance from the fort.

Then from the garrison from Zli Dol several guns were fired : and a volley was discharged also from Ognianoff's fort, at his command. A cloud of smoke covered the trenches, and the mountains echoed with the report.

Several men in the front ranks of the column were seen to fall.

At that moment Ognianoff caught sight of the heads of three men stealthily making for the path towards the Stara Réka brook. These were insurgents deserting the fort under cover of the smoke and general confusion. Ognianoff instinctively recognised in the fugitives his neighbours of the previous evening who had planned their flight aloud.

He leapt to the verge of the rock down the side of which they were descending. The fugitives were climbing down one after another by a steep rocky path hollowed out by the winter torrents.

"Back—back to your places, or I'll fire," he cried, pointing his gun at them.

The fugitives turned round and remained fixed to the ground as if petrified. They had left their guns behind them. In one of them Ognianoff recognised Deacon Vikenti, shaved and in peasant dress. The lad blushed to the eyes for very shame ; it was his voice that Ognianoff had tried in vain to recollect the night before.

The fugitives turned back mechanically.

"Father Marin, take these cowards and put them to work in the trenches. If one of them attempts to escape, blow his brains out," and Ognianoff returned hurriedly to his post.

"Why, you wretched cowards, you might have fired off your guns at least before trying to cut it," grumbled Father Marin, as he led them to the trenches with his gun pointed at them.

The commander's vigorous action calmed the remainder of the insurgents. They repressed all tokens of fear, but for a few minutes only. Their lips were tightly clenched, and the panic would soon become general.

The Turks had not yet fired off a single gun. The fall of their comrades occasioned by the first volley from the fort had for a moment thrown confusion into their ranks. They carried the wounded into the rose-gardens close by and retreated hurriedly. This first success emboldened the insurgents, who kept up an energetic fire upon the enemy. The whole mountain seemed to tremble under the uninterrupted firing. White puffs of smoke hung over the various peaks and showed where the forts were. The fire was kept up even when the Turks had retreated out of range. Far away behind the horde could be seen a knot of horsemen. These composed Tossoun Bey's staff. The fugitives approached them and formed a thick group round them, which remained there for some time. Evidently the plan for the attack was being concerted. Soon a movement was noticeable in that armed throng : it formed into several groups, which separated the one from the other. Then, as if at a given signal, all these groups rushed forward with wild and excited cries. Some advanced along the bare summits towards the mountain, others towards the heights of Zli Dol, others in the direction of the Sredna Gora towards the valley of the Stara Réka, through which lies the pass to Klissoura, and others again towards Ognianoff's fort. The insurgents greeted their advance with a volley while they were yet far distant, but the Turks reserved their fire till they came within range.

In a few minutes the fort was completely hidden in clouds of smoke from the constant firing, but the numbers of the garrison decreased steadily every moment. Ognianoff, black with powder and mud, with the bullets whistling round him, rose every moment to discharge his Martini, and then sank down again into the trench.

From time to time he cried without turning round : " Let 'em have it ! fire ! courage, brothers ! "

Suddenly he heard Father Marin's voice near him ; the old man was saying to some one :

" Stoop down, lad, can't you ? you'll be hit ! "

Ognianoff involuntarily turned to the right and saw through the smoke an insurgent who was firing away at the enemy, bolt upright, and completely exposed to their fire. Such boldness was perfect madness.

Ognianoff, to his surprise, recognised Kandoff.

So struck was he that he went mechanically towards him, and held out his hand through the smoke, saying :

" Give me your hand, brother."

The student turned, threw a calm, icy look at Ognianoff, but pressed his hand warmly. The greeting exchanged by the two rivals was a sign of reconciliation before their bleeding country—perchance an eternal farewell.

A drop of blood fell on Ognianoff's hand as he held Kandoff's—it flowed from the student's arm.

Ognianoff noticed the blood, but it did not surprise him,

Q

nor did he think at all about it. What most astonished him was Kandoff's presence there.

In truth the student, who had been sent with the reinforcement on the previous evening, had not yet been noticed by Ognianoff in his feverish excitement and agitation. Kandoff was the nocturnal somnambulist who had made the unsuccessful attempt at suicide with his eyes fixed on Rada's dwelling.

Ognianoff turned away and looked round him.

He then saw to his dismay that the trenches were almost deserted. The insurgents had vanished from the fort. Only five or six men still remained and kept up the fire, which was gradually dying out on the other forts as well, also deserted by their defenders. The enemy's bullets now poured in still more frequently, and it was an enterprise of great peril to show one's head above the trenches.

Ognianoff, despairing, beside himself with rage, maintained with his few brave comrades the unequal combat, resolved to die at his post. It was the only fort which still continued to fire.

Suddenly he heard a sharp cry of pain beside him.

Ognianoff looked round trembling. Close to him lay Vikenti, lifeless. A stream of blood was pouring from his breast and reddening the earth beside him. That blood had washed away his disgrace.

Father Marin carried the body under cover, where it might be taken by others and carried into the town. But there was no one there. The heights were deserted.

A deadly silence prevailed in the empty trenches. Only a few shots fired now and again from the still garrisoned forts to the north and west of the town made an echo, perfectly useless to all intent, to Ognianoff's fort, which now attracted all the enemy's bullets. The Turks continued to advance, firing unceasingly. They moved cautiously through the vineyards and rose-gardens which were still between them and the fort, stooping behind every chance shelter, for fear of a sudden attack from the heights above them. One by one they reached the forts deserted in the panic. In place of insurgents or their bodies they found arms, knapsacks, cartridges, and other munitions of war. They found even the cherry-tree cannons which had been carried up the day before—two or three to each fort. These were still loaded, no one having thought of firing them in the panic of the moment : this was also the case in Ognianoff's battery.

The Turks had now reached the heights over the town itself. They were fired at from the streets—their standard-bearer and another fell. But the fate of the battle and of the town itself was now decided in favour of Tossoun Bey's horde. They poured down the cliffs towards unhappy Klissoura like a black swarm of crows upon a fresh carcase.

CHAPTER XIX : RADA

As soon as the first shots on the heights above Klissoura announced that the fateful battle had begun, the towns-people, overcome with wild panic, began to flee towards Koprivshtitsa, through the Vrlishnitsa, a narrow pass over the Sredna Gora, with a brook of the same name, that eventually joins the Stara Reka, flowing through it, on the south-west side of the town.

Gospoja Mouratliska, in whose house Rada was staying, hurriedly collected together her children and the most precious of her possessions and prepared for flight with the rest. She went to Rada and sought to persuade her to accompany them. But in spite of all her entreaties, the girl remained firm. She refused to leave the house. Kind Gospoja Mouratliska besought her, on her knees, with tears in her eyes, to leave at once ; she could not abandon her to such a terrible fate. The Turks were already to be seen on the heights over the town, and every moment was precious.

"You go, Anitsa dear ; take the children, but leave me alone, I beseech you ! " cried Rada, urging her hostess to fly.

Gospoja Mouratliska looked at her terrified. She clasped her hands in despair. Through the window the Turks could be seen already nearing the town. She did not know what to do.

Evidently it was only despair that could strengthen Rada in her unreasoning obstinacy ; and, in truth, she was a prey to deep despair.

Since that terrible encounter between Ognianoff and the student, she had remained overwhelmed by the crushing contempt of her lover. In her agitation she was unable to justify herself, and since then she had not seen him again ;

so that Ognianoff still persisted in his terrible infatuation, with his heart filled with hatred and aversion towards her. If he was killed in the fight, he would die with a curse on his lips and with cruel sufferings at heart. The thought filled her with dismay. She had not a moment's rest. Her conscience upbraided her for doing nothing when she had it in her power to comfort and convince him. The poor fellow would die resolutely, desperately ; he had gone to seek death—he was not afraid of it. It was her duty at least to make his death less painful, to quiet and comfort him with the thought that he died beloved and idolised. Perhaps she might even rescue him from the jaws of death, for then he would seek death no longer. She might preserve him for herself and for the country. But he had never once come down into the town. In vain she had tried several times on various pretexts to visit the trenches and see him just for once, even though she drew down his wrathful glance on her. Access to the fortifications was ruthlessly denied her. Her only consolation lay in the visits of Staïka, Kill-the-Bear's bride, and her neighbour. Kill-the-Bear had three times come down to the town on various errands, and each time had paid his wife a flying visit and brought some news of Ognianoff. Thus by means of Staïka, Rada had learnt that Ognianoff was well in health, though much dispirited ; but that was all. During those six days, which seemed to her as long as centuries, her love for Boïcho increased with her sufferings—he was so brave and so unfortunate. She almost worshipped him now. He appeared to her such a chivalrous nature. She saw him in the full beauty of his manhood, armed, and with the aureole of glory round his brows, meeting death on those heights yonder with a bitter smile on his lips, never turning back to cast one last look, to whisper one last farewell to her who could not live without him, and on whom he had trampled with scorn. The night before, when she had met Ivan Kill-the-Bear for the first time, she had been unable to restrain her feelings, and had wept bitterly before him. The good Ivan had consoled her as best he could, and had promised to take a letter for her to Boïcho, which she had at once hurriedly scribbled off in pencil. (For reasons which we have already seen this letter reached Ognianoff only as the fight began.) But she had not received any reply, not even a verbal message ; and her grief and despair knew no

bounds. She felt that life would be impossible for her if
Boïcho should carry his scorn with him to the grave, to
which she had so evidently driven him. Life appeared to
her hateful, since the source of love and happiness was now
eternally dried up. What was now left to her ? Hopeless
sufferings, bitter sorrow, the contempt of the world, and
despair—everlasting despair. What was her life worth now ?
To whom could she turn without humbling herself to the
dust ? Bela Cherkva now appeared to her black and
hideous as the grave. Should she go and abase herself
before Hajji Rovoama again ? or go and beg Marko to
protect her ? She would have died with shame rather than
face that good man now. He had surely heard foul
calumnies about her, and doubtless regretted the good he
had done her. No, no, Boïcho alone could console her and
save her, and he would die up there ! This Mouratliska
was quite right in her desire to live. She had something to
live for ; she had some one to mourn for her, for there was
some one who loved her. But she, Rada ! She could not
bear the burden of her unhappiness ; she was too weak.
She had nothing left in this cruel world, to which no ties
now united her. Yes, but if Boïcho survived ? How
terribly he would despise her for not being able to justify
herself ! All the appearances were against her. His wounded
vanity could not pardon her. The blow dealt to his heart
and to his pride was a crushing one, and Boïcho would
never, never see her again. She knew that he was not to be
moved on the point of honour. No, no, she must die
Now she might meet an easy and even a glorious death
under the ruins, the noble ruins, of that heroic town. Let
Gospoja Mouratliska go her way ; she would stay there to
die ! Yes ! since Boïcho had not bidden her to live—had
not honoured her with a single word of response—she must
die. And if death should spare him, let him know that
Rada was an honest girl, that the Bulgarian maiden does
not fear death, and that she had sacrificed herself to her
love for him.

These or such as these were the thoughts, begotten of
despair, in a tender and sentimental soul, overwhelmed with
grief, which hovered like clouds in poor Rada's head while
Gospoja Mouratliska begged and entreated her with tears
to follow her. But Rada was immovable.

At that moment cries were heard in the street. Gospoja

Mouratliska looked out of the window : she saw the in-surgents in full flight : she called to one of them :

" Why, Christo, what's going on up there ? Where's Ognianoff ? Where are you all running to ? "

The insurgent replied, panting :

" It's all over, Anichka, we're done for ! Ognianoff—he's still there, poor fellow ! The whole world's topsy-turvy. Fly at once towards the Vrlishnitsa ! " and the insurgents vanished from view. Evidently Christo was from Ognia-noff's fort. Rada shrieked like a madwoman. Then Gospoja Mouratliska, seeing that all efforts were useless, left the house.

It was high time, for not long after Rada heard women's despairing shrieks from the northern side of the town, which was now overrun by the Turks. As she stood overwhelmed with grief and terror she saw from the window a crowd of bashi-bozouks rushing down a street with drawn swords in their hands : they caught up two Bulgarians, who were at once cut down. She saw perfectly plainly a red flood gushing from the fallen. She saw death—terrible death, in its most repulsive form, and was seized with wild fear. The desire of life awoke with redoubled force in the young girl, and overcame all other feelings, paralysed all her resolutions to die with which despair had inspired her.

She attempted to escape, to save herself from death, or from the life these lewd and bloodthirsty assailants might have granted her. She opened the door to fly downstairs, but at that moment she heard the door of the courtyard burst open with a loud crash and through the branches of the fruit-trees she saw an armed bashi-bozouk followed by another figure hurrying towards the stairs on which she was standing transfixed with terror. She turned, fled back to the room, bolted the door, and half dead with terror tried to conceal herself in the opposite corner. She had scarcely done so when a loud knock was heard at the door and a fierce frightful voice began to roar outside. As the door was not opened the person who sought to enter began to kick and hammer at the door. Gradually it cracked and yielded on one side : the barrel of a gun immediately protruded through the chink, and the door began to be forced open. Rada heard the boards crack as they yielded, she saw an enormous foot pushing its way through; the assailant was almost in the room.

Then inexpressible terror overcame all her other thoughts. Death appeared to her a thousand times preferable to the terrible moment which was approaching. She flew to the eikonostasis, lighted a taper at the lamp burning before it, and hurried to the corner. There on the table stood a sack of gunpowder which had evidently been forgotten by the insurgents. Rada sat down beside it, took the taper in her left hand, and with her right thumb began to force open the mouth of the sack : she soon penetrated the coarse sacking.

Just then the door fell to the ground with a loud crash and a giantic figure burst into the room.

Ivan Kill-the-Bear stood before her.

Behind him was Staïka.

Rada did not see them—she approached the candle to the gunpowder.

CHAPTER XX : THE TWO STREAMS

AT that very moment Ognianoff was far off in the mountain.

He was the last to leave the fort, the rampart of which the Turks were already scaling : he had escaped death by a miracle : his cap had been pierced in two places. He sought for death, but the instinct of self-preservation, stronger than any other feeling, had saved him.

Now he stood on the summit of the Vrilshnitsa, on its left ridge, beneath which flowed the streamlet.

Tears were coursing down his blackened, blood-stained face. Ognianoff was weeping.

He had stopped to see the terrible picture of the wreck of the revolution. He was bareheaded.

Below him in the valley a panic-stricken throng of insurgents, women, and children fled with wild terror towards the mountain. The shrieks and groans of these unfortunates were clearly audible where he stood.

On the opposite rock Klissoura in flames lay before him.

Suddenly his glance fell on his right hand, which was blood-stained. He remembered that the blood was Kandoff's. And Kandoff reminded him of Rada. His hair stood on end : he sought in his pocket and drew out Rada's crumpled letter, which he opened.

He read the following lines, written in pencil in a weak and trembling hand :

" Boïcho ! You left me in scorn. I cannot live without you. I entreat you to send me one word in reply. If you wish it, I will live—I am innocent. Do answer me. Boïcho, I'm suffering agonies. If you won't, then farewell, farewell, beloved ; I shall find a grave beneath the ruins of Klissoura.   RADA."

Inexpressible pain was depicted on Ognianoff's countenance. He glanced towards the town, where the flames were spreading rapidly. At different points of the town fresh flames were bursting from the roofs ; their pale red tongues shot out and seemed to be licking the air. Dense black smoke rolled behind the town and mingled with the clouds which had now covered the sky : this made it grow dark earlier. The flames spread with great rapidity on every side. Their ruddy glare lighted up the valley, the slopes of the Ribaritsa, and the waters of the Stara Réka. Ognianoff was trying to distinguish the two-storeyed house where Gospoja Mouratliska lived. He soon found it out and recognised with terror the two windows of Rada's room. The fire had not yet spread to the house, but around it all was ablaze, and it would soon be in flames.
" Poor girl, she's there ! oh ! it's horrible, horrible ! "
And he flung himself down the slope towards the stream. He rushed madly down the ravines and thickets and sped back towards the mouth of the stream, towards Klissoura.
The narrow pass of the Vrlishnitsa was blocked by fugitives of every sex, age, and condition. That terrified human mass, extending along the whole course of the river, resembled another stream flowing in the opposite direction. The panic had in an hour emptied Klissoura and filled the mountain pass. Every one fled panting and panic-stricken, as if the pursuer was already close behind. Some had hastily snatched up a few clothes as they fled, others carried various articles of furniture or other household goods, sometimes most useless and cumbersome. The effect was occasionally almost comic. Thus a wealthy citizen who had left house and home was flying with a large Dutch clock under his arm. Further on a woman was carrying her sieve, which considerably impeded her flight. Old women and girls might be seen flying barefoot over the rocks and carrying their shoes in their hands, so as not to soil them. Ognianoff at every moment came into collision

with these terrified groups, or tripped over women who had
fallen fainting to the ground, and were shrieking desperately
without any one coming to their aid. He saw all these
horrors as he fled wildly towards the town, bareheaded and
bewildered with only one thought—to save Rada. Instinctively he sought her among the fear-distorted faces of
the women and girls whom he met, but in vain—he fled
on again. These people were strangers to him—they were
phantoms—they did not exist for him. He could not even
understand why they were flying—he did not think about
them, nor did they think about him—no one wondered or
asked why he was going back when they were all going
forward. At every step the scenes of horror became more
frequent and more terrible. At a turning in the pass he
saw a little girl who had been thrown down in her flight
and had fallen into the river, where she lay shrieking
wildly for aid. Further on a baby was crying bitterly for
its mother, who had apparently deserted it as an encum-
brance in her flight. Old women, men, mothers passed by
the poor creature, but no one saw or heard it. Every one
thought only of himself. Fear hardens the heart and is the
highest and most loathsome form of egoism. Shame itself
does not so abase the human countenance as terror.
Ognianoff mechanically stooped, picked up the child, and
went on his way. In a thicket at the side of the path a
woman lay groaning in travail with a face distorted with
suffering. She held out her hands to implore the passers-by
for aid. Groans, piercing shrieks, and the wailing of
children filled the air. As if to crown all this misery rain
began to pour in torrents. The storm increased in fury
every moment : foaming streams soon flowed down the
slopes towards the river, drenching the feet of the unhappy
fugitives, while the rain beat against their faces and soaked
their garments ; children dragged along by their mothers
uttered heartrending shrieks as they slipped and fell in the
torrent. The cries and lamentations grew louder and louder.

The rocks on each side of the pass reverberated the
wild echo, to which the roar of the swollen river was now
added. Suddenly Ognianoff recognised a woman in an
approaching group of fugitives—the first person he had
noticed in that procession. It was Gospoja Mouratliska,
with one baby in her arms, and three older children following behind.

" Where is Rada ? " he asked.

She was unable to speak, and could only point in the direction of the town.

" In your house ? "

" Yes, yes, make haste," she could hardly mutter.

Weak as she was, Gospoja Mouratliska kept on her way energetically, though her face showed how exhausted she was by the almost impassable path. But energy replaced muscular force with her, and she had inspired her children with it.

" Where are you carrying that child to ? " she asked in a faint voice, scarcely audible in the turmoil.

Ognianoff looked down. He hardly knew he was carrying the child, and had no recollection of having picked it up.

He looked at Gospoja Mouratliska, bewildered.

" Give it to me, give it to me."

And she took the child from Ognianoff, pressed it to the left side of her dripping breast, on the right side of which nestled her own child, and went on. It was quite dark when Ognianoff reached the mouth of the Vrlishnitsa.

From there the whole of Klissoura was visible. The rain had extinguished most of the fires, but here and there flames still flickered under the roofs and threw from the windows a lurid glare upon the town. Now and then a house would fall in with a loud crash, and the flames shot out and spread to other houses. Suddenly Ognianoff saw a new fire break out in the southern part of the town. Great flames and showers of sparks burst forth and scattered in every direction. Ognianoff recognised Gospoja Mouratliska's house in the midst of the flames : just then the upper storey fell in with a cloud of flames and yellow smoke. Rada's room was there !

He flung himself like a madman into the flaming streets, filled with infuriated Turks, and was lost to sight.

PART III

CHAPTER I : A RETROSPECT

IN a few days the insurrection * was everywhere stamped out.

The contest died away—its place was taken by panic fear. The revolution ended in capitulation. History furnishes examples of risings as sacred and as ill-fated, but of none so tragically inglorious.

The April insurrection was like a still-born child, conceived under the impulse of the most ardent love, and stifled by its mother in horror at its birth. It expired before it was born.

The insurrection has no history—it was too short-lived for that.

Golden hopes, profound faith, gigantic strength and enthusiasm, the heritaeg of centuries of suffering, all vanished in a moment. It was a terrible awakening.

And how many martyrs it caused—how many victims—how many deaths and downfalls ! Ay ! and some slight heroism—but what heroism !

Peroushtitsa was its Saragoza. But Peroushtitsa has no place in the history of the world.

Batak ! † that is the only name which has shone out amid the struggle ; out of the flames and the smoke it has blazed forth over the whole world, and has perpetuated its memory among the nations.

Batak—a worthy characteristic of our revolt : fate sometime perpetrates such puns.‡ But if the rising gave us Batak, it also raised up for us Alexander II.

If this movement, and its ill-fated results, had not brought on the war of liberation, then it would have been pitilessly

* The three places where the revolutionary movement was most serious were : Panaghiourishté (in Turkish Otlouk Keui), Koprivshtitsa (in Turkish Avrat Alan), and Peroushtitsa. According to the official report by Mr. Baring (see the Blue Book, issued in 1877, p. 149), at Panaghiourishté 760 Bulgarians were killed, 14 Mussulmans having been slain there at the beginning of the outbreak ; at Koprivshtitsa, 130 Bulgarians fell, while 72 Mussulmans were first killed ; Peroushtitsa, after some resistance, was captured and burnt by Rashid Pasha on May 12, 1876 ; 750 Bulgarians are officially reported to have fallen there.

† At Batak the terrible massacre of almost the entire population was treacherously effected by Ahmed Agı of Tumrush.

‡ The Turkish word " Batak " means a snare, a pitfall ; *lit.* marsh.

condemned on all sides ; common sense would have stigmatised it as folly ; nations would have set it down as a disgrace, and history—a meretricious harlot that bows only before success—would have branded it as a crime. Poetry alone might have forgiven it and crowned it with the laurel of the hero, in memory of the patriotic infatuation which urged the humble Anatolian cloth-workers to take their stand on the heights of the Sredna Gora—those sublime heights ! —with their hollow cherry-tree cannon.

It was a poetic folly : for young nations, like young people, are poetical.

*   *   *   *   *

Ognianoff had for three days and three nights been wandering upon the Starna Planina. He kept on towards the east, so as to reach Bela Cherkva, being quite ignorant of what was going on there. It is a six hours' journey from Klissoura in ordinary times, but for a rebel flying from the gallows sixty hours are insufficient.

During the day Ognianoff crouched in the woods and thickets ; he slept in copses of trees, like a wild beast, to avoid being seen by the patrols ; and at night he wandered along the dark and deserted paths, at random—sometimes going backward instead of forward. He lived on grass—that is to say, he was as hungry as a wolf. He did not dare to beg for hospitality at the sparsely scattered huts on the Balkan —the probability was only too great that he would be roughly repulsed, through terror, or else betrayed to the Turks.

Often as he shivered on some mountain peak he could see a red glare in the sky, to the south. First of all he took this celestial phenomenon to be the after-glow of the sunset. But as night went on the glare became still brighter and extended over a still wider horizon. It was like the reflection of an aurora borealis appearing in the south.

It was caused by the flames that reduced many a flourishing village to ashes.

It was a terrible but majestic sight.

Through a gap in the Balkan the view to the south became more extensive. Ognianoff saw with horror that the Sredna Gora was in flames. It was like a volcano emitting fire from twenty craters at once. The whole firmament was lit up by the fires.

Ognianoff tore out his hair.

" It's the ruin, the ruin of Bulgaria ! " he said in despair as he saw the flames. " This is the result of our sacred efforts. This is what our ardent hopes have come to : blood and fire ! My God ! my God ! And there," he added, pointing towards Klissoura, " there my heart lies under the ruins. My two ideals were scattered at the same time—the two idols I worshipped. I am like a lifeless phantom, that cannot find its grave ! "

He resembled, if not a phantom, a skeleton. To every sheepfold and Bulgarian hut strict instructions had been given not to afford hospitality to any suspicious-looking wayfarer. The Bulgarians did even more : they pursued all such and hastened to inform the patrol ; indeed, their zeal often went so far that they finished off with a bullet some wounded or half-starved insurgent. A fortnight before, these same shepherds had welcomed the apostles as the dearest of guests. The Stara Planina, that kindly mother of brave lads sung of in many a brigand song and old legend, proved herself a cruel stepmother. The panic and cowardly baseness of cities and villages had migrated to her most deserted glades, and taken up their abode in her brigand fastnesses and wildest solitudes.

CHAPTER II : A SHEPHERD'S HOSPITALITY

THAT night Ognianoff slept in a thicket which covered the northern slope of one of the spurs to the east of the bare Ribaritsa.

He was emaciated by hunger and exhaustion—he had eaten nothing but grass and herbs during those three days, and a hundred yards away he could see a sheepfold, where bread, cheese, and milk were to be had. He was in the position of Tantalus, condemned to eternal thirst before a cold stream of which he could not drink.

But the wolf never dies of starvation when there is a flock of sheep to attack. The teeth of the watchdogs are not so sharp as the pangs of hunger. Ognianoff resolved to follow the wolf's example. He left the thicket, crossed the brook, and walked firmly towards the shepherd's hut.

There were two women in the hut, the shepherd's mother and his wife, mending clothes, and two boys, engaged in plaiting something. The dogs were probably with the herd somewhere close by.

The women screamed when they saw this stranger,

bareheaded, blood-stained, with his eyes starting from his head.

"What do you want ? " cried some one from outside.

A tall, grey-haired old shepherd appeared with his gun on his shoulder.

Ognianoff recognised him as the Greek shepherd Yani, who often came down to Bela Cherkva to sell his butter, and who knew him quite well.

" Good morning, Master Yani ; give me a piece of bread, in God's name," said Boïcho hurriedly, to show his pacific intentions.

The shepherd examined him from head to foot. Whether he recognised him or not, the scrutiny seemed to displease him. He entered the hut with a frown, broke off half a cake of bread, and at the same time whispered something to one of the boys.

"There, you'd better be off, or there'll be trouble. Some one'll see you here, Christian," he said sternly, as he gave Ognianoff the bread.

Ognianoff thanked him, and hurried towards the stream to hide himself again in the thicket where he had spent the night.

" My God ! " he thought to himself with bitterness, " this half-savage Greek had pity on me, while the Bulgarians drove me from their huts yesterday with their dogs, like a wild beast."

Ognianoff swallowed his bread hurriedly and greedily, while his eyes lighted up with eagerness. Famine had dimmed the noble fire of his glance, which had become dull and fierce as a beast's. At that moment Ognianoff would have refused to share his bread with his father, for hunger is a more savage counsellor than despair itself.

Boïcho quenched his thirst at the stream, and began to make his way up the slope towards the thicket. He felt the beneficent action of the food ; his forces seemed to be returning. But just as he had reached the cover the sound of distant voices made him turn round. From the hill on which the sheepfold stood, a band of Circassians were rushing towards him, and beckoning to him to stop. Before them ran several dogs. (As is well known, the patrols at this terrible time consisted chiefly of Circassians, who were accompanied by hounds trained to follow the track of a man and to hurl themselves at him.) On the top of the hill stood

Master Yani, in his white wrapper of coarse homespun, watching with curiosity the chase he had prepared ; for, while breaking off the piece of bread he had given the fugitive, he had sent his boy to give notice to the nearest patrol.

Hospitality and treachery—these two harmonised simultaneously with the cunning nature of that semi-savage nomad. He had carried out both with perfect conscientiousness. In feeding the hungry he had accomplished a duty of humanity ; in betraying the rebel he had relieved himself of all unpleasant consequences. He now watched the result quietly.

Ognianoff saw the danger that awaited him. With his unfailing presence of mind, which so often deserts one at moments of danger, he began to calculate his chances. Across the stream there was a slight acclivity which might conceal him for a minute or two from the eyes of the patrol while they rushed down the slope on the other side. During that time he might gain the thicket ; but that would avail him nothing—they would soon reach him there. It was hopeless to attempt to escape by flight from the bullets and the hounds. In the brook itself there were low bushes between the two steep banks ; but he could not conceal himself there, for, even if he escaped the notice of his pursuers, the dogs would soon find him out. Everywhere there was destruction for him ! But there was no time to hesitate—he must make up his mind. Instinctively he chose the brook, and dashed down the slope like lightning. In a moment he was wading among the bushes in the brook, the banks of which were rocky. At the foot of the rock deep cavities gaped, as if they had been dug out. Ognianoff crept into one of these lairs, and determined to sell his life dearly.

For some seconds he listened, revolver in hand : those seconds seemed hours. The barking approached—then grew fainter, and gradually died away. He waited. What could this mean ? The patrol had evidently lost his track, but not for long. Ognianoff guessed that they were looking for him in the thicket, and that, not finding him there, they would naturally search the stream, where the dogs would at once discover him. The animals' instinct would not be at fault a second time. How long his agony of anxiety lasted he never knew. His eyes were fixed on the stream, with its scanty bushes which rustled in the water. Every moment he expected to see the muzzles of the hounds—the animal seemed to be fatal to him—plunged into the cave where he was, or to hear their bay.

Suddenly he heard a dog bark. His eyes swelled out and grew fierce ; his hair stood on end ; he clutched his revolver convulsively.

CHAPTER III : TO THE NORTH

THE barking which Ognianoff had heard close by to the right was not repeated. It was replaced by another sound, the sound of human footsteps. Several men were coming that way, down the hill, for the ravine crumbled beneath their feet, and pebbles rolled down to the very mouth of the cave where the fugitive was secreted. Soon he saw two sandalled feet pass by the opening—two more followed, and were succeeded by a third pair : these all passed silently and noiselessly. Yet a fourth appeared. But instead of going by he stopped and stooped down. Ognianoff saw the profile of an enormous elongated head—the head of a gorilla : the owner of the head was tying up the fastening of his sandal, which had become loose and was dragging.

Ognianoff remained like a statue, with his revolver pointed towards the outlet.

The head looked into the cave : then it was raised, and a shrill whistle sounded. This was evidently a signal for the others to return.

The head again bent down and peeped in—Ognianoff resolved to fire.

" Who's there ? " asked a sonorous voice.

" Ivan ! " cried Ognianoff, thunderstruck.

For in truth it was Ivan Kill-the-Bear.

" Why, it's the teacher ! " cried the others, who had now come up. Ivan Kill-the-Bear, without waiting to be asked, crawled into the cave and pressed Ognianoff's hands with tears in his eyes. The other three followed. They were all from Klissoura.

Boïcho's first question was : " What was that dog barking ? "

The Klissouriots answered :

" There wasn't any dog—it was Kill-the-Bear."

Ognianoff smiled as he remembered the giant's peculiarity. He assailed them with questions.

"We've made a pretty mess of it God bless its soul," sighed Kill-the-Bear in a voice of thunder.

"Courage, Ivan my boy! God won't desert Bulgaria!"

"Yes, but Klissoura's done for," declared one of the Klissourists, gloomily.

"There's nothing left of it but ashes," added the second.

"Dear! dear!" sighed the other.

"What's the good of crying over it now, brothers? We did our best—and failed. Courage and patience. Our sacrifices won't have been useless. . . . Have you had anything to eat?"

"We haven't seen a piece of bread since we took to the mountain," answered one of them, almost tearfully. Indeed, there was no need to say it: Ognianoff saw their famished and emaciated countenances. He divided what was left of his bread and gave it to his three guests.

They fell to ravenously. Only Kill-the-Bear declined.

"Keep the bread for yourself—you want it. I've got my dinner here;" and Kill-the-Bear took from his bag a hare, skinned and bloody. He pulled off a piece, dipped it in the salt, and began to devour it with his sharp teeth.

"Yes, but it's raw?"

"Raw or not, it's all one to a hungry man. Flying rebels can't light fires," said Kill-the-Bear, as he munched the tough flesh. "These Christians turn up their noses at meat; they'd rather feed on grass, like tortoises," he added, wiping the hare's blood from his lips.

"How did you kill the hare? Did you fire at it?" asked Boïcho with some curiosity.

"I killed the hare because 1 didn't fall in with a wild boar; if I had, I'd have caught that and throttled it."

In truth, Kill-the-Bear had surprised and caught the hare in a thicket, without firing at it.

"But what made you get into that bear-pit?" asked the giant, looking round the cavern.

"There was a Circassian patrol after me, and how they lost my trail I can't think: they had dogs with them."

"Oh, that's why you asked about the barking, is it? Well, the dogs must have come upon the scent of some other game—a hare, likely; take my word for it, they went after that. Kill-the-Bear knows something of that kind of thing. . . ."

"That must be the heathens we saw right away over there on the other side," said one of them.

R

" May God destroy them ! You can't show your head for
fear of patrols ; the Balkan's black with Turks and Circassians. God bless you for the bread, Ognianoff. I'd
have been done for without it."

Ognianoff began to feel relieved. He saw that he had
been saved only by a miracle, not for the first time in his
life.

" Where are you going now ? "

" We'll try to get through to Roumania. And you ? "

" For the last three days I've been making for Bela
Cherkva, and you see where I've got to."

One of the Klissouriots remarked :

" Ah, they're a cunning lot at Bela Cherkva : they
haven't risen, not they—they know better than that."

This was said in tones of anger : not so much because
Bela Cherkva had not revolted, but more from envy that it
had not suffered like the rest. Alas ! such is human nature:
all sufferings are endured more easily when one knows
they are shared by others, even though these be one's
friends and relations. It is that cruel feeling, so strongly
developed in our hearts, which stimulates the soldier to
heroism and gives him unflinching courage in the presence
of death while his comrades fall right and left round him.
Leave the hero by himself, exposed to danger, and he will
fly in panic fear. One of our proverbs says : " What's for
the whole world is like a marriage-feast."

" Have you heard anything about Bela Cherkva ? " asked
Ognianoff.

" Don't I tell you ? They've shown themselves very
smart. We were the only ones ready to liberate the
Bulgarian kingdom ! "

" It's wonderful—wonderful ! " said Ognianoff, thoughtfully. " Everything was prepared, and they were all so
keen at Bela Cherkva."

" Well, never mind—it's better so. What'd be the good
of their being burnt down too ? "

" I say, have you seen the sky at night—how red it
is ? What a heap of villages they must have burnt," said
another.

" Yes, yes, I've seen it," said Ognianoff, gloomily.

" The world's topsy-turvy. Call that a revolt ? It was
a disgrace ! And we, poor fools, we're still in for it. Let
them as deceived the nation give an account of it to

God ! Why couldn't they keep quiet till things were ready ? ''

Ognianoff listened silently to these reproaches. They grieved him, but he could not resent them. If not quite justifiable, they were at least most natural in the mouths of the poor ruined victims. He himself had in his mind more than once reproached the people, just as they reproached their leaders : such are the sad but logical consequences of failure.

"Come, it's no good snivelling—God knows what's happened. It was written by God and the Blessed Virgin : if Klissoura's lost, Bulgaria isn't lost, is it ? " said Kill-the-Bear, trying to console them.

"I say, Ivan, what's become of the wife ? Where have you sent her to ? " asked Boïcho.

"Staïka ? Oh, she's all right, God bless her soul. I took her to Altinovo, and from there—— Well, I never. I forgot to tell you about the schoolmistress ! "

Ognianoff started at these words. He had a presentiment of Rada's fate, but did not dare to ask about the terrible story. He had seen in the night how the house fell in ruin, with the flames around it on all sides ; the girl must have been crushed to death there—if, indeed, she had not put an end to her life before. He had come too late to save her, and this thought lay like a terrible weight on his soul. Besides, some other feeling he dared not analyse agitated and tortured his whole soul.

"It was touch and go with her, bless her pretty soul."

"What !—is she alive ? " cried Boïcho.

"Yes, yes, teacher ; but if it hadn't been for Kill-the-Bear——"

"Where is she now ? " asked Boïcho, excitedly, as if he wished to read the whole story in a moment upon Ivan's great, rough, kindly face.

"Don't be afraid—she's in good hands," said Kill-the-Bear, reassuringly.

An ineffable feeling of relief came over Boïcho. His face beamed as he said with emotion to the giant :

"Thanks, thanks, Ivan ! You've relieved me of a frightful torture ! "

"Well," added Ivan, "it's a good thing Staïka told me in time. You see, Anichka met Staïka as she was leaving the house, and said to her : ' Staïka, tell Ivan (that's me) that

Rada won't fly, for all my begging her ; but don't leave her there, poor thing ; take her away by force.' When I heard that, God bless its soul, what was I to do ? When I got in, she locked the door. I hammered and shouted ; she wouldn't open—I had to break the door in. What do I see ? There she was at the table, holding a lighted candle to a canvas bag."

"The bag of gunpowder ! " cried Ognianoff, shuddering as he thought of the death Rada had prepared for herself.

"That's it—the gunpowder. Enough to blow the whole place up to the sky in a thousand pieces. There's a silly girl for you ! But I didn't know it was powder," continued Kill-the-Bear ; "and I went straight up to her. Well, whether God did it, or whether there was a draught from the door, the candle blew out. ' What are you doing there, teacher ? ' says I. ' Everybody's off to the mountain. What are you stopping here for ? ' And I takes hold of her, and off we go to the Balkan, with Staïka following behind. Staïka kept telling her it was all right, while she cried and groaned. My stars, teacher, how she did cry for you ! I made sure you were killed, but I wouldn't tell her so. I said, ' The teacher's safe and sound, teacher ; never fear, teacher.' But we were late ; the Vrlishnitsa was full of Turks ; there was no getting through. Here's a fix—what's to be done ? Well, we took to the mountain, and got to our village at midnight. I took the teacher and Staïka to our Vlko—my brother-in-law—and made for the Stara Planina. And here you are alive—God bless your soul ! "

Ognianoff silently pressed Kill-the-Bear's hands.

"I left them at Altinovo, but they must be at Bela Cherkva by now. Vlko was going to take them there in the morning, dressed as Turkish women. It's frightful just now with the Turks at Altinovo ; but they say things are quiet at Bela Cherkva. When you get there, teacher, find out Staïka—my wife, that is—and give her my kind love. Say you saw me here, fit and well, and living on roast hare and white bread, so as she shan't fret."

"Yes ; but I don't think I shall go to Bela Cherkva now, Ivan."

Kill-the-Bear looked at him in surprise.

"What ! You're not going ? "

"No ; I don't want to, now."

"And where are you going, then ? "

" We'll see."

" Then come with us to Roumania."

" No ; you'd better go by yourselves, and even separate. It doesn't do for too many to go together."

The darkness of the night had now spread over the valley and penetrated the cave. The brook rippled past mournfully. The fugitives could hardly see one another. Kill-the-Bear and his comrades rose to go.

" Come, teacher, let's kiss each other before we go. God knows which of us 'll survive ! " said Kill-the-Bear.

They took leave of each other, and separated.

Ognianoff remained alone. He threw himself on the ground, face downwards, and sobbed like a child.

The long pent-up volcano of suffering now burst from his heart in a flood of tears. It was the first time that that man of iron had ever wept aloud. His strength of mind had given way. Suffering, cruel disappointment, the pangs of conscience, regret for the countless victims sacrificed so uselessly; his love destroyed without hope of revival ; grief, inconsolable grief at his solitude, and detestation of life—a whole series of reminiscences, some bright, others gloomy, but all bitter alike : all these flowed forth in his tears. He had encouraged those poor people who had lost their all in the fire kindled by him and his comrades, while he himself was crushed and disconsolate. He had tacitly brought down this terrible punishment upon them. He had made an effort to restrain himself before the Klissouriots, while blood was flowing from his heart, which throbbed within him like a wounded snake. And that Rada, too ! He could not forget her—she had wept also. He was vexed with himself for thinking of his own personal sorrows before his country's ruin ; but he could not help it. Never mind ; that was all over now. Every tie was broken. He would never return to Bela Cherkva—the cradle of his love. It appeared him black and gloomy as a grave now. He had told her at Klissoura that all was over between them : he had withered her with his glance, trampled upon her in scorn. True, he had risked his life in the flames to try and save her, but he had done so through some other impulse— not from love ; perhaps from a feeling of chivalry—almost unconsciously. No, he would not go there to gaze upon his fallen idol—not even from afar : his pride revolted at the thought. He would make for Roumania ; he would get there somehow, like so many others. At Bela Cherkva he could only hide himself like a wild beast, at the risk of being betrayed by his enemies ; besides, there was nothing for him to do there. In Roumania, that hospitable land of freedom, he might still work for Bulgaria until her wounds were healed : there he could breathe freely once more. To the North—to the North !

And Ognianoff turned his steps northwards.

The sky was cloudy. Utter darkness reigned over the silent solitudes of the mountain.

All night he wandered over the peaks and across the valleys, avoiding as far as possible his former direction. His new resolution gave him redoubled strength, which the food he had eaten contributed to increase.

At dawn he stood on a mountain peak : before him stretched a broad green plain to the south. He recognised the valley of the Strema. Bela Cherkva lay at the foot of the mountain. He bowed silently to destiny.

CHAPTER IV : THE FLAG

OGNIANOFF, as though awakening from deep slumber, saw too late that he had come to the very place he was seeking to avoid.

He had taken the wrong direction : he was on the bare rock above Bela Cherkva, far from any thicket or other place of concealment : to seek to retrace his steps would be madly to rush into destruction. The only thing left for him to do, was to plunge into the deep valley of the Monastery stream, which afforded a good shelter, and from thence to make his way as best he could.

But when he reached the springs from which the Monastery stream takes its rise, and saw the scanty fir-thickets on the rocky slope, the sight of these familiar scenes at once changed his resolution.

" No ! " he said, " I'll stop in this brushwood all day and start back again to-night. I'll manage to get a change of clothes in some Balkan village, and then off to Roumania. Never, never again to Rada ! "

And he lay down to rest beneath the pines, in the tall weeds and grass which rendered him invisible. For hours he lay there patiently waiting for nightfall.

Late in the afternoon Ognianoff suddenly remarked on the

heights behind him something black streaming and fluttering in the wind. It resembled some gigantic bird waving its motionless wings in the air. He gazed at it with surprise.

"It's a flag !" he said in amazement. He saw that it was a red banner planted among the rocks at the summit. The wind was peacefully waving the flag, which must be easily visible at Bela Cherkva.

No one was to be seen near the flag. Who could have planted it there ? For what reason ? Was it a signal of revolt ? Ognianoff took it to be the latter. There could be no other rational explanation of its presence there.

Ognianoff could no longer restrain himself. Dismissing all thought of further precaution, he hurriedly left his hiding-place, hastened up the heights from whence he had descended, and gazed attentively towards Bela Cherkva. It seemed to him that he could hear distant reports of guns being fired. Where could they be coming from ? He strained his eyes in the direction of the town. Thanks to the extraordinary clearness of the atmosphere, he was able to discern white puffs of smoke, such as are emitted by firearms, at the upper end of the town.

"It's a revolt—a revolt at Bela Cherkva !" he cried joyously : "my true comrades Sokoloff, Popoff, and Micho haven't been standing with their arms folded. The revolt must have broken out in other places as well. This flag must be the sign agreed on. The smouldering flame has burst out at length. My God ! there's still some hope left!" And he flew down the steep cliff as though he had wings.

CHAPTER V : THE SLAIN

It was completely dark when Ognianoff emerged from the black and rocky valley of the Monastery stream.

He passed by the Monastery, but did not think it necessary to look in to see Father Natanaïl : it would have been a loss of precious time. The thought that the revolt had at last broken out at Bela Cherkva had as it were galvanised him and restored to him all his moral and physical forces.

He took the main road to the town, and soon distinguished in the dark the black outline of the familiar houses, chimneys, and trees. Then he left the road and climbed the hillock which rises above Bela Cherkva to the north, and at the foot of which the schoolhouse lay.

From that height he searched the city with his gaze ; all seemed wrapped in slumber ; there was no light anywhere ; he could discern no noise or any other sign that a revolt had broken out in the town ; the only sign was the usual barking of the dogs. This surprised Ognianoff : he began to wonder what was to be done. To go down into the town and knock at a friend's door seemed to him imprudent, to say the least. He resolved to go to the boys' school, which was close by : the old caretaker could give him such news as she had of what was going on in the town. He hastened down towards the western side of the school, and climbed the fence which surrounded its enclosure. On examining the place, he found that he was in the cemetery, which took up the greater part of the yard. In the middle the ancient church loomed tall and silent, itself like a gigantic tombstone. At the end of the courtyard could be seen the black mass of the school buildings, all plunged in darkness and slumbering. This deadly silence which greeted Ognianoff, instead of all the noise and confusion to be expected in a revolted city, took him by surprise and inspired him with the gloomiest forebodings. A cold wind seemed to issue from the terrible quiet and darkness of the gravestones : these loomed silently before Ognianoff's eyes with those mysterious shapes which night lends to every object ; they seemed like living creatures, or like the dead emerging as far as the waist from the graves. He could not restrain a painful feeling at heart—a secret desire to leave as soon as possible that chilly abode of darkness and mystery. At such an hour the human soul is overcome with involuntary terror. Our nature cannot endure any contact with the other world without a cold shudder. The coffin-lid which falls over the corpse divides the two worlds, which do not recognise one another, which are at enmity together. Mystery and darkness instil terror. Night is an enemy, a grave is a mystery. Few are so brave as to pass unmoved through a cemetery at night, or so impious as to laugh at such an hour—their very laughter would appal them. Who knows if Hamlet would have jested so airily upon skulls if alone at night in a graveyard ?

Suddenly, through the dark, to which his eye had now become accustomed, Ognianoff remarked a dim, motionless light, almost like an eye, issuing from the church itself through the low window. It must be a candle or a taper. This faint light was a welcome break in the darkness, the only sign of life visible in the town—it flickered so hospitably and almost gaily.   Impelled by an invincible curiosity, Ognianoff advanced over the tombstones, approached the window in which the light was shining, and looked through.   The candle was burning in the great brass candlestick near one of the columns of the church.   Its dim light scarcely threw a faint flicker a few feet round the candlestick on the floor.   The rest of the church was in darkness. Within that dimly-lighted circle Ognianoff remarked certain indistinct forms laid out.   There was something there. What could it be ?   He pressed his forehead to the glass and peered in.   Then he saw what it was.   Three human figures lay there on the matting—three corpses.   Upon them and on the matting were deep stains of blood.   The candle threw a tremulous and shrinking light upon the scene.   The faces, distorted, and with gaping mouths, bore the signs of a painful death.   The eyes of one of them, staring wide, seemed to be looking fiercely and reprovingly at some point on the dark ceiling of the church.   The other had fallen forward.   One eye on which the candle-light fell seemed glaring straight at Ognianoff's window.   The apostle's hair stood on end.   Yet he could not tear himself away from the window.   The dead man's glance held him there transfixed—like a living man's who recognises you and wishes you to recognise him.   Suddenly Ognianoff started with a cry.   It was Kandoff.   There was a deep wound under his chin.   He was killed.

Ognianoff left this terrible sight and hurriedly retraced his steps.   How could Kandoff have come, wounded, to Bela Cherkva ?   How had they been killed here, he and the others ?   Had there been a revolt in which he had fallen a victim, or else had he simply sought death—simply revealed himself and been killed ?   What was the meaning of the flag on the Balkan and the firing in the town, and this silence now ?   Ognianoff could not think of any answer to these questions.   Clearly some great misfortune had happened. He pondered over what he should do next.   To enter the town now at night and knock at any door, in his complete ignorance of what had taken place, would be reckless.   This death-like silence which prevailed at Bela Cherkva froze his very soul.   It was more terrible than the most unwelcome sound.   He resolved to wait for dawn in the Monastery valley, and to see what was to be done in the morning.

And he

CHAPTER VI : THE MESSENGER

OGNIANOFF spent that night in a deserted mill on the Monastery stream.

Very early in the morning he climbed up the slope behind the sacred spring,* where the great rocks lay scattered about as if they had been thrown down there. He lay hid among these unperceived ; from that height he could see everything that went on below.

The valley was still deserted. The stream murmured as it flowed between its banks of granite : the mills and a few water-wheels groaned and rumbled. The heavens were clear and blue ; the first rays of the morning sun had just reached the top of the Balkan ridge. The early swallows flashed through the air, pursued each other in twittering zigzags and bathed in invisible water. The morning breeze rustled among the weeds with which the rocks were overgrown : over the green plain the golden rays of the sun gradually spread—they reached the black clump of pines, penetrated the weeds, and gilded the height on which Ognianoff stood. But as yet no one appeared on the path. Ognianoff was weary of waiting in that place : the uncertainty began to be insupportable. He fixed his eyes on the valley in the hope of seeing some one from whom he might learn what was going on, and, if possible, beg a change of clothes, so as to make his entry into Bela Cherkva less perilous. But no one appeared, and the fugitive was growing more impatient every minute. Only the noise of the stream replied to his disquieted soul.

At last his eyes flashed with satisfaction. The door of a mill opened ; a little girl came out and began to bathe her face in the stream.

" It's Marika ! " cried Ognianoff joyfully, for his piercing glance had recognised the girl as poor old Stoyan's orphan daughter. He now remembered that since her father's death she had lived with her uncle at the mill. Providence was coming to his aid.

In a moment he had made his way down to the river, and crouching behind a rock, he called her by her name.

Marika was already drying her face with her apron. She

* Sacred springs (ἀγίασμα) are common in the East, and much resorted to on the special saint's day to whom they are consecrated, by votaries of all creeds.

turned round and recognised Boïcho at once. She ran towards him.

" Is that you, Boïcho ? " she asked.

" Come here, Marika," cried Ognianoff from his hiding-place.

The girl looked at Ognianoff with eyes wide with pleased surprise. His face was terribly emaciated, his clothes ragged and blood-stained, he was bare-headed, exhausted, as is natural in a man who for ten days and nights has battled with hardships, sleeplessness, pursuers, the elements, hunger, want, and danger at every step. Any other person appearing at that hour and in that solitude would have frightened the girl, but Ognianoff exercised a strange fascination over her.

" What's going on in town, Marika ? " was his first question.

" The Turks are there, Boïcho."

Ognianoff clasped his forehead with both hands and began to think.

" What was the firing about yesterday, do you know ? "

" Yesterday, Boïcho ? I don't know, Boïcho."

" Didn't you hear the guns ? "

" No, Boïcho, I wasn't in town yesterday." Marika did not know what to answer, but Boïcho now saw what had happened. There had been an attempt at insurrection, which had been immediately stamped out by the Turks, who were now masters of Bela Cherkva. He had come too late. An hour or two earlier, perhaps, his presence might have given affairs a different turn. This delay was one of those fatalities which sometimes exercise an influence on the destinies of nations.

After two minutes' thought, Ognianoff asked :

" Is there any one else at the mill, Marika ? "

" Only Uncle Mancho—he's still asleep."

" Marika, do you know where Dr. Sokoloff lives ? "

" Yes ; at old Mother Yakimitch's."

" That's right. And do you know where Brzobegounek's house is—the Austrian, I mean—with the whiskers ? "

"The man who makes the little black people ? "

" Yes, yes, that's right, dear," said Ognianoff with a smile at this innocent satire on the poor photographer.

" Do you think you could go and take a letter to them, darling ? "

" Oh, yes, Boïcho," answered the girl, joyfully.

Ognianoff drew from the pocket of his tunic a pencil and a piece of paper, much crumpled. It was Rada's letter. The sight of it filled him with dismay. With a trembling hand he tore off the blank part, and, spreading it on a flat stone, wrote a few words on it, after which he folded it up.

" Now, Marika, you're to take this letter to Dr. Sokoloff : if he's not at home, take it to the Austrian. Put it away carefully in your pocket.

" Yes."

" If they ask you where I am, you can tell them—but only those two, do you hear ?   Say I'm in the empty mill, behind the Hambaroff Mill."

Marika glanced towards the northern side of the valley, where the solitary mill lay, half in ruins.

Ognianoff had not put his name nor his hiding-place in the letter, fearing lest by some mischance the paper, instead of reaching its destination, should fall into dangerous hands. He was quite convinced of Marika's devotion, but dared not entrust her with a verbal message, lest in her simplicity she might make some slip, of which the consequences might be fatal.

To impress still more deeply on her mind the importance of her errand, he added quietly :

" Because if you lose the letter, dear, or tell any one else by mistake that you've seen me, or where I am, the Turks will come and kill me.   Be careful, darling."

At these words Marika's face assumed a grave and frightened look, and her hand involuntarily sought the place under her arm where she had inserted Boïcho's letter under her dress.

" I'll go and tell uncle I'm going to fetch the bread."

" That's right, Marika—mind you remember what I told you."

Marika went into the mill.

Boïcho returned to his hiding-place behind a rock, and waited to see Marika start.

He waited for a whole hour, with terrible impatience.

At last he saw the girl picking her way barefoot across the stones in the path : he watched her disappear in the direction of Bela Cherkva.

CHAPTER VII : MARIKA'S FAILURE

WHEN she reached the meadow before the Monastery, Marika stopped, out of breath, and looked anxiously round ; but she saw that she was unobserved, and continued her journey hurriedly. All the way to the town she did not meet with a single person ; the fields were deserted, as also the street which the orphan was about to enter appeared to be. Suddenly Marika stopped. She saw three Turks coming towards her from the other end of the street. Filled with terror at the sight of these men, she turned round without hesitating, and fled down into the rose-gardens, intending to enter the town by the other street on its western side. This was going considerably out of her way, and increased the distance between her and Sokoloff's house. At last Marika reached the western side of the town. To the right stretched the great bare plain ; to the left was the town, with its narrow street, and the row of low shops on either side. The shops were completely deserted ; neither Turk nor Bulgarian was to be seen there. All the shops, doors, and windows that had shutters were closed : this solitude encouraged the poor girl, and she ran down the street. But she had hardly advanced ten paces when something made her turn back : she remained transfixed with surprise. Not far away on the plain a huge cloud of dust was rising, from which proceeded a confused clamour of heavy footsteps, trampling of horses, and loud human voices. Soon, through the dust, could be seen the origin of all this disturbance. It was the horde of Tossoun Bey, returning victorious and triumphant after three days' plunder from the ruins of Klissoura. Men on foot and horsemen advanced in inextricable confusion, loaded with arms and booty. Soon the throng surged like a wave into the street, which it completely filled, and passed through it with wild clamour. It was only a part of the horde, consisting of a few hundred Bashi-bozouks, all natives of the neighbouring villages to the east of Bela Cherkva. They were now marching in triumph, with their banners displayed, to the sound of music and with such trophies as they could bring with them. The rest was stored in the endless line of waggons which came behind. For the sake of ease, the Bashi-bozouks had put on the most precious clothes plundered from unhappy Klissoura, so that the bloodthirsty array had in some respects a comic appearance—it resembled a carnival procession, in Asiatic taste. Many had put on women's valuable fur jackets, fine shirts, and quilted satin vests, in spite of the heat. Some Bashi-bozouks had even decked themselves, doubtless in contempt, in rich ecclesiastical vestments stolen from the churches at Klissoura. Their leader, Tossoun Bey, wore a magnificent European dressing-gown of grey cashmere, lined with red cloth, with long hanging red tassels. Evidently Tossoun Bey was unacquainted with the use of this garment, which he took to be some luxurious overcoat, most appropriate for his return to Bela Cherkva.

It was a repulsive sight.

But Marika hardly saw it. At the very moment that the horde came into sight she disappeared from the street and passed through others still more silent and deserted. At last she reached Sokoloff's door. She knocked : there was no reply. She knocked again and again.

"Who's that knocking ? " asked the old housekeeper from inside.

"It's me. Open the door, mother Yakimitch," was all the girl could say.

"What do you want here ? "

"Dr. Sokoloff. Open the door—do ! " cried the girl tearfully.

The old woman muttered something angrily, but opened the door.

"What do you want ? He's not at home," she said curtly.

"Where is he, mother? "

"Tell me, and I'll tell you. They've been looking for him since yesterday, and there's not a sign of him. Be off with you."

And the old woman slammed the door.

Marika stood in dismay outside.

She ran back. The photographer's door was close by : she knocked at it.

"What do you want, little girl ? " asked a woman in rags, haggard, and sorrowful.

"The Austrian."

"What do you want him for ? "

"Let me in to see the Austrian ! " cried Marika, as she tried to force her way past the woman.

" Are you mad, child ? Haven't they killed the Austrian ? " answered the woman wildly, pushing Marika into the street.

These words terrified the poor child. She now began to think that Boïcho would be killed too, that the Turks were after him, and that they would take the letter away from her, because some one had told them she had got a letter from Boïcho. What could she do ? She looked round her, and noticed that the street was quite empty, and that there was no one there. She became frightened and began to cry. Just then some one stumbled against her from behind. She looked round : it was Kolcho.

" What are you crying for, my dear ? " asked the blind lad, fixing his sightless eyes upon Marika, as if he sought to recognise her.

If Marika had known Kolcho better, she would have transgressed Ognianoff's orders and told him the whole story : Kolcho would have replaced Sokoloff. But she was afraid of this strange man and fled down another street.

" Stop, stop, Marika ! " cried Kolcho, who at that minute, through his wonderful faculty, recognised by her weeping that it was old Stoyan's daughter. He had knocked immediately after her at Sokoloff's door, to ask the old woman about the doctor : from her he had learnt that a little girl had just been to look for him. Some presentiment told him that the girl was Marika, and that if she was looking for the doctor it must be for some very serious reason, as indeed was shown by the fact of her crying because she had been unable to find him. Who could have sent her to Sokoloff at such a time as this ? Only some one who did not know what was going on—some stranger. Could it have been *he* ? Since the previous evening a rumour had been current that Boïcho had not perished, but had escaped to the mountains, and was probably in hiding there now. Perhaps it was Boïcho who had come down to the Monastery stream, where Marika lived at her uncle's mill, and had sent her to inform Sokoloff of his arrival. Yes, yes, this Marika was an instrument of Providence. The supposition strangely excited Kolcho. He cried, advancing in the direction the girl had taken :

" Marika, Marika, come here, child."

But there was no answer.

Kolcho groaned in despair.

By that time he had reached the market-place.

This at least was not silent nor deserted : loud talking and the trampling of horses' hoofs could be heard.

It seemed like a procession.

Every one was talking Turkish. What could this be ?

Kolcho stopped, astounded, near the café, and listened to what was being said.

He heard a loud voice inside, saying, in Bulgarian :

" There, just think of it—it's shameful: to try and burn the town down over our heads ! It was touch-and-go they didn't kill every one of us, like dogs, and not leave one stone standing on another. Where are the brigands now, I should like to know : bring 'em here and I'll read out their sentences for 'em. Revolt, indeed ! Against whom ? Against the Sultan, their father and benefactor, who watches over us as the apple of his eye, to see that we come to no harm. So many hundred years we've been under the shadow of the Sultan's throne, our grandfathers have prospered, and our fathers, and we ourselves—aye, and our grandchildren'll be put to it to find anything better. Let's have a little common sense, bother you all ! Whoever isn't comfortable here can go to Moskovia. We're all right."

Kolcho recognised Chorbaji Yordan's voice.

" Long live His Majesty the Sultan ! " cried another.

This time Kolcho recognised Fratio.

These two expressed the panic which had overwhelmed the town. The former was hateful only, for he was sincere in what he said—he had spoken and thought thus even before the outbreak ; but the other was repulsive, for he was actuated only by cowardice. His cry met with no response, but he found it in the very silence which followed. In such times as the present, the Yordans were right and the Fratios honourable. Every outrage upon the fallen was permissible—every brutality of the victor condoned. *Væ victis.*

The April insurrection was less terrible in its massacres at Batak than in the baseness of its downfall.

Kolcho sighed deeply.

He turned back towards Mother Ghinka's house.

CHAPTER VIII : THE MEADOW

THAT day, about noon, a family was to be seen sitting in a delightful meadow, under the shade of the green trees, just outside the town. At the southern end of the meadow rose the stone fence round a garden, the gate of which opened on to the meadow : to the north stretched the panorama of the Stara Planina, with its gaunt, spare peaks, steep slopes seamed by the ravines, and the picturesque and blooming plain below.

The meadow and garden belonged to Chorbaji Yordan, whose family it was sitting there. With this exception, not a soul could be seen stirring outside the town ; for although since the capitulation things were quieter and some life appeared in the streets, no one ventured abroad either on business or simply to enjoy the beauties of nature. Only Yordan's family could hope to do so unmolested.

For Yordanitsa had fallen seriously ill in consequence of her grief at Lalka's death, and had been confined to her bed for many days. The doctor had insisted on the necessity of a change of scene for the sufferer, and, as the streets were not quite safe, she had been conducted through backyards and gardens to Yordan's plantation in the suburbs, where she could breathe in and enjoy the pure fresh air. The change at once revived her. From the garden they had ventured out into the meadow, where two great buffaloes were grazing, also Yordan's property.

A zaptié sitting some distance off protected the party from insult or annoyance.

There were amongst them two who did not belong to the family : these were a stout and lusty peasant girl, and Rada.

The peasant woman was Staïka, Kill-the-Bear's bride, whom Ghinka had engaged to help in the house-work : she had also extended a hospitable welcome to Rada ; nor had this given rise to any objections on the part of Yordanitsa or any other member of Yordan's family. On the contrary, the sight of Rada, their lost Lalka's dearest friend, seemed to afford them a sweet but painful consolation, and their former contempt and hatred gave way to more humane feeling towards the poor homeless girl.

We have already seen that Staïka and Rada, who had become friends at Klissoura, had both alike suffered in the ruin of that town. ·Thanks to Staïka, Ivan had been in time

s

to save Rada. On the way, she had done her best to console the weeping girl, and when they arrived, two days before at Bela Cherkva, refused to be separated from her. Simple, half wild as she was, she understood, nevertheless, Rada's painful position, and shared her woes. There had been some talk just before of Boïcho, and Sister Hajji Rovoama had averred that he had been killed in the fight : this had made Staïka look pitifully at Rada's face, which grew pale at the news ; and she conceived a violent hatred for the nun who spoke so calmly of Boïcho's death.

" One 'ud think she'd seen the teacher killed with her own eyes. Why should she be glad, the old owl ? " whispered Staïka angrily to Rada.

" Hush, hush ! " Rada answered softly.

Staïka listened for a while to the conversation, and then whispered again to Rada : " Rada, the old cat's got whiskers. Why doesn't she shave them ? "

Rada smiled involuntarily. " Hush, dear."

It was the first time Staïka had seen sister Hajji Rovoama: she did not know she was her mistress's aunt. To be revenged on her she had slily cut the string of the nun's rosary and stolen some of the amber beads ; and she was now watching with glee the discomfiture of the old woman as she looked for her missing property. At last Staïka nudged Rada and burst out laughing.

" What are you laughing at, Staïka ? " asked Ghinka.

" Why, at the fuss the old crow's making over a couple of grains of maize."

" You mustn't say that, Sister Hajji Rovoama, dear," whispered Raja, correcting her.

Fortunately, Staïka's uncomplimentary expression passed unnoticed : just then every one turned to Stefchoff, who had come from the town.

He at once began eagerly to describe the doings of the deputation in which he had taken part. This deputation, headed by Yordan Diamandieff, had been sent that day to meet Tossoun Bey, who was on his way to attack the city as having revolted, and to entreat him to spare it. After much trouble, the deputation had succeeded in saving Bela Cherkva from the fate which had befallen Klissoura, but upon three most onerous conditions : 1st, the town was to pay down on the spot one thousand liras * to Tossoun Bey as

* A lira is about 18s. 6d.

a compensation to his band, thus baulked of their promised spoil; 2ndly, all weapons, down to the very penknives, were to be handed over to him ; and 3rdly, all suspected persons were to be given up to the authorities.

This complete capitulation, which was powerless to save Batak from Ahmed Aga of Tumrush, saved Bela Cherkva. Tossoun Bey entered only with a part of his forces, to take over the arms. Hence Chorbaji Yordan and in some measure Stefchoff were now looked upon as the saviours of the town. As he explained all these doings with pride, Stefchoff cast from time to time a spiteful glance at Rada, who did not even look towards him. But the presence of that hated man weighed on her like a heavy burden. The harsh tone of his voice affected her nerves : every sound of it awoke a painful echo in her heart. She saw personified in him the fatal ruin which had befallen her dearest hopes, and he inspired her with nameless fear and aversion. My God, she thought, so many good people have been killed, and this monster lives and rejoices ! He's honoured and looked up to—why ? Because he's so bad and vile ? But suddenly she turned towards Stefchoff with a look of interest, because he was now talking of Boïcho, and more gleefully than ever before when he had mentioned Boïcho's name.

"What ! do you mean to say the scoundrel's alive ? " asked Sister Hajji Rovoama, doubtfully.

"Yes ; he's fled to the mountain," said Stefchoff ; " but whether he's still alive I can't tell. Perhaps the vultures have picked his bones by this time."

Rada pressed her hand to her heart with a painful emotion.

"I tell you the Count's alive—he's not dead," said Hajji Simeon. "He's been dead so often, and comes to life again every time. I don't believe it. It reminds me, when I was in Moldavia they all said the brigand Yankulesco was dead ; the newspapers wrote about him. Well, we all said ' God rest his soul,' when one day, as I was travelling near Tourgou Namtsou, whom should I meet but Yanku-lesco—curse him ! ' Good morning, Domnule Yankulesco,' says I : he just took my watch—as a keepsake, he said. What I mean is, he didn't kill me, as he might have done. I mean to say a brigand never dies."

And Hajji Simeon winked in a friendly manner at Rada,

as much as to say, " Take my word for it, the Count's alive."

" Provided the ruffian doesn't come here and burn the place down, like Klissoura."

" Come ? I wish he would come, that's all, and that confounded bear-trainer too. I should like to get hold of him and settle his business, like Master Kandoff and the others," said Stefchoff.

" Ah, it's a pity, but somebody must be sacrificed to save thousands," said some one.

" Of course. What do they come here for, the vaga-bonds ! "

" What for ? Why, to hide themselves," answered Ghinka, eagerly.

Stefchoff stared at her with astonishment.

" Well, Ghinka, I suppose, according to you, Father Yordan's done wrong ? "

" No—he's done well ; you've both done well, you and father ! My word ! one would think you were Jews or Turks, not Bulgarians ! Don't you ever think what made the poor fellows go out on the mountains to die ? " Ghinka's face flamed, and her eyes flashed.

" You're mad, girl, you're mad," said her sick mother.

" As for these friends of yours," sneered Stefchoff, " these patriots : to hear you talk, we ought to go out to meet them, to send the school children to sing hymns when they come, to open our doors to them and cook sweetmeats for them, like some people, who baked biscuit."

" Yes, I know, I know," interrupted the enraged Ghinka : " betray them to the Turks, kill them, shoot them, drink their blood, like you did to those poor lads yesterday ! When I think of Kandoff's poor mother, how she shrieked and fainted in the middle of the road ! Ah ! Lalka, dar-ling ! My God—my God ! "

And Ghinka sank down at the foot of a walnut-tree and sobbed aloud, with her handkerchief to her eyes. Her sudden outburst was caused by the thought of the insur-gents who had been shot the day before, but those present attributed it to Lalka's death. Rada hastened to her side to comfort her. The mention of her daughter had also dis-turbed Mother Yordanitsa, who began to cry.

Their grief drove Stefchoff wild : he guessed them to be crying over the insurgents.

The zaptié, who understood something of what was being

said, approached Stefchoff and Hajji Simeon, and said in a low voice :

" Have you heard ? There's another Koumita from Klissoura come down the mountain to the Monastery stream."

'' What ! Who told you so ? " asked Stefchoff with a start.

" The gipsy woman Arabia ; she saw him while she was gathering herbs."

" When ? "

" To-day, at noon."

" Has she given notice about it ? "

" I don't know."

" Oh, we must see to this at once," cried Stefchoff, snatching up his fez from the grass : " we were all but being put to fire and sword to-day, and here comes another bandit upon us."

" That's the man, I'll be bound," said Hajji Simeon suddenly.

" Who ? " asked Stefchoff.

" The Count—didn't I say he was alive ? "

" So much the better—there'll be more butchery."

Hajji Simeon was now frightened at his own words, spoken without meaning any harm. He grew pale.

" Kiriak, are you going ? "

" Yes, of course."

" What business is it of yours ? Let the poor fellow alone," said Hajji Simeon, in tones of entreaty : " we'll find some corner in the whole town where he can remain hidden. Every one likes the Count."

" You're mad, Hajji," cried Stefchoff with a sudden flash of anger. " Bela Cherkva must be saved."

And without bidding farewell to the company he hastened towards the town, continuing his whispered conversation with the zaptié, who accompanied him as far as the garden wall.

Hajji Simeon stood as if petrified.

CHAPTER IX : AN ALLY

STEFCHOFF'S sudden departure had scarcely been noticed by the family, who were all busy round Yordanitsa, trying to comfort the old lady.

" Missus, you'd better be off into the garden. I see our Turks are beginning to come this way through the orchards," said the zaptié, who approached and took his rifle before joining Stefchoff, who was waiting for him.

Mother Yordanitsa rose to go into the garden. Ghinka supported her under the arms as she walked, the others followed. Last of all came Rada, and Staïka : Staïka pressed her friend's hand warmly and said, " Rada, the teacher's alive, did you hear ? " But Rada did not answer, being seized by new terrors. For some presentiment told her that this fresh victim of the disaster of Klissoura, who had come down from the Balkan that day, and whom Stefchoff was eager to betray with a light heart, was no stranger to her—that it was he himself ; and her heart throbbed with inexpressible dismay.

" Why, look at that little girl running alone barefoot," cried Staïka, pointing to a little girl who was darting across the meadow.

It was Marika. The child was returning disconsolate, after trying vainly for several hours to find out where Dr. Sokoloff was. With delight she saw Rada, the only friend of Boïcho's whom she knew, and who could assist her. Though she had not forgotten Boïcho's instructions, Marika felt that Rada would not be dangerous, that Boïcho had most likely forgotten to say she might tell Rada, and that there was no harm in trusting to her.

Rada rose to meet her.

" Come here, Marika. What is it, dear ? "

The little girl stopped, looked round her timidly, and asked :

" Rada, dear, do you know where the doctor is ? "

" Sokoloff, dear ? No, I don't know. Is anybody ill ? " Marika shook her head.

" Who sent you for the doctor, then, dear ? "

" Rada, dear ; it was—Boï——"

Marika in her terror did not venture to complete the name.

But Rada understood. She grew pale, and tears started to her eyes. At the same moment Stefchoff returned, and fixed his piercing eyes on Marika. He had noticed her, and come back for that reason.

" What have you got in your hand, little girl ? " he asked.

Marika trembled. She started back guiltily, and hid her hand in her dress.

" Give me the paper ; I want to see it," he said, advancing towards her.

The girl shrieked wildly, and fled across the meadow towards the rose-gardens.

A dark suspicion formed in Stefchoff's mind. He guessed that there was some important secret in the letter the terrified child was trying to conceal : he had also recognised old Stoyan's orphan. Why had she come to Rada, and who could have sent her with a letter at such a moment ? Could it be from Ognianoff, and was he the rebel who had come down from the Balkan ? The thought made his face beam with evil joy, and he hastened after Marika.

Rada, sighing deeply, followed Marika, who, seeing the buffalo drover in the way, turned back and fled in the opposite direction : this would throw her right into Stefchoff's arms, who was running towards her.

Marika saw this new danger and shrieked aloud, as if to implore assistance against her cruel pursuer.

Staïka was watching this scene with much surprise. She could not understand why Stefchoff was so anxious to secure the paper, but from Rada's face she saw that he must at any cost be prevented from getting hold of it. The moment she understood this she ran like a hare across the meadow, and seizing Stefchoff by the coat-tails, held him firmly, so as to give the child time to escape.

Stefchoff turned round and saw the peasant-woman. Her boldness surpassed all belief.

" Guv'ner, what are you chasing the girl for ? " asked Staïka angrily, holding him.

" Let me go, you pig," shrieked Stefchoff in a fury, struggling to get free. " Ah ! I see it all ; she's sent you, you infernal village hussy. Kosta, Kosta, confound you, catch hold of her ! " he cried to Yordan's drover, who had been startled by Marika's screams. He cut off her flight. The poor girl stopped in terror when she saw this fresh pursuer, turned back like a frightened fawn, and hid herself between the buffaloes, as if to beg for protection against her fellow human creatures.

Staïka, whose wild instincts had been roused, tried to throw herself upon Stefchoff and the drover at the same time ; they stood before her like hens facing an eagle, but a despairing sign from Rada held her back.

The amazed peasant girl did not dare to go on. She

sorrowfully watched the poor child, half dead, as she fell fainting on the grass by the buffaloes. Ever since that terrible night in the mill Marika was subject to hysterical fits whenever she was frightened. One of the buffaloes, who was standing upright, bent his great head over the motionless girl, sniffed gently and compassionately at her face, and raised his damp nose again, looking round quietly and unconcernedly out of his wide blue eyes.

Stefchoff hastily searched Marika's dress, for he had seen the child put the letter away there as she fled. But he could not find it. They hunted all over the field, but the paper had vanished, as if it had sunk into the ground.

Stefchoff turned round angrily.

" I wonder if he's swallowed it," he said, looking savagely at the buffalo.

Golio, as if he understood that he was suspected of theft, opened his huge mouth wide ; only a few half-munched blades of grass were to be seen in his capacious jaws.

Stefchoff was bewildered. He could not understand what had become of the letter.

" No doubt the little devil has dropped it somewhere in the field," he said, and he and Kosta began to search again.

Marika soon came to herself. Her first impulse was to feel in her pocket ; she began to cry when she found nothing there. The poor child rose and went away sobbing.

Stefchoff and the drover searched for a long time. At last Stefchoff went off hurriedly to the town. He had probably found the letter. As he passed by Rada he muttered with a savage look : " We'll see his head stuck on a pole to-day."

Rada, overcome with dismay, was unable to move. Staïka stood bolt upright by the buffaloes. She shared Rada's fears, but could not understand why she had not been allowed to help Marika to escape. She still looked fiercely in the direction in which Stefchoff had disappeared, while she unconsciously stroked Golio's shaggy neck.

Golio sniffed at the hand of this stranger who was caressing him, and turned away.

" Here's the letter, Rada," she cried, picking up a muddy scrap of paper which had been concealed under the beast's hoof. Golio had indeed placed his foot upon it while sniffing over the fainting Marika.

Rada seized the letter, unfolded it with a trembling hand, and glanced at it hurriedly.

" From Boïcho ! " she cried.

She pressed her hand to her heart, overcome with emotion. The letter consisted of two lines only :

" I've come down the Balkan. Bring or send me clothes and news at once."

There was no signature to the letter.

Rada read it over again and again : she noticed with emotion that these words were written on the blank portion of the very letter she had sent by Kill-the-Bear at that frightful moment. Her signature " Rada," in pencil, was still on the other side. Her tears flowed afresh.

" What does it say in the letter, Rada ? " asked Staïka.

" He's alive—alive, dear," exclaimed Rada with a sigh.

Staïka's broad face grinned all over with joy.

" Teacher's alive, is he, Rada ? Didn't I tell you the old cat knew nothing about it, for all her talk about the teacher ? "

" He's alive, dear, he's alive ; tell Ghinka I'm not well, and that I've gone home. Don't say a word about the letter ! "

And she went towards the orchards.

CHAPTER X : LOVE AND HEROISM

WHAT Rada required above all was time to collect her thoughts, and to take a rapid decision. She crouched behind some neighbouring bushes, which concealed her from view, and began to think earnestly what she should do. Things were most critical. Boïcho's life hung on a single hair, and he suspected nothing, for it could only have been Boïcho whom the gipsy had seen ; yes, yes, it must have been he. He must at once be informed of the danger, and be supplied with the means of escape. For her, for a girl, this was no easy task : the fields were now deserted except by occasional Bashi-bozouks prowling round in search of plunder. She shuddered at the thought that she might encounter some of these semi-savages : but Boïcho's life was at stake, and she must risk everything. Her love would brave all the cruelty of fate or of man. Yes, she must start at once. But he asked for clothes, ordinary clothes of course, the clothes of some peaceful citizen, so as to avoid arousing suspicion. Properly disguised, he might even enter Bela Cherkva. This was a great difficulty. Where could she find such clothes ? Who would incur the evident danger of lending his ? Where could she search for clothes when every moment was precious ! Then another thought struck her, which ought to have occurred to her from the first : where was Ognianoff hidden ? The letter did not say. Probably out of precaution he had enjoined Marika to reveal the secret only verbally to Sokoloff. And now Marika was gone ! Oh ! why had she not thought of asking her just before where Boïcho was ? Thank God, at least she knew he was in the valley of the Monastery ; she had heard the zaptié say so. The valley of the Monastery was immense, but she would find Boïcho if she had to search every inch of it. But, oh dear ! his enemies would not lose all that time ; they knew exactly where he was waiting for the reply to his letter. But she would find him ; she would get there before them, long before, for her feet would be winged. If she could only have found the clothes, and they were the most necessary of all ! My God ! and time was going by so fast, and there was no one to advise her.

All these thoughts presented themselves to her in a moment with lightning rapidity. She resolved to leave her hiding-place, and hasten towards the valley of the Monastery. But first of all she looked carefully through the bushes towards the garden. By the gate she saw a man standing in a tall fez, dressed in a suit of grey tweed. She took him at first for Stefchoff. But no ; this was a shorter man, and quite different in appearance. She recognised blind Kolcho. Her heart quivered with joy, although Kolcho, being blind, could be but of little service to her. But at least she would discuss the matter with him. God alone could have sent him there.

But she saw with dismay that Kolcho was already passing through the gateway into the garden.

She called aloud:

" Kolcho ! Kolcho ! stop ! " and darted towards him.

Kolcho heard her cry, and stopped.

In a moment Rada was at his side.

" Kolcho ! "

" Rada ! I was looking for you," said the blind lad.

And drawing near to her, he whispered :

" Boïcho's alive ! "

" Yes, yes ; I know he is, Kolcho," said Rada, panting.

" He's in the mountain," added Kolcho.

" No, Kolcho ; he's come down into the Monastery valley."
Kolcho started.

" What do you mean, Rada ? "

" He's there, he's there now, Kolcho ; I've just had a
letter from him. He wants clothes, Kolcho, he must have
clothes. They've brought word to the Turks ; the gipsies
saw him. But I'll fly to him and warn him. He'll escape.
They won't catch him ; but wherever he goes they'll know
he belongs to the rebels, because of his clothes. My
God ! my God ! and there's no time."

While Rada sobbed out her broken ejaculations, Kolcho
was thinking : he had hit upon a plan.

" There's clothes to be had, Rada," said he.

" Oh, Kolcho, tell me where. Where can we find them ? "

" Close by, at a friend's house."

" Quick, quick, dear ! "

" Wait here half a minute."

And Kolcho hurried away.

Rada waited impatiently hidden among the bushes. Not
more than a minute or two passed, but they seemed to her
hours. Moreover, she was trembling lest some one should
come out of the gardens and find her there alone and in
that state of excitement.

She groaned aloud.

But at that moment a little girl came towards her carrying
a bundle.

The blind lad had placed in it a fez, a long coat and a
pair of trousers of grey tweed. He had been wearing them
a moment before. His tender solicitude had also thought
of two other things which Rada in her confusion had forgotten : in the pockets he had put a loaf of bread and a
hundred piastres.

But Rada did not even look at the bundle : she took it
from the little girl and hastily went northwards, through the
orchard.

" My God, my God ! " she thought to herself bitterly, " he
doesn't want to see me any more ! What have I done to
him ? And I love him so."

As it has already been stated, the fields were deserted,
not a single Bulgarian dared to venture outside the town :
only Bashi-bozouks were occasionally to be seen lurking

there ; and for a lonely girl the danger was still greater and more terrible.

But Rada did not even think about it.

Love has only one thought—self-sacrifice.

CHAPTER XI : THE BASHI-BOZOUK

OGNIANOFF, hidden in the deserted mill, was awaiting the appearance of some friend, or at least of Marika.

The dilapidated mill, which was crumbling in ruin, stood solitary at the topmost end of the stream, not far from the thundering waterfall : beyond it there was no other building.

In its walls were great chasms, where the doors and windows had formerly been, and a part of the roof had been carried away by the wind.

The breaches in the walls served Ognianoff as portholes through which he could watch the path which followed the stream up to the very waterfall, where it crossed to the other side and wound up the slope to the mountain.

Ognianoff was much disturbed. The terrible feeling of uncertainty grew stronger every minute : his anxiety and dismay were increasing. He could not understand the reason of this delay. But his worst fear was lest Marika should not have succeeded in finding either the doctor or Brzobegounek, who were perhaps obliged to remain in hiding. He never for a moment suspected the terrible danger which was threatening him. He could not guess that his presence there was now known to friends and foes alike, and that his fate depended upon the solution of the question who should arrive first, the former or the latter.

He saw some one coming up the path, to his dismay. It was a Turk, tall and powerfully-built, with a green turban round his fez ; a long yataghan gleamed in his belt ; he was dressed in a blue jacket and breeches, and carried a bundle on his back. It was probably one of the Turks of whom Marika had spoken, a Bashi-bozouk.

But what could he be doing there ?

Ognianoff drew his revolver and watched the stranger carefully.

The Bashi-bozouk continued up the path, walking with very long strides.

He gradually approached the deserted mill, but at

fifty paces from it he turned off and passed to the other side.

Ognianoff was astounded ; but he was obliged to remain silent and motionless. He could only wait and look on.

The Turk kept on his way up. He crossed the stream on the stepping-stones, passed through the tall spreading weeds at the foot of the cliff, and stopped. Ognianoff noticed that he stopped at the very place where the path up the mountain began. He grew pale. This path was the only one by which he could escape to the Balkan in case of need. The steep and jagged rocks were quite inaccessible elsewhere. Could this man have come to cut off his escape ? was he followed by others ?

Just then the Turk took off his turban, one end of which had become unrolled. The whole of the Bashi-bozouk's face and head were thus discovered to Ognianoff's gaze.

He now saw a young and handsome face with a broad white forehead, over which the thick fair hair fell in curls.

Ognianoff involuntarily uttered a cry of surprise—then, standing at the empty-window frame, he put two fingers to his mouth and whistled.

The shrill sound was echoed by the rocks.

The Bashi-bozouk fixed his eyes on the mill from whence the sound came ; he saw Ognianoff beckoning significantly, and hastened forward. It was Sokoloff.

The two friends embraced each other warmly.

" What, Boïcho, Boïcho ! you're alive, brother ? what are you doing here ? " cried Sokoloff moved to tears.

" And you, doctor, in this get up ? "

" What are you doing here ? when did you come ? "

" Last night—what kept you so long ? "

" Kept me ? " asked Sokoloff with surprise.

" Yes—couldn't Marika find you at first ? "

" Marika ! who's she ? "

" What—didn't she find you ? " cried Ognianoff. " I sent her to you with a letter this morning."

" She didn't find me—nor any one else either—I was in hiding," answered Sokoloff.

Ognianoff looked at him with surprise.

" What for ? where are you going ? "

" I ? I'm flying."

" Flying, doctor ? "

" Yes—can't you see by my clothes ? "

" And when did you leave Bela Cherkva ? "

" I managed to get out last night. I've been hiding all day in the Hambaroff mill."

" Fancy ! we've been close together all day without knowing it. How strange ! But what can have become of Marika ? " said Ognianoff, who was again becoming anxious ; " and where are you going now ? "

" To the mountain. ¯I've been waiting till now for my passport and some money. But now I won't leave you— we'll live or die together. Ah ! Boïcho, Boïcho, what terrible misfortunes have come upon our country ; who'd have thought it, brother ? "

" Sit down, sit down, and let's talk."

CHAPTER XII : THE HISTORY OF AN UNREVOLTED CITY

CROUCHING together in a corner, the two friends related to each other respectively what had happened at Klissoura and at Bela Cherkva during the last nine days. From Sokoloff's words, or more properly report, everything now became clear to Ognianoff. Bela Cherkva had in truth not risen immediately after Klissoura. It had not risen like so many other towns and villages as well or better prepared for the revolt—everything had been lost through the premature outburst. At the first news of the movement at Klissoura, the committee had split up into two parties—the first anxious to avoid an attack being made on the town, against which they would, however, defend themselves, but determined to rise only in case reinforcements were sent to them from outside ; the second of opinion that the standard of revolt should be raised at once, come what might. But the majority of the townspeople decided to capitulate. The extreme members of the committee, who wished for immediate action, that is to say, the doctor, Popoloff, and Bezporteff, were decoyed into Pope Stavri's outhouse and locked up there, and a deputation, headed by Chorbaji Yordan, was sent to K. to express submissive and loyal sentiments on behalf of Bela Cherkva, and to ask for a garrison to protect them.

The Government, somewhat dismayed at the revolt, joyfully accepted this offer and sent fifty Bashi-bozouks to Bela Cherkva to collect all the arms in the city and defend it against attack. Soon a whole heap of guns, pistols and daggers were piled up in the courtyard of the Konak. This lightning conductor—the capitulation—saved Bela Cherkva. Only one victim was sacrificed—Marko Ivanoff, who was carried off to Philippopolis loaded with chains on account of his cherry-tree.

Five days later, a banner appeared on the summit of the Balkans : this gave rise to various conjectures, explanations and rumours, and fresh hopes were aroused. There was great excitement : it was said that several thousand insurgents were marching from the Balkan to the rescue of Bela Cherkva, headed by Russian and Servian officers. No one knew positively from whence this unexpected succour was coming : it seemed to be falling from the sky. Kableshkoff had so often spoken of a mysterious army ready to appear at the appointed time, that the most sceptical began to believe. Every one looked hopefully at the banner on the summit of the Balkan. Some even averred that they could see men with guns on their shoulders on the mountain ridge—they took the bushes for an army. Others whose eyesight was still sharper could distinguish Russians among them by their great shaggy kalpaks. Then Pope Stavri came and unlocked his outhouse, and said to the captives :

" It's a sin to keep you under lock and key any longer, children ; Micho was right ! Come and see what there is on the mountain."

The three prisoners rushed from the door. Half an hour later they had taken possession of the Konak, Bey, arms, garrison and all. The whole city was in ecstasy. Bela Cherkva had revolted. But almost immediately terrible news came, which struck dismay into the hearts of all. A cattle drover had come down with all speed from the mountain, and brought word that there was no one at all on the Balkan. And Tossoun Bey had already started for Bela Cherkva, to level it to the ground. Meanwhile the panic was doubled by the news of the fall of Klissoura, brought by three fugitives, who had come down from the mountain and taken refuge at the school in the upper part of the town. These were Kandoff, who was wounded in the arm, and two others from Klissoura. The old housekeeper took them in and concealed them in the rafters of the school house. She had also provided them with bread, for they had for two days eaten nothing but herbs ; and at their request given notice of their arrival to Brzobegounek, who had brought them clothes, fezzes, and tobacco.   They had not finished their first cigarette when through the chinks in the roof they saw that the school was surrounded on all sides by Turks.   Brzobegounek happened to be still in the rafters.   There was no hope of escape.   The Turks began to fire at the roof from outside, through the windows.   The two men from Klissoura, being wounded, fell down and gave themselves up.   They were cut to pieces on the spot. Brzobegounek managed to fire his revolver twice, and wounded a Turk, but fell at once pierced by a dozen bullets. He was also despatched.   Kandoff alone remained.   Every gun was levelled at the spot where he was expected to appear.   But he did not show himself.   Suddenly the rafters, which were rotten, gave way, and Kandoff fell to the ground.   He rose to his feet, folded his arms, and cried : " Fire, I'm ready for you ! "

The Turks thought he was the commander and had surrendered, as he spoke in Bulgarian and they had not understood him.   They waited.

" Fire, you savages, other Bulgarians will still remain ! " he cried again.   This time they understood what he meant. In reply thirty guns were fired at once, but not a single bullet seemed to have touched him.   He rushed down the steps and made for the church through the courtyard. Again they fired without effect.   He had reached the church door, when two bullets struck him and he fell in the church itself.   They despatched him with their yatagans.   From there they hastened in search of the doctor.   Several citizens joined the Bashi-bozouks.   Dead or alive, he must be found, to avert Tossoun Bey's wrath from the city : the doctor must be sacrificed to save Bela Cherkva.   In the dark the terrified landlord of the house where he was hidden turned him out.   The band of pursuers caught sight of him in the street and followed in his track, but he managed to get a start of them.   As he fled along the long Moukliss street he tried the doors which he passed in the hope of being able to slip into one of them ; but every door was firmly barred, and he continued his flight.   When he reached the market-place it seemed to him that there were now two bands pursuing him, for he saw a dozen men ahead of him barring the road.   He turned to the left and flew down a side street : his pursuers lost sight of him and he was able to stop for a few seconds to rest himself. But the danger was as great as ever. The band would not be long before searching that street also, and at best there was but little chance of his escaping their bullets, thanks to the clearness of the night.

To try to get out of the town was hopeless. Every outlet was closely guarded by sentinels. There was only one hope of safety—to take refuge in the house of some friend. Fortunately he remembered that Pope Dimcho's house was close by. He hastened to it and knocked at the door : it was opened by Pope Dimcho himself, a member of the committee.

" Pope, hide me ! " said the doctor.

" Impossible, impossible, doctor ! You'll be seen coming in : it'll only ruin me as well," whispered the pope, as he gently pushed him from the door. In truth, Sokoloff could hear the patrol advancing in the street opposite. He fled wildly back, and turned into a blind alley, where one of his relations lived. He knocked at the door, and implored to be admitted.

Necho, his relative, who let him into the hall, at once saw the gravity of the situation.

" Are you mad, doctor ? Do you want to burn my house down over my head ? You know I've got a wife and children." And with these words he opened the door and led him out. The doctor hastened out of the alley into the Petkanoff street. Fate brought him face to face with his pursuers.

" If you don't stop we'll fire ! Stop, doctor ! " cried one of the constables to him from behind. In truth Sokoloff did stop, but not, however, where the zealous Bulgarian constable ordered him to. He knocked at Saratoff's door— he was his family doctor and one of his best friends, and resolved to try his luck there also.

" Who's that knocking ? " asked Saratoff.

The doctor answered.

But Saratoff's only reply was to bolt the door more carefully, and not another sound was heard from inside.

T

CHAPTER XIII : THE HISTORY CONTINUED

" WHAT a disgrace !   My God ! " groaned Ognianoff, much distressed.

" I tell you there's a panic in the town, brother ; nothing but cowardice and treachery on every side.   It's no longer the same Bela Cherkva," said Sokoloff gloomily.

Ognianoff drew a deep sigh.

" Cowardice and treachery, you say ?   They're the natural offspring of our ill-fated revolution.   They follow behind it, as wolves and crows do the battle army.   And who put the flag on the top of the mountain ? "

" I don't know."

" Who do you think did ? "

" The Turks, they say."

Ognianoff looked at him with surprise.

" Yes, the Turks," continued the doctor, " because it was seen on the previous day, when Tossoun Bey left Klissoura to fall on Bela Cherkva with the intention of destroying it.   He was heard threatening to do so before he left Klissoura : he was only looking out for some pretext.   No doubt it was for the same reason that they spread reports of the great army that was coming to relieve us, instead of which we got Tossoun."

" Then he's at Bela Cherkva to-day ? "

" Yes."

" No doubt frightful scenes are going on there ! " cried Ognianoff excitedly.

" Well, more shameful than frightful," replied the doctor " the man I sent to the town to-day brought back word tha Tossoun Bey had spared Bela Cherkva because they sen a deputation to receive him in state.   He saw them piling up a whole heap of arms in the courtyard of the Konak brought in by the townspeople themselves—the cherry-tre cannon was there too.   Ah ! poor Marko !   I'm sorry fo him most of all ! "

Ognianoff sighed.

" Yes, poor Marko ! that's the worst of all.   He was th victim of some loathsome treachery—so was Kandoff," added Sokoloff.

" Yes.   Who betrayed Kandoff and his comrades ? asked Ognianoff, while deep wrinkles formed on his brow.

" I forgot to tell you—it was Yordan Diamandieff ; th

stupid old woman went and told the pope secretly, and the pope told Yordan. He stood there himself, urging on the bashi-bozouks—'Fire, what are you waiting for ? We won't have brigands and traitors in our city.'"

"My God, my God ! Poor Kandoff ! I saw him fighting at the fort at Klissoura like a hero; and like a hero he fell ! What a frightful shock it was when I saw his corpse last night ! But how did you get away, after all ?"

"I managed to get taken into a house at last. By this time I expect they've got the hue-and-cry out against me at Bela Cherkva. Let them catch me if they can !"

"What are your intentions now, doctor ? where are you going ?"

"To Roumania, of course."

"Yes, I'd thought of going there too, but the flag made me come down from the mountain."

"As it's made me go towards it. But you can't go in that cloak, and you've got no hat !"

"That's why I sent Marika to you with a letter asking you to bring me things to go in. It's strange she should be so long."

"That doesn't matter," said the doctor. "As soon as it's dark we can go to the Hambaroff mill, and old Lilko will give us everything we want. Fortunately, I happen to have an old passport ; that'll do for you. And there's food in the bundle."

"That's splendid. But I didn't come here to escape again. I came in the hope of finding a rebellion."

"Well, it's missed fire," said the doctor, bitterly. "All we could do was to get into this mess."

"Haven't you any news from elsewhere ?"

"Only vague rumours : there's the same tale on all sides. The revolt didn't spread, and ended in disaster. You know more about it than I do."

"Yes ; from this mountain I've seen twenty villages blazing at the same time," said Ognianoff.

"Ah, brother, the nation wasn't ripe for this kind of thing. We made a terrible mistake," said the doctor ; "and Bulgaria's paying dearly for it now—so many victims, and all in vain !"

"Mistake ? of course we were mistaken. But the revolution and the victims were bound to be. I could even have wished they were more numerous and more terrible. We can't destroy Turkey by force of arms, but we can gain the sympathies of the world, at least, by our frightful sufferings, by our martyrdom, by the rivers of blood that are now flowing in Bulgaria. It's a sign of our existence, at least. No one troubles about the dead—only the living have a right to life. If the Governments of Europe don't take action on our behalf, they don't deserve to be called Christian and civilised. It's all the same—if nothing had happened we should have had nothing to regret. We've carried out a human obligation ; we tried to purchase our liberty with our blood—we failed. It's matter for regret, but there's nothing to be ashamed of. The shame, the crime, will be for us if we remain with our arms folded—if we trample on our fallen idol—if we forget the blood and the flames that cover Bulgaria to-day ! "

" Ognianoff," said the doctor after a short pause, " it seems to me that there's no one who thinks so except us two : the whole of Bulgaria is cursing us as the authors of her misfortunes. Or, listen—everybody thinks Stefchoff the real liberator."

CHAPTER XIV : A SERIOUS CONVERSATION

THIS was the first time Stefchoff's name had been mentioned. Ognianoff frowned.

" Do you mean to say that contemptible creature's still alive ? "

" Contemptible creature ? Stefchoff's the wisest, the proudest, most respected man in the town now," said the doctor. " He and Yordan are triumphant—he passes as the saviour of the city, while they'd shoot us down like dogs if they saw us."

" Never mind, he's a base and cowardly creature. How unhappy poor Lalka must be."

" What ! don't you know ? Lalka's dead."

- " Dead ? you don't say so ! "

" She died on the 18th of April," muttered the doctor !

" How much sorrow in such a short time ! He must have killed her, the scoundrel ! " cried Ognianoff.

" Yes, he killed her—a few months with him were enough."

Ognianoff, much moved, seized him by the hand.

" Ah ! brother, we're both equally unhappy."

The doctor looked at him inquiringly.

" Lalka, the being you loved is now in the grave," added Boïcho, sorrowfully ; " and the other being I loved is in the grave, lost to me for ever."

" No, your Rada's alive, she's at Bela Cherkva ! " cried the doctor, eagerly.

" Alive ? yes, she's alive—but dead to me."

The doctor looked at him with surprise.

" Yes, dead to me for ever," repeated Boïcho, gloomily. " Poor Kandoff ! God rest his soul ! Why did I survive him ? "

The doctor's astonishment was increasing.

" Boïcho, do you mean to say you quarrelled with Kandoff at Klissoura ? "

" Yes, to the death."

" About Rada ? "

Ognianoff frowned.   " Don't let's talk about that," he said.

" Are you mad, Boïcho ? To suspect Rada ? The thing's absurd ! "

" Absurd ? I thought her innocence itself, brother—and what was the end of it ? " groaned Ognianoff. " I believed in her. I loved her so ardently. My country seemed dearer to me then, my confidence in myself greater, my courage unbounded ! And what awakening ! Just fancy. Well, I need only tell you that I fought at Klissoura, not with the hope of repulsing the enemy, but to meet death in the field. Don't talk about it ! " and Ognianoff bent his head to the ground.

" You're deceived. Rada loved you faithfully, and still loves you ; but she's very unhappy, and unjustly accused— by you first of all," said the doctor with displeasure.

Ognianoff threw a reproving glance at him.

" Doctor, for the sake of poor Kandoff's memory, don't talk any more about this sad business."

" It's precisely Kandoff's memory that I wish to clear from your suspicion. Don't imagine that he acted treacherously. True, he fell in love with Rada. As you know, he was passionate, and easily carried away. His inexplicable infatuation made him give up society, the committee, and everything—but all this had no effect on Rada's feelings, and he never insulted her with any improper proposal. She never told you of it from feelings of modesty, but she often complained to Lalka of Kandoff's platonic attention. Ah! now I think of it, here's the letter he wrote her on the 19th of April, the dáy he followed her to Klissoura. Netkovitch gave it to me. Read it."

And Sokoloff drew Kandoff's letter from his pocket-book, and gave it to Ognianoff.

Boïcho glanced hurriedly over it. His eyes filled with tears. An expression of joy at once lighted up his face.

"Thanks, Sokoloff, your words have taken a terrible load off my heart. This is not the language of a favoured lover; it's the despairing confession of one who knows he has no hope. How could I ever have suspected her? Thanks, thanks, you have restored me to my senses; you've given me new life."

"Poor Rada, how happy she'd be if she knew. I wasn't able to see her, but I heard she was in despair for you, of course, since, like every one else, she thought you dead. Write her a line or two before we go, to comfort her, poor thing."

"How do you mean write to her?"

"Why, humanity demands it."

"No, humanity demands not that I should write to her, but that I should go to her and ask pardon of her on my knees. I've been cruel to Rada to the degree of cowardice," cried Ognianoff.

"Yes, I'd have advised the same, only now it's impossible."

"Impossible or not, I'm going," said Ognianoff resolutely.

"What, you'll go to Bela Cherkva?" cried the doctor, astounded. "Oh! it's absolute madness. I tell you the town's ablaze. Yordan and Stefchoff are saviours there now. You're only exposing yourself to certain destruction!"

"Doctor, you ought to know that I care little for my life when my honour's at stake. Tossoun's entire army couldn't keep me back. I must beg pardon of my suffering Rada for my cruel conduct, which led her to the desperate resolution of putting an end to her life in the ruins of Klissoura."

And in two words Ognianoff described the incident.

"Then I won't restrain you, brother," said the doctor, with emotion.

Ognianoff thought for a moment and added quietly:

" Besides—that's not all: Rada's mine; I plighted my faith to her before I left her here for the last time. I plighted my faith to her before God, and instead of a 'ring we exchanged solemn vows. I can't leave her, you see, and if I should reach Roumania safely I should send for her to share the poverty, want, and sufferings which make up the life of an emigrant. Oh! how gladly she would come to share my lot, as she shared it here. She's a heroine in her love, doctor, and I wouldn't give up her heart for the whole world."

The doctor's emotion was visible on his face.

" As soon as it's dark I'll be off, and this very night I'll be back again, safe and sound, I promise you. Now I don't want to die, doctor, for Rada still lives for me, and Bulgaria is not yet freed! "

CHAPTER XV: THE MEETING

THE doctor was peering through a hole in the wall.

" There's some one coming," he said; " it must be Marika."

Ognianoff turned and glanced down the valley.

" No, it's not Marika; she's not so tall, and had a blue dress on."

" This one's in black, carrying a bundle."

" It's Rada," cried Ognianoff with a start.

The doctor shared his surprise.

Ognianoff drew himself up at full length in the doorway of the mill, and beckoned with both hands.

Rada, who for some time had been wandering over the rocks, hunting for Boïcho, now caught sight of him. She flew towards him, and was in the mill in a moment.

" Rada! " he cried.

" Oh, Boïcho, Boïcho! " she sobbed, half fainting, pressing her lips to his cheek. The doctor watched the scene with deep emotion.

" And how is it you're here, Rada darling? " asked Ognianoff as soon as he had mastered his feelings.

" Marika brought me the letter you'd given her for the doctor. Ah, Boïcho! why are you so cruel to me? " said Rada, amid tears of joy. " You're not angry with me now, are you? You'd no right to be angry, you know, don't you? "

" Forgive me, pet, forgive me! " and Boïcho kissed her

hands. "Sokoloff's just been showing me how mad I've been : it's terrible to think of ! I was coming to the town to ask you to forgive me for my cruelty. I'm unworthy of the love of an angel like you. But you'll forget and forgive, won't you, Rada ? " And Ognianoff gazed anxiously at her eyes, moist with boundless love and devotion.

But Rada suddenly grew as pale as a ghost, started up from Boïcho's side, and exclaimed :

"Fly, Boïcho ! I forgot to tell you. Fly ! You've been seen here, the Turks are coming ! "

Ognianoff and Sokoloff were thunderstruck.

"Quick, quick, fly to the mountain ! " cried Rada in terror.

"What ? " cried Sokoloff, who could not believe his ears.

" A gipsy woman saw you and came and brought word, before I even met Marika. As I was coming here I saw a whole band of bashi-bozouks going towards the vineyards ; they've blocked the road, they're coming after you, Boïcho. My God ! I forgot to tell you, the first thing. I lost a whole hour looking for you in the valley. We'll meet some other time. Fly, fly ! "

In spite of the presence of mind for which Ognianoff was remarkable at critical moments, he was quite overwhelmed by this terrible news coming at such a joyful hour as this, at his unexpected meeting with Rada, comelier and more charming than ever in the light of her heroic love : he was unable to take a rapid decision. He felt powerless to part from her at such a moment. And time was precious.

" Fly—yes ! but what about you ? " said Boïcho.

" Never mind about me ; I shall be all right—only fly, quick ! Take this, the clothes are in it, but fly, Boïcho ! Farewell, we'll meet again, if you'll only fly. Boïcho, dear Boïcho—farewell ! "

And Rada, handing Ognianoff the bundle, seized him by the arm and forced him to the doorway.

" No," said Ognianoff resolutely ; "I can't leave you like this. If these savages get hold of you——"

" Oh ! Boïcho, they're coming ! "

" Yes, and if they find you alone in this wild spot, those brutes ! No, better die here defending you ! "

But Boïcho saw at once the madness, the complete uselessness of this desperate resolution. He asked Rada abruptly :

" Rada, will you go with us ? "

To this most unexpected proposal Rada replied with rapture :

" Of course, Boïcho ! I'll go with you to the ends of the earth. Let's fly, Boïcho ! "

Ognianoff's eyes flashed.

" If we can only get to the ' Little Chair ' behind the waterfall, I can keep them there the whole evening, while you take Rada up the mountain," said Sokoloff.

In truth behind the waterfall there was a narrow pass, strewn with sharp jagged rocks, and known as the " Little Chair," from which a well-armed man could keep a whole battalion at bay ; it was the only path up the mountain.

There was no time to be lost.

" To the mountain ! " cried Ognianoff.

And he was the first to reach the doorway, from which he cast a searching glance round the valley.

CHAPTER XVI : THE PARTING

It was too late.

On the opposite bank the sharp rocks were black with Turks. They were taking up their position behind the boulders and bushes there, and only their heads and the barrels of their guns were visible. On the summit stood a figure in white trousers pointing towards the mill. It was the gipsy woman. The Turks were already swarming up the cliff on which the mill stood.

Ognianoff and the doctor saw that they were surrounded, and did not even think of escaping—it was impossible.

The Turks continued to advance with precaution, taking advantage of every shelter afforded by the rocks and bushes : there were about a hundred of them.

The path leading down to the valley was still open.

Boïcho turned to Rada and said :

" Rada, go down the path along the stream."

But just then a terrible thought darkened his face, and he said :

" No, better stay here."

The same decision was expressed on Rada's face.

" With you, with you, Boïcho," she faltered, with her hands folded across her breast.

So much grief, love, and devotion could be read in her moist glance !   Such readiness to die !

Ognianoff and Sokoloff counted up their cartridges.

" Eighteen," said the doctor.

" Enough to die honourably," said Ognianoff in a whisper.

Tossoun Bey commanded the attack in person.   Before appearing on the cliff he had placed a guard in the valley, and so completely surrounded the rebels, or rather the rebel, for he was convinced that only Ognianoff was inside.

Before giving the word to fire, Tossoun Bey ordered a final appeal to be made.

" Surrender, Konsoloss Komita," was cried in Turkish.

Only the echoes replied.

Rada crouched half fainting in a corner.

" Courage, Rada," said Boïcho mournfully.

She made a motion with her hand, as though to say " I was afraid at Klissoura because I was outcast and alone. Now I'm not afraid of dying with you, as you love me. You shall see."

Boïcho understood the heroic meaning of this dumb answer, and his eyes grew moist.

Meanwhile the moments were passing by.   Ognianoff and Sokoloff, leaning closely against the walls for protection, held their revolvers tight.   They glanced towards the two cliffs, from which they expected every moment to hear the report of the guns.

A minute passed by, evidently the respite allowed by Tossoun Bey.

Then from the eastern and western sides of the gorge alike there was a roar of musketry.   The besieged heard the bullets whistle over their heads and through the holes in the masonry, and fall flattened at their feet.

The valley of the Balkan re-echoed the sound.

Suddenly the firing ceased.

In spite of its many breaches, the building had sheltered the three unfortunates.   Not one of them had been touched.   Only Rada had sunk to the ground, unconscious : the poor child's courage had deserted her.   Her hood had fallen off, and her dark hair rolled in waves over her shoulders and in the dust.

A second volley would not be long in coming, and Rada, as she lay there, was exposed to the bullets.

Ognianoff stooped, raised her in his arms, and carried her

into the most sheltered corner, where he laid her, placing
the bundle under her head ; but she did not recover—she
lay unconscious and insensible of all that was going on
round her. And before that fair pale face, with its closed
eyes and bloodless lips, that graceful and charming figure
lying in the dust, a terrible inexpressible sorrow filled his
heart as he thought of the fast approaching moment when
he must part for ever from the hapless girl who had united
her lot with his own, and whom his hand could soon no
longer defend from the unutterable fate which was in store
for her.

" Hadn't I better kill her myself ? " he thought.

As no reply was received from the mill, the besiegers
became bolder, and advanced to the bottom of the cliff.
The circle round the mill was growing narrower, and the
moment for decisive action was rapidly advancing.

" Surrender, Komita ! " they cried again.

There was no answer.

Suddenly a storm of bullets burst upon the mill. As
the volley grew louder the Turks approached still nearer.
From the continued silence, they came to the conclusion
that the concealed rebel was unarmed. Bullets rained upon
the walls.

The Turks were now quite close. The time was at hand.
Ognianoff stood upright at one window, the doctor in the
doorway.

They looked at one another, and each discharged his
revolver into the surging mass of the enemy. The unexpected rejoinder brought three Turks to the ground, and
revealed the force of the mill. The Turks saw that there
was more than one rebel there. This confused them, but
only for a moment. The victors of Klissoura rushed with a
shout at the building. Some aimed from the banks at the
openings in the walls, so as to prevent the defenders from
appearing there and firing at the attacking party. The
struggle could not last.

" Doctor, we're done for : farewell for ever, brother," said
Boïcho.

" Farewell, brother ! "

" Doctor, not one of us must fall into their hands alive ! "

" No, not one of us. I've got four cartridges left. I'm
keeping one for myself."

" I'm keeping two, doctor," and Ognianoff involuntarily

turned towards Rada. She lay there still, but her face had become deathlike in its pallor ; from her left breast a thin stream of blood was quietly trickling down over her dress. A bullet had glanced off the wall and struck her. She had passed from unconsciousness into eternal slumber.

Then Boïcho left his post and drew near to her : he knelt down, took her cold hands in his, and imprinted one long kiss on her icy lips ; he kissed her forehead, her wondrous loving eyes, her hair, and her wound where the blood was flowing. If he uttered any sound, murmured a last farewell in that last kiss, whispered a " Good-bye till we meet again, Rada," it could not be heard in the roar of the guns outside and the pattering of the bullets within. He wrapped her in his cloak. When Boïcho rose, tears were flowing down his cheeks.

A whole ocean of sorrow was in those tears.

Perhaps—who knows ?—there was mingled also a warm feeling of gratitude to Providence !

CHAPTER XVII : DESTRUCTION

DURING this last mute farewell, which lasted only half a minute, Sokoloff was facing alone the hundred assailants. Suddenly he turned round and saw Rada. Then his hair stood on end, his eyes flashed like a tiger's, and heedless of the danger, he drew himself up at full length in the doorway, as though mocking at the bullets, while he cried in the purest Turkish :

" You cursed dogs ! you shall pay dearly for every drop of Bulgarian blood ! " and he discharged his revolver into the thick of the crowd.

With redoubled frenzy the horde now rushed at the impregnable fortress—for such the ruined mill seemed to have become. A wild shout, followed by a fresh volley, cleft the air.

" Ah ! " groaned the doctor, flinging away his revolver. A bullet had pierced his right hand. Inexpressible terror and despair were depicted on his face. Ognianoff, still firing at the crowd, and also covered with blood, noticed this and asked :

" Are you in pain, brother ? "

" No, but I've fired off my last cartridge—I forgot."

" Here, there are still two left in my revolver, take it,"

said Ognianoff, handing the weapon to Sokoloff. "Now they shall see how a Bulgarian apostle dies!" And drawing the long yataghan from the doctor's belt, he rushed from the door into the crowd, dealing frightful blows left and right.

     *   *   *   *   *

Half an hour later the whole horde, triumphant and ferocious, was marching with demoniacal glee from the valley with Ognianoff's head on a pole. The doctor's head, slashed to pieces by their knives (it had first been shattered by the doctor himself with a bullet), could not serve as a trophy. So also Rada's head was left behind for reasons of policy : Tossoun Bey was more cunning than his colleague of Tumrush.

A cart behind conveyed the killed and wounded.

With savage shouts of triumph the band reached the town. It was more silent and deserted than a graveyard. They set up the trophy in the market-place.

Only one man was moving there, like a ghost.

It was Mouncho.

When he recognised the head of his beloved "Russian," his eyes flashed with a fierce unreasoning rage, and he broke out into a colossal and appalling blasphemy against Mohammed.

They hanged him by the butcher's shop.

The idiot was the only man who had ventured to protest.

BALLANTYNE & COMPANY LTD
TAVISTOCK STREET COVENT GARDEN
LONDON

Lightning Source UK Ltd.
Milton Keynes UK
UKHW021913071222
413554UK00005B/170